Me and Matilda

Across Australia

MARY SEATON

SWEETSPIRE LITERATURE
—— MANAGEMENT ——

Other Books by the author

The Overlanders

Mary Of The Shanty

The Ringer Jack

Tales From The Sand Hills

The Power Of The Mage's Staff

I have a song here in my heart as I waltz along that dusty track.

And I am very seldom lonely for I have Matilda on my back.

I keep the road in front of me and the river left or right'.

After all my wandering I sleep with Marilda every night.

So close that door a gentle in my face and don't be shaming.

I am a son of this here country and I'll be there in the naming.

I am Walter Simon Earman I am swaggy extraordinaire.

And with Matilda on my back there we make a damn fine pair

So, take up your Matilda friend and go and find your track.

If the way be hard and long just, lay your head upon your sack.

I am thankful for the sun the moon the stars and for the song inside my head,

For the rivers and the fish and my full belly, and warm bed

For all that life has given me now, I say thanks from me and Matilda

For Tracey and Joseph

CHAPTER 1

Wally jumped down onto the tracks from the train and somersaulted a couple of times before landing on his feet. As the guard's van went passed Wally was hit on the head by a half a loaf of bread the guard had thrown at him.

'Next time you bastard, I'll get you next time.' He laughed at Wally and saluted him as the train rushed on down to the station. It was Jerry the guard's job to prevent these blokes from hitching a lift on the trains, but he never did. He liked most of them and he knew better than anybody what it was like to be homeless, and even penniless. He knew the hunger that gnawed at you all night long and the cold that tormented you.

'Thanks mate' sang out Wally lifting the bread with his good arm, a huge grin on his face. It seemed like a half a loaf could mean life or death out here on the road. It was a hard lesson, this swaggies life. But Wally would eat well tonight he had a potato and a slice of bacon in Matilda. He had done some work the week before for a farmer and had been paid in food. He also had tea and sugar and now, a half a loaf of bread. A meal fit for a swaggy king.

Wally had a small pension which helped; but some of the poor beggars had to do just that to survive. Mostly they worked at odd jobs along the way, but often times they had to resort to begging. Wally was well off compared to some, but he helped where he could. In fact, he helped to such an extent that the last week to pension day he was usually stoney broke and he sometimes relied on handouts himself. Here he was three days to pension day and he was almost broke. He'd need to be near a government office and a bank.

He hitched his pack up higher on his back. He had a swag and a piece of tarp which he used as a ground sheet or a tent cover depending on the weather. He had a pot in his pack and some spare underwear and a shirt. Hanging by his side from his belt was his billy with tea and sometimes sugar riding in it. He also carried a water bag and he carried most of his personal belongings in a sugar bag which rode on his back in the swag, covered by the tarp.

His kit was heavy, and he liked to catch trains or hitch a ride sometimes when he could. Though Wally did love to walk along the riverbanks and enjoy the sights and sounds and smells along the way. And Wally did also love to be out in the weather. He found that mother nature thrilled him and at the same time made him feel like he belonged. Waltzing with Matilda eased his heart and stilled his mind.

With him Wally carried a small black and white photo of his home and his extended family. It had all but broken his heart to leave them, but Wally was on a mission. Every night he took this small photo from his wallet and kissed it, then went off to sleep.

Like most of the other swaggies Wally followed the rivers as closely as he could. Water could be hard to find out in this country and these men stuck close to a good source. He also carried a handline and hook and when he could he did a spot of fishing. He had a trap with him also and had been able to supplement his tuckerbox with a rabbit here and there. He reckoned the bit extra weight was well worth it when he sat down to rabbit roasted on the coals. Sometimes when his sack was full he carried it in his hand.

Wally walked to the town centre, and walked into the first pub he came to. From the vehicles out the front he had a pretty fair idea he would find a few locals in there. This was Swan Hill on the banks of the mighty Murray River in the great Murray Valley of the great Murray basin.

Wally hoped he would find some work and the pub was the best place to find it. He was making his way to Albury Wodonga. He did hope to make enough to get him there on a steamer though he could follow the mighty Murray most of the way, on foot if needs be.

Wally wanted to make it to Queensland, but for now, he just relaxed and enjoyed the countryside and the different towns. He loved the excitement and the sense of freedom he got and waltzing with Matilda left a glow inside him. He also loved camping out and sleeping under the stars. And Wally liked almost everyone he met. There had been the odd times when other swaggies had looked after him.

Wally sat on a bar stool and ordered a schooner of VB beer; it was his, what they called 'entry fee'. It gave him licence to sit in the bar until he drank it. Wally hoped he wouldn't have to buy too many he was a bit short on cash. He had ten-shilling note and a two-shilling coin left which would do him nicely, if he didn't spend too much in the pub.

The barman, a big fellow, grinned widely at him and said, 'haven't seen you in here before young fellow, you just passing through, are you?'

Wally smiled and said, 'I was really hoping to find some work, I need to make some money and get to Albury.'

'Plenty of work out on the mine mate.' He leaned across the bar a little, 'see the old bastard at the end of the bar there with the black hat? He's the man you gotta see. Come on down here young'un and I'll introduce you if you like.' The barman gestured for him to come while the old man in the black hat sat waiting.

Wally was introduced to the man called Eric, with a long grey beard and a black battered hat on his head. The barman told the older man that Wally needed some work and then went off to serve someone. It was a busy Saturday afternoon in the township of Swan Hill.

The older man looked Wally up and down he noted the slouch hat and his heavy army jacket. His swag was pretty much army issue to. He liked what he saw and grinned.

Wally noted his sharp blue eyes behind an easy grin. He held his hand out to Wally and the two shook hands. Wally knew from old that this was a way of sizing him up. But the man nodded at Wally's arm and asked him straight out if it was a problem digging with it.

Wally grinned and shook his head, 'I can dig as fast as most blokes, and I can go all day.'

'Good on you son. Well, I do need a couple of blokes on shovels, so I tell you what. I'll give you a go. Be on the highway out to South Australia Monday morning at around about five, wait there at the city limits. I'll give you a fair go, how's that mate? If you can do the job, you've got it. I appreciate your service to your country.'

The grin Wally bestowed on the man brought an answering grin from him as it always did with people. 'Sit down son I'll buy you a wee drink.'

After they'd finished their drinks, Wally got his wallet out and lifted his hand to signal the barman.

The older man whose name was Eric watched him pull a ten-shilling note from an otherwise empty wallet. He put his hand gently on Wally's crooked arm. He smiled at Wally and said gently, 'no son, no. You hang on to your money lad and buy me one back at the end of the week. That is if you are still talking to me hay?'

Wally looked down at his ten-shilling note and shook his head, 'I must buy you a drink, I must.'

The older man realized that Wally would be shamed if he didn't buy him a drink back, so he removed his hand. 'Well okay son but make it a wee one hay. A butcher would do nicely I have to be home for teatime solid and sober or my dear old mum will kill me. And thank you lad you are a fine man. How'd that arm happen, in the war, was it?'

Wally nodded, 'took a bullet in New Guinea. I can do most types of work with it though. I have worked on a farm most of my life.'

That night the old man Eric took Wally home for dinner with him. Eric's mother who was seventy-two immediately liked the young man. She fed him until he could eat no more. After tea they asked Wally to stay the night, but Wally loved to sleep out. He left promising he would meet Eric out on the highway on Monday morning.

'Oh yeah before you go, there's a bit of a campsite out at the mine where some more blokes like you stay. It saves them having to cope with the ten-mile hike into town and back every day. So just make sure you can take a bit of tucker with you lad. Theres' water and laundry facilities as well out there and a bush shower and dunny. And there's a big shelter where you can get in, out of the rain. Alright then good night son, see you Monday.' The old man grinned up at him now, 'I sleep out there me self quite often. I like it son. You can get a ride in to town with me whenever you need to hay? And don't worry mate if you can dig the jobs yours. We bloody appreciate what you boys did for us by Christ.'

Wally thanked him and then said good night to his mother. 'What will you do all weekend' she asked?

'I like to fish Missus; I have fished everyday nearly from the Murrumbidgee for the last twelve or so years. Apart from the couple of years I was overseas.' He smiled at her, 'I carry a fishing line and a trap with me always, and it keeps me from starving. Thanks again for that lovely meal.' Wally dropped his head and said softly 'it has been a while.'

The old woman smiled gently at the big man in the doorway. 'Oh, the Murrumbidgee, I have relatives on that river. Well good night my dear I'm for my bed.' The old lady had brought her hands from behind her and handed Wally a calico bag tied at the top. 'For Matilda' she said with a smile.

'Thank you very much from the both of us. And if I get any fish, you shall have one.' He held his hand out to her and bestowed on her his most precious gift. He grinned from ear to ear, and she did the same back.

'God bless you son' she said and went inside. Eric saw the tear spring into the young man's eye and smiled at him 'good night son' he said softly.

Wally turned and waved at the front gate. 'If you head off down that way son' called Eric pointing, 'you'll come to the river. Just a little to your left when you get there is a tree which will house you just fine, I think. I have slept under it myself lad.'

'Thank you, sir, I will follow your heed.' And Wally was gone into the night. He did follow instruction and did indeed find one such a tree. It would be his palace for the night, Probably for the weekend he thought.

Wally made camp under the tree which was just out along the river towards the mine. He picked a sheltered spot under the huge tree with its thick foliage. It looked like that tree would hold back the cold rain and the hot sun.

Wally took off his billy his waterbag and his little fire lighting bag. Next, he took Matilda from his shoulders and lay her gently on the ground. He scrounged up some wood and lit a small fire.

Wally sat for a while looking into the flames, letting their mesmerising dancing take his tired mind and sooth it. He smiled to himself now as he thought of home and Dan. He had had to promise Dan faithfully that he would return once more to the banks of the lovely Murrumbidgee River. And of course, he would, for he had promised this. And Wally knew his heart lay with the Murrumbidgee and the people he loved there. He had assured Dan he would be back in a year or two.

He had waved goodbye as he walked down the road towards town. Most of the people there had wept openly including Dan. But alas Wally suffered from the same complaint as Jack had. Only no one knew about him, he'd always kept that tucked away.

Wally picked up a stick now and poked the fire with it and made sparks fly into the air. How he loved it, loved the freedom and the peace. He had seen Jack had found peace and had wanted it for himself.

Eventually Wally got up and spread his swag out. He took off his jacket and rolled up his sugar bag for a pillow. Wally put anything sweet or good to eat in the billy, put the lid on and hung it in the tree in case of ants.

As he lay his head down, he pulled his jacket up over his blanket for extra warmth. He said his usual silent prayer for everyone at home. He'd only been away six weeks, but it felt like six months. Wally closed his eyes and let the gentle night take him to other places. Wally didn't ever know why it was, but he never seemed to suffer with the flashbacks and nightmares that other blokes suffered with.

And as ever Wally looked forward to exploring his new backyard in the morning. He hoped the river would give him some fish and the land would give him a rabbit. He prayed for this only, for himself. And thanks to the generosity of the two people Eric and Gladys, he still had food. He also had a fruit cake for the first time in a long time, bread, and some thick slices of cold roast meat he'd found in the little bag. He smiled to himself as he lay there, people were kind, good. Life was good and it made him feel good.

Wally wasn't naïve he slept with his back to the tree trunk, even though he had never experienced anything but friendliness and kindness on his journey. But he wasn't naïve.

The murmurings of the night gave way to the hustle and bustle of sunrise. Birds sang as they got ready for the day. Wally sat up and grinned at the river; it was a beauty this Murray River. He loved it and went about getting ready for the day himself.

Wally ate sparingly at breakfast finding he had no appetite for food at that time much. He ate mostly at lunch time and then ate sparingly again most nights.

Wally had a handgun which Mary had slipped him when he left. He had just twenty bullets for it, and he had never used it. And because Wally wasn't naïve, he slept with it under his pillow.

How he missed her he thought now. But missing her was preferable to the gut-wrenching need in him when he was close to her. He remembered how Dan had looked at him when he said goodbye with tears in his eyes and said softly 'must this love of mine come at such a cost Wally?'

Then he had shaken his head and pulled Wally into his embrace and held him and sobbed, unashamedly the man had sobbed. Mary and Ron had had to help him inside.

As soon as he could he'd write. He'd buy some paper and an envelope stamped and he'd get the lady at the post office to write the address on it. He started sorting his things. He wanted to get down to the river to fish, of course, Matilda would have to go with him. Matilda was all he had. Wally carried a knife on his belt and his gun in his pocket. He'd gotten plenty of practice with guns, so he was a damn good shot. You had to be in the commandos. Wally carried the gun where he could get at it quickly in case, he spotted food on the hop.

He opened the little calico bag and smiled, fruit cake. Almost a whole fruit cake. There were also an apple and an orange along with the meat, enough meat for three or four days probably. Yes, he would go fishing today for as long as it took, he had to take Eric's mother Gladys a fish.

Wally finished his coffee; he had found a tiny packet of that in the calico bag to. When he was packed up, he shouldered Matilda and went down to the water's edge. It wasn't long before he found a nice patch of worms and sat down to fish.

Wally loved fishing even when he didn't catch anything. He had sat there for over an hour, dreaming of catching barramundi in Queensland, when he landed his first fish. It was a good-sized Murray cod, well over a foot long. He gutted it and took the scales off and sat down to catch another. By lunch time he had caught three, so he went to cook one for his lunch. He still had his potato though he'd scoffed the piece of bacon at breakfast. He hadn't wanted that to go off.

After he'd eaten his lunch, he walked along the river until he found a likely place to set his trap. There were signs of much activity in the rabbit community and a dung hill, so that's where he set his trap. When that was set, he got the fish from the tree branch and went off to give Eric's mother Gladys, the fish he'd promised her. He had two for her wrapped in some newspaper.

He always carried a little newspaper with him, it was so handy. He carried some in his fire lighting bag in his sugar bag under the tarp which, when scrunched up made fire lighting much easier. Wally bought a newspaper when he was unable to find one so he could keep up with the world news.

Wally loved the feeling of being aware of what was going on in the world around him, and Dan had loved teaching him the finer points, explaining to him about politics and such. Thanks to Dan and his radio that Mary had given him, he could hold a conversation now, just about anywhere.

He had developed a love of sports to, and he and Dan had done a lot of screaming at the various umpires and such on the radio. To the point that they had been kicked out of the long hut by the women once or twice. But they had been allowed back in, promising their behaviour would improve.

Back home Dan had got him used to keeping up with the latest news, current events, and trends etc. Wally had begun a love affair with music from that radio also. He and Dan and some of the others, sometimes sang along to the songs they knew. It was a Saturday night favourite thing to do, and it was mostly country music.

And of course, on those freezing nights when the frost came calling, Wally used newspaper in his bedding under his army great coat. It was a trick he'd learned from Dan when they'd been on the road. Newspaper was quite an effective insulator he'd said.

Wally walked the distance to Erics house with a song in his heart. It was a beautiful day, and the birds were singing. He knocked on the door and Gladys answered.

She was ecstatic when she saw the fish. 'You really do look after yourself. I admire you.' She wiped her eye and said, 'come into the kitchen and I'll make you a nice cupper.'

'Oh, thank you for the coffee I had it for breakfast and some fruit cake. Thanks very much. A bit extra food comes in mighty hand out on the road.'

'You are welcome, dear. You know my other son died over there in New Guinea. He was about your age and size. I have a shirt of his you could probably get some use out of.'

'Oh no Missus I couldn't.'

'Nonsense, I know how much Eric will work you. You will need a couple of extra shirts and they are warm. Wait here and get him anything he wants Eric.' She cast a stern eye at her son though the love in it was not lost on Wally. He smiled at the man who got up to get him a cup of tea.

'Yes milady' he mumbled and shot a grin at Wally.

Gladys came back with two checked shirts one which was brand new. Wally's eyes were shining green, and Eric smiled. 'Go on son take them, I'll get payment out of you.'

Wally grinned and picked up the red and black shirt, he held it for a while and put it down. He had a lump in his throat as he thanked Gladys. He looked up at her now and said softly, 'could I trouble you for some help Missus?'

Gladys sat down 'of course love, whatever you need.'

Wally cleared his throat and shuffled his feet before speaking. 'Well, I need to write home and I would need someone to address the envelope so as I know it will get there. If that's alright.'

'Yes of course it is love, no problems, I would be glad to. And you can write the letter yourself?'

'Yes, thank you. I'll organise that next time I come into town. I'll need to go to the shops next time I can get into town, probably. Anyway, that would be great.' He looked down at his lap, 'it will be a hard letter to write.'

Gladys nodded her eyes full of compassion she said softly, 'alright then, I have paper and a pencil, and I have envelopes if you like.' She put her hand on his briefly, 'so you can get started whenever you wish. Here take some' she handed him pages from a writing pad and some cardboard to rest it on. Next, she gave him a pencil. 'Here' she said and handed him a rubber. Smiling she said softly, 'I have written hard letters myself dear and I know roughly how many pages you will need to write to get the one you want.'

'Thank you very much, from the bottom of my heart. You know, I am glad I came on this journey now and found out how much goodness there is in the world.'

'I just hope you still feel that way come Monday night son' put in Eric with a smile.

Wally excused himself after a while saying he had to organise his tea and check his trap. He thanked them both at the front door and remembered the calico bag. He got it out and gave it to her and thanked her again for the food. Wally remembered how important calico bags were up on Mable Downs.

She thanked him for the fish and watched him leave. She knew she loved him, and she also knew she would lose him. He would move on someday, but something told her that she and Wally would always be connected. Like mother and son, they would be connected. Eric saw it and was surprised by it. He knew his mother was a very fine judge of character and he was well pleased.

Wally also knew he would forever be connected to these people. He'd never had a mum, not that he could remember anyway. He trudged along the riverbank, a smile on his face and a song in his heart. He loved this life, loved this waltzing with Matilda. And he loved the river. Rivers had been bloody good to him he thought now. As he thought about the things, he'd gotten from rivers the smile grew broader on his face. 'Thank God for rivers' he murmured shifting his pack a little higher.

Wally detoured a little leaving the town limits he checked his trap. He had a rabbit for his dinner and doubting that he would catch another he pulled his trap up and went back to his camp site. He fished for and hour catching five fish.

Throwing his swag on the ground and hanging his billy he set about lighting a fire. As he gutted and skun the rabbit he decided to keep it and eat a fish.

Rabbit would keep better than fish and tomorrow he had a long way to go.

He hoped he would not be a disappointment to Eric and in turn his mother. They had been very kind to him, and he felt he owed them.

When he'd finished his dinner he took the rabbit to the water where he washed it. Back at the tree he hung the rabbit to freeze.

CHAPTER 2

Wally was waiting on the side of the road for Eric on Monday morning and threw his swag in the back. 'Climb in the front here young fulla.' Wally opened the door, 'too cold up in the back this morning son.'

Wally settled himself in the front and listened to the older man talk about the mine. He was glad to get in the front seat out of the cold wind. As if mirroring his thoughts, the old man said now 'hope you got a nice warm swag there young un. There's some spare kit laying around out there in the shed, some of the blokes have grabbed an extra blanket. You're welcome to grab one and make it yours mate okay. Nights are bloody cold out here mate.'

'Thanks Eric I appreciate everything you've done for me. I'll try not to let you down.'

'I know mate, I know. I know because mum knows.' Eric smiled at the younger man. 'You sure made an impression on her. You are a lot like my brother who never made it home from the war. He was a lot younger than me; he was my half-brother. My mothers first husband was killed when a tree fell on him, he was a lumberjack in the Victorian highlands.'

'I'm sorry to hear that,' said Wally.

The sun was lighting the sky in the east and Wally was excited. Today he'd find out if he could cut it out here in the world of the working men. He'd been surprised when he and Dan had got home from Queensland and Dan had started giving him more responsibilities.

The first of these new responsibilities had been digging holes and he soon got the hang of it and could keep up with Dan. He'd been a big help digging in the gardens to and then at harvesting the paddocks. Wally was a driver and Dan had recognised it immediately. And Wally operated machinery better than most.

So, Dan had also taught him to drive the tractor and to plough the paddock. When he'd mastered that he had taught him to drive the truck. Wally was quite capable of driving the truck and tractor and the car and he was also a natural with the horse and cart much to Mary's delight. Wally was also capable of baling hay and slinging it up in the back of the truck using hooks.

Dan knew that Wally, a naturally powerful man, had lost a lot of the power in his left arm. But Wally's right arm had gotten stronger to make up the difference. Wally had never behaved as a man with no left arm and the fact that he used it, though less now, kept him in the game. Dan was very proud of Wally. Dan had taken him to a physiotherapist and Wally had always done his exercises which helped him immensely. Yes, Dan was very proud of the young man and he told him so often. Dan also came down on Wally, not so much for failing but for giving up.

Dan had also taught him to shear the sheep and to slaughter and butcher. He had also gotten Wally up on Lilly and taught him how to ride and care for her. These things were now commonplace to him, and he was grateful for it. Yes, he owed Dan a lot and he'd come back to him one day as promised.

But for now, there were things he needed to do. Things he needed to get out of his system. And there were all those rivers out there, what better place to practise. Wally thought he'd try to remember all of this when he wrote his letter, he didn't want Dan to worry. He loved Dan and thought of him as his father. Yeah, he'd send a letter off at the end of this week he promised himself now.

Eric had asked him what he could do, and Wally told him of all the things he was capable of. 'I do have my licences for a car and a truck.'

'Do you think you could handle a bulldozer son?' Eric was surprised himself, by the question he'd just asked.

'I know I'd be willing to try, I had no trouble with the truck and tractor. And I can drive a grader as well.' Wally smiled at Eric and shrugged, 'I got on well with the grader driver on the highways back in Balranald.'

'Good, because our bloody bulldozer operator up and took off last week, I never liked the man anyway. Come the end of this week we are gunna need a driver for that. So, I'll get you up on it to practice a little. See what you can do hay? It's having some repairs done to it but by about Wednesday I'll get you up in it.'

'No worries. I'll do my best Eric.'

'I know.' Eric fell silent for a little while then asked 'where are you headed Wally? You strike me as a man who has a plan. I mean most swaggies wander aimlessly, waltzing along the highways and river ways with Matilda on their backs. But not you I think.'

'I want to go to Queensland I have a brother up there. Me and Jack were close before the bloody war. He found peace up there and well . . . . But first I want to travel these rivers a bit. Then I'll come back to the Murrumbidgee, she saved my life. Her and a man called Dan and a woman named Mary. The Murrumbidgee will always be my first love.'

'There's a story there, Wally? During the depression, was it?' And quite a story to I'll bet thought Eric.

Wally nodded; a bout of homesickness had grabbed him in the belly. How he missed them, not even in the war had he missed them so much. In war time you never looked ahead far enough to get homesick you just tried to stay alive for today. Eric was talking again.

'Oh yeah mate, she was a tough time all round. I did travel the Murray to Goolwa in my youth. And then I travelled back up the Lachlan to Sydney. Well Cowra anyway. I've been up and down the Murrumbidgee a few times to, lovely river. Yeah, I travelled those rivers on a steamer, only way to do it mate. I think some of em still run and you can get jobs on them. I have a mate who is a captain on the Murrumbidgee Princess, I think they are mostly passengers now. People still like to go by river when they can and there are still those who like to send goods up and down on the river.' Eric shrugged, 'a habit, I guess, that and it's a nicer ride. If you ever want to you can give me as a reference mate. Yeah, go and see him and then maybe look at working your way up the Lachlin.'

'Thanks Eric I will Look into that. I'll get his name before I go if you don't mind. But for now, I have a bulldozer to master and before that a shovel to operate. I really appreciate the chance here mate and I hope I don't let you down. I will do my very best.'

'Like I said, I know son. So, are you thinking of traveling the rivers all the way up to Queensland? There are some mighty fine rivers to travel mate. I once went up the Paroo to the Barcoo and I stopped by the Bulloo River on my way and fished her for a time and Coopers Creek. I came down through Queensland to South Australia along the Diamontina. Best years of my life by a long shot. I am a river man myself mate so I know how it gets you. I envy you.' Eric slowed up, 'anyway here's the turn off.'

Ten minutes along a rough corrugated road and Wally got his first look at the mine, it was a dismal sight. Off to their right Wally saw the shelter Eric had spoken of under some trees. He noticed there were about fifteen men standing around drinking from white mugs.

'That's the shelter I told you about son. See that shed over there, well every morning I will lock all your possessions and theirs in that shed while you are off working and you get them back at knock off time. Too much stuff has gone missing and too many fights over it.' Eric smiled at Wally, 'your Matilda will be safe in there, mate.'

At the shelter Eric introduced Wally to the other men who handed them both a mug of coffee. Wally found he liked most of them. After he'd had his coffee Eric opened the shed. Looking at Wally he said, 'you'll need to take lunch with you mate we won't be back here until after work. I'm sorry I should have told you; I hope you have some lunch.'

'Thanks, yes I do.' said wally and grabbed the sandwich he'd made with a little bread which he'd bought in town and the slices of lamb Gladys had given him. He'd bought potatoes and tinned meat and two tins of vegies with him. He'd got some tea and sugar and flour also. Wally had become quite adept at making scones and fried scones. If he could catch a couple of rabbits, he'd have plenty of food until he got to town. If not, he'd tighten his belt.

Wally smiled he had a candle in Matilda and the writing material Gladys had given him. He'd get started writing a letter to Dan. A daunting task but he would just have to remember it was Dan who would be reading it, and he would be happy he'd got a letter even if he couldn't read it at all. Maybe he'd get Gladys to look it over before he sent it.

Wally followed the men to the worksite. Some of them looked a little doubtfully at Wally's arm and Eric noticed it, he just hoped Wally was as good as he said he was. Eric knew he would keep his word to the man no matter what.

Somebody handed Wally a shovel and told him where to dig. Then they all set about watching him while pretending not to be. Wally knew it and he didn't blame them. He didn't want to let the side down, wanted to show them. But Wally was no fool and he knew he had to be there at the end of the day. So, he'd need to pace himself, need to find his stride.

Nodding to Eric, Wally lifted the shovel and started to dig. Eric grinned. He watched the younger man for a while. His style was a little awkward because he couldn't extend his arm all the way out and he did have a tendency to toss the dirt clear over his shoulder. But by hell he could dig.

Eric watched in amazement for a while as the big man settled himself into a rhythm. He walked over and told Wally he'd be back in an hour or so. He said softly, 'can you really do this all day young un? Fair dinkum?'

Wally nodded, he'd have to take care to settle his swing and his breathing down. He had about three quarters of the physical ability that the others had in their arms, so he'd have to make up for it with sheer grunt. But he was no stranger to this battle. He was glad now that Dan had been hard but fair, mighty glad.

Wally relaxed a little and smiled faintly. As the old man walked off, he'd mumbled 'you'll do lad.'

And when Wally finished the day at four thirty, he had a deal of grunt left and after he got his stuff out of the shed, he walked off to set his trap. He had two fish and a rabbit in the meat safe which he knew wouldn't last so he took one for his tea and handed the rabbit and a fish to the hungry men and got huge grins in return. 'Fresh rabbit and a fish' exclaimed an old prospector swaggie they called Freddy. 'Lovely' he ginned at the fish.

'I've got some veggies we can have with it' stated one of the men and another offered a bit of bread, and so on it went. Wally grinned at their excitement; they were hungry. Wally knew hungry when he saw it. These men were thin and gaunt looking and he vowed he would try to help them.

Wally told Eric that he would be back in the morning in time for work. 'Righto lad, a bit after daybreak would be good mate.' Wally nodded and smiled; he knew exactly what time it was because he wore a watch. They started at seven, he'd be here at seven.

Wally took Matilda with him and most of his food, his waterbag and billy. He hoped to catch a couple of rabbits and share those as well in the morning, these men worked bloody hard. He told them he'd be back in the morning.

They watched him go, the man was a marvel, and they knew it. Wally didn't know it, but he'd softened the hardest of hearts in the camp. Eric smiled softly; he saw it. He was staying the night at the camp and found he was a bit disappointed that Wally was not. But Eric thought he knew what the young man was up to and smiled as he left.

When Wally got back the next morning, he had two rabbits. He gave one to the blokes and they all put these rabbits in the meat safe. Wally was given a mug of coffee by one of the older men who said, 'hell of a job you did yesterday, Wally.'

The other men without exception grinned and nodded their approval and admiration. Wally knew he'd been accepted. 'If it suits you all I'll make a stew out of these two rabbits tonight, and we can all share it.'

That night Wally was amazed as the men handed over vegetables to contribute to a sizeable stew. Wally made a damper as well and stuck a few potatoes in the pot and thickened it with a little rice. That night they all ate like kings. Swaggie kings, and as such they left enough for the next nights tea.

Eric was impressed with the young man and was saddened to think they would lose him. But Eric knew that this man's major contribution to this raggedy group would certainly live on in their hearts. For he had contributed a great and needed dose of humanity.

On Wednesday morning bright and early, Eric came and got Wally, it was time to get up on the dozer. Wally was eager but his heart was in his mouth and his left hand shook a little as he climbed up in the seat. He looked at the controls and knew he could do it.

He grinned at Eric and the blokes who had stopped work to watch in awe as the young fulla with a severely disabled arm, sat himself in the dozer seat. Some of the blokes gave up trying to look busy and leaned on their shovel. All watching a young bloke who had restored something in these men. They weren't sure what it was, but they knew they'd lost it a long time ago. And they also felt glad to have it back. They hadn't felt pride like this in more than a decade. And now the young bloke was starting up the dozer and to a man they were pulling for him.

It took Wally a few minutes to sort it all out and he looked down at Eric and nodded. Eric gave a sweep of his hand to indicate a marked-out area. 'Just start digging when you're ready lad. Probably just take it down a couple of feet today if you can manage it.' He strode off to leave the man to get the feel of it. He was already impressed.

When Wally gave it plenty of throttle to make his first cut, he was astounded. He'd watched the highway dozer operator and had a pretty fair idea how it all worked. The power of the machine left him exhilarated but a little nervous.

And so, with a loud 'yeeha', he dropped the blade. Eric grinned and turned to watch, he had to. Something in that 'yeeha' had got him in his middle and he knew he'd been right in his choice.

Wally made his first pass; the cut was clean and steady and even. Wally was a natural, somebody had taught him well. Eric walked away that day wondering about the man, and he did wonder about this man called Dan he talked about.

By the time Wally went back to town with Eric some of the others went to. They all needed to get some stores, so they took a few hours to go into the shops. Wally had been out there for two weeks now, and they had managed on the rabbits and dampers and whatever else they could scrounge up. Although they were down to one feed a day at times. So, they had given Wally what they could afford, and he had done the honours.

Wally had been out trapping and fishing some nights after work, along the river. One night he had come across a bush turkey which he'd shot, he couldn't believe his luck. He had cut the head off so as to disguise the fact that he had a gun. That could fall into the wrong hands if they all knew he had it.

When Wally had returned with it a cheer went up and though some shot him quizzical glances, not one man questioned him as to how he had caught it. They were just so glad that he had.

The week before, Eric had taken Wally and dropped him at the river to fish and he'd come back the next day with ten good sized Murray cod and a large wombat which would feed them for a few days. Again, he cut the head off the wombat and again no one questioned him.

The weather was bitterly cold, and Wally was glad of it as the meat lasted for several days in the meat safe. Wally had also realised how lucky they were to have the rough shelter that they slept under each night. When it rained, they all stayed dry and warm. Wally had had a good look around and he thought they could probably scrounge up enough material to put a second wall on their shelter. If he built it on the east side, he would cut out most of the cold wind he thought. He had also looked into installing a bit of a chimney and have the fire inside; he'd talk to Eric.

He and Eric had gone into town and came back with more flour and potatoes and a huge fruit cake from Gladys. They made do as these men were experts at doing. They also came back with bags of rice and cereal, milk powder sugar and tea. Wally found a sheet of tin and made a cover for these bags of precious produce. He put four legs on it and fashioned empty tins to them to keep the mice and rats from getting into the food.

After his second week on the dozer Wally had found he needed to start his letter to Dan, he was proud of himself. Sadly, Gladys had been right, and he had started three letters before he found his mark. And that wasn't counting all the rubbing out he did. Eric watched him from the fire and wished he could help. Almost to a man, they wished they could help. But they knew the only help they could offer him was to leave him in peace with it.

On the third letter Wally felt he had it sorted out in his mind what he wanted to say. So, armed with the first two pages he began his long and laborious letter to Dan. He wrote it on his bit of cardboard table, in his best handwriting. He was most glad of the cardboard and smiled as he thought of her. She had given him ten pages; plenty he thought now.

He settled himself down in the light from his candle. He began.

7/6/1954

Dear Dan,

I hope everybody is well there Dan. I am not far away; I'm working on a mine outside of Swan Hill. Probably closer to Echuca. I need to make some money to travel up to the end of the Murray to the Snowy River. I do wish to travel the length of the Murrumbidgee to, and then possibly back up the Lachlin to Sydney.

I am operating a dozer here Dan thanks to your teaching. I do find that I love it and will stay for a few months at least. So, if you have a mind to write to me you can send mail to the mine care of the Swan Hill post office. I just need to know you are alright Dan. I promise you I will be back some day, I could never just leave you and the Murrumbidgee Dan. I love you all and I say a prayer for you every night.

I must tell you Dan, that I have met only nice and good people. I don't want you to worry about me though old man I am nobody's fool. Thank you for taking the time to teach me to be a good and productive man, a decent man.

I have some things I need to do Dan; I need to get some things sorted and out of my system. I do love rivers and I want to see and experience some before I settle down in one place. Thank you for my love of them to. I wish I was better with words so I could make you understand. But here is what I need no help with. I love you Dan, you are the only parent I ever had. And I know you love me to. I'll be back Dan, I give you, my word. You always told me Dan, that a man is only as good as his word.

Please tell the others I love them and miss them as I miss you. I am experiencing some devilish home sickness. But I am loving it to Dan. I love this life and the rivers. I met a man who has been up the Paroo and the Barcoo and the Bulloo rivers. I hope to see these to. He is a good man, is Eric my boss.

I must go now Dan, Early start tomorrow. I was shovelling first few days Dan, and I was able to keep up easily. Thanks again. I will say good night now from me and Matilda. I await word from you.

All my love

Wally XX

Wally folded his letter carefully and when he looked up it was to see the softly smiling face of Eric. Wally held up the letter and grinning he waved it about as he got to his feet.

'You made it Wally' said Eric relieved. Every man there felt gladdened.

'I did Eric. Could you look it over and make sure it is good enough to read.'

'Certainly son.'

Wally handed the letter to Eric along with his candle and he went off to relieve himself ready for bed.

Eric read the letter by the light from the candle and the fire. He was impressed and he was moved. For a few moments he thought he might cry. He had never read anything so simply beautiful. Just like the man who'd written it.

Wally returned and Eric handed the letter back, 'it is perfect son. Any man would be proud to get that.'

Wally smiled and put the letter in an envelope, He owed Dan a lot. Just the fact that he could send a letter was thanks to that man. At odd times Wally wondered why he had left him. Then Wally remembered.

By the end of the second week Wally was operating the dozer as if he'd been doing it for years. At days end Eric usually came up and stood with him as he checked his motor and refuelled it. Eric had noticed how the man took care of his machine. And Wally was never hard on his machinery, making sure to never ask too much of a load from it. And yet the man always seemed to get the same amount of work done if not more than anybody else. He spent a lot less time going back over his work to fix it, Wally did it once.

'I am going to be sad when I lose you young Wally. You have worked hard; none harder son and you have brought about change here. Hard to explain but it is good change, very good. Gladys was right at the faith she had in you. She is seldom wrong about people.'

Wally grinned at Eric in his open friendly way as he clapped the older man on the shoulder. 'You feel alright Eric?'

Eric gave a hic of a laugh and shaking his head he said, 'yes son I am alright. What have we got for tea tonight, Wally? What culinary delights have you got in mind?'

'No Eric I thought I'd just cook some food hay.'

Eric looked at him and noted the crooked grin that Wally always wore when he was taking the Micky. 'Okay you just do that lad.'

Wally turned serious now, 'thanks for everything that you have done for me Eric.'

'You're thanking me son? Huh.' Erics voice was gentle, and Wally walked on in silence for a bit.

Wally said, 'Got a nice bit of beef I scored from Ned over at the smelter. Thought I'd make a stew with it. You know, just for a bit of a change like.' The two men laughed.

Eric said, 'you helped me out of a bit of a bind mate, I was wondering who I'd get to drive the damn dozer and here I am, got a cook as well. We'd all be hungry without you mate.' Eric glanced sideways at the big man he had come to admire.

'Well Dan always says one good turn deserves another.'

'I'd like to hear more about this Dan and your large family on the Murrumbidgee. I reckon there's a story there, son and it must be bloody good one to, because you came out of it.'

That evening the two men talked and Wally told Eric about his large family back home on the banks of the Murrumbidgee River, a stone's throw from where she flows into the Murray River. He told Eric of the long trek to the Murrumbidgee and the people they'd lost along the way. About the starvation and the cold that took them. About the hopelessness of it all as they roamed the countryside looking for work. And when they did get work there was never enough money for housing, so they lived in the tents. Those who were lucky enough to have them.

He told the story of how Dan had picked him up lost and alone on the side of the road. Had loved him and cared for him. Had made him know that he was part of a very large and very loving family and for that, he should count himself amongst the very lucky. And Wally recalled how it wasn't long before he believed it.

Wally relayed to these men that Dan was the first human being he could ever remember hugging him. And Dan had stood by him from that day on, he had promised him this, that day on the side of the road. The others followed Dan's lead as ever and accepted him and loved him. And eventually over time, Wally had begun to realise just how lucky he really was.

The men all listened quietly by the fire light; they loved a good story. Most of them had done it bloody tough during those dark years before the war and they understood. And to a man they all knew just how lucky young Wally had been.

Wally told them of the man called Dan who brought the men and anyone else who were without shelter into his tent at night when sleeping outside may have brought more death upon them. Along the way some of the men had managed to get some work, and they handed whatever they made over to Dan. It was Dan they looked to for leadership; Dan who would get them through. It was Dan who loved them.

He mentioned how Dan's wife had died of cancer and left him with two boys to care for besides the rest of them. How the man had loved them and had loved each and every kid in that camp, always making time for them all. The one never more important than the other. And how his people loved him back and respected him, trusted him.

He had saved every bit of money he could to send these kids to school dressed as well as any other kid. Wally went on now 'and he had said that they must have a bag for their little backs and all the pencils and food they needed. They were not to be inferior if we were to turn out highly skilled professionals. He would say this as he watched them play.'

Wally smiled here as he retold of the man's fierce pride in them all. Wally told how every adult in the long hut had pitched in to teach these kids schoolwork and many other skills. To get them ready for school. 'Even the old men taught them their knowledge and trades. That camp has turned out soldiers, officers, lawyers, doctors, and farmers. Even a girl who is now a test pilot. And in Dan's eyes, never was one better achieved than the other. Dan used to say you had to be at the top of your game not somebody else's.'

Wally went on, talking about the council moving them on and the despair that was creeping in on them. The despair that the people who lived there in the town didn't want to know about them, didn't care about them and there was nowhere to turn. No one to turn to.

But Dan, well he just kept on fighting for them and worked tirelessly to feed them and keep them warm and happy and to keep their self-respect intact. How government aid was dwindled down to almost nothing, but the old blokes and anybody else who got jobs here and there, gave Dan whatever they had. And Dan kept none for himself, no one did Wally told them how in those early days, they had watched their children grow thinner and more despondent. And in an emotionally charged moment he gave voice to the love they had for each other. Yes, and how an empty belly seems to deepen your heart. Some eyes had begun to sparkle with tears, at that glowing and warming fire. The fire of kings.

But when Wally brought Mary into the story they were astounded. Some were almost inclined to doubt the young bloke's word but somehow, they didn't. This was Wally. But they'd never heard of such kindness, such love, such insight, and such bravery. Even Eric sat astounded at the story Wally told and to a man they knew they listened to the truth. A legend was born on this night at this here fire.

The story of Mary who rode up on her cart one day and saved them. Taught them to grow their own food and gave them the means and land to do it, and they were never starving again. No more children died from that day forward, nor for that matter did any old people die.

Dan had worked tirelessly and had gone on to help feed the town during the worst of the years. He and Mary took food into the town markets and Dan had not only never raised his prices but had dropped his prices to feed these people and their children. These people to fell for him.

Mary had given them the ability to fish the river and had given them a couple of traps to get rabbits and a gun to get pigs, the feral pigs which roamed the Murrumbidgee. And they had walked back from a very cold hard place together. And Mary and Dan led them away from it.

Then when the council threatened to move them on again, they had been devastated. But Mary stepped in once more and she had given them some more land to build a dwelling on. She had taken them in her cart pulled by a big loving horse named Lilly to the dumps for materials and they had built the long hut. And they had moved in just before the long dark winter, and a terrible winter it had been. But nobody froze to death again, and their gardens grew and flourished as the children did.

They had put the families at one end of the long hut and the men at the other and they had put the kitchen and the fire in the middle. The fire kept them warm. There were around thirty people in all, and beds were made for everyone and as time went by, they got new mattresses.

All family sleeping areas were petitioned off for a little privacy with walls of mostly hessian or tarpaulin and a curtain door. Everyone inside, fed, and warm. Alive!

By the end of the story these hardened men found they loved and admired the woman and Dan and all the others who had made a happy home out of cast offs from the dump. Made a happy, secure home all living in a long hut. They had saved lives as surely as night follows day. And Mary, well she'd given them the ability to save themselves and others. And they had thumbed their noses at a cold cruel council.

Wally told the story of how Mary had put a table on the side of the highway and kept it stocked with bits of food all through those days of the starving swaggies. Food which was always gone within a day or two. The legend grew.

But Wally was not yet finished and the night animals, the sounds of the bush and the fire were the perfect back drop to this fine story. This emotional roller coaster of a story. Wally was looking into the fire as if he saw it all, and they looked into the fire and they to saw.

Mary who was not afraid to stand up to hard hearted councils. Added to that was Dan's patience with a towns people who just didn't understand them, needed time to understand them. Hell, Dan hadn't ever given up on these townspeople and Wally had watched him weave his magic on them. They now loved and respected him and made sure at the same time, to never mess with him or his loved ones.

Wally talked very fondly of the woman who had engineered their rescue together with the man who upheld the order, no mean fete with that many people. And Wally said these two people eventually got married and Mary signed four acres over to the people of the shanty for their own security. Wally smiled a far-off sort of smile. 'We were lifted from beggars to privileged overnight and we knew it. We had become land owners no less and it was a glorious thing.'

Throughout the story of his people, Wally had the men about him laughing at times and wiping their eyes at others. Some had tears spill down their somewhat hollow, weather-beaten cheeks as the harrowing emotions that had them crippled, began to exit their own hearts. Trapped within their tears, the sorrows of their lives that had held them captive for so long, began to leave them. Began to free them.

They sat now like kings around the fire in their raggedy clothes and listened with their hearts to Wally's story and were themselves lifted. They were warm and with full bellies, but they remembered, and they understood alright.

Most of these work weary men knew of the hardships about which Wally, their newest member spoke. They hadn't forgotten and to most of them those days were hovering over them still. Starvation was just a pay away and they were to a man, already homeless. And more than a few of them realised that they had made a home here, living all together under this shelter consisting of a roof and one wall. And hadn't this young man promised he would build yet another wall.

Yeah, they were a family, and they'd made it work. A family with no blood cementing them together; just love and a need to belong. Men around the fire lifted their hands to brush away a tear or two.

And with his usual understanding of people and a bit of a flair for the magic himself, Wally mentioned this now. He concluded, 'three times in my life I have been lucky enough to be a part of a large family with no blood binding them to each other. Just love, a need for peace, and a will to survive.' He sighed and went on.

'The long hut taught me this and the army reinforced it as we depended on each other for our very lives. All this as we marched through hot deserts, steaming jungles and freezing cold, far-off lands singing Waltzing Marilda as we went. And now we have been thrown together here in this place and just think what a stroke of luck that was.' Wally grinned around at the faces at the fire. The grins that answered his made his heart soar and the men saw the wonder on Wally's face and were lifted yet higher.

'Here, here' said Freddy from the back of the group. A murmur to that effect went round the men there. 'Thanks Wally' he said and the rest nodded. Yes indeed they all reflected, what a stroke of luck.

Eric lay awake that night and wondered if he'd been wrong about God. He had blamed him for taking away his brother and leaving his mother in tatters. But his mother had done no such thing, she had blamed no one.

'It is written in the stars', she would say. And then she would smile at him and say 'there is too much to be done to sit about and be sorry for ourselves Eric. Your brother is gone forever I know, and we must do his share until God sends another in his stead'. And she worked tirelessly still at her various charities. Eric imagined she would do that until God took her.

And she had accepted Wally as some sort of gift from the almighty. Well, Eric wasn't quite ready to do that. Was he? And yet here was Wally when they needed him, and right when they needed him. And Eric thought that the young Wally had not yet even begun.

Eric turned over and pulled his blanket up and his tarp up over that. He had never gone through that sort of starvation that twisted your gut until it hurt like hell. And he had never been bone shivering cold. Maybe Wally was a gift from God, maybe he'd been sent to bring empathy to him. Maybe to all people. Maybe he was meant to bring all things needed to all people who needed it.

Eric sighed deeply. Under any circumstances philosophy was not his strong point.

Eric had an epiphany in that moment, and he somehow knew he had to let Wally go. Wally had a purpose on his journey that no man should interfere with. For what Wally had to give, Wally got back.

Eric was sad but he was strangely elated, and he was grateful for the time he'd been given with Wally. For in the grand scheme of things a bloke like Wally coming into your life for just a moment was a grand occurrence. And anybody lucky enough to have that bestowed on them ought to treasure it. His mother had known. Yes, she had, thought Eric now.

Eric started to warm up and grow drowsy. As he closed his eyes, he knew in his heart that to be given the opportunity to help such a man on his quest was a duty. And for the first time in many years a thrill surged through Eric.

Most of the men thought for a little while that night about Wally. About the story the young man told that was so similar to their own. Most of these men had lost people back then or had come across bodies.

Bodies of the poor miss begotten and dispossessed souls who had succumbed to hunger loneliness and the loss of hope.

You could die from hopelessness, from lack of love as sure as you could die from lack of water food or warmth. But Wally had brought hope to them, a hope for the future and a renewed interest in staying alive. By God he had.

Wally had brought to them the realisation of the importance of being connected. To some one, to each other. They realised that blood had precious little to do with the sort of connections that saved lives. And Wally had given them their very own legend. The legend of Mary passed on through Wally. The son of Mary. So, in their eyes they were blessed.

Wally lay in the dimming glow of the fire and thanked his God for the gifts which had been bestowed upon him. For Dan and Mary who he had left home to avoid disrespecting. Who he loved more than he loved himself. He loved them more than life itself.

Silently he offered a prayer for his family back there on the Murrumbidgee. And he offered a prayer for this family he had here near to the banks of the mighty Murray River. He thanked them also for finding Eric and his mother and the love they had for him.

Most of all now Wally thanked God and the universe for the love he had in his heart for others and the fact that he seemed to have enough to go round. Wally hoped he could be the man Dan was someday. And Mary, who did he thank for her?

Wally didn't see himself as being on a mission or looking to save souls. Souls were somebody else's job. But he knew the importance of a healthy body. He knew you had to start there, and if he could help with that then the rest would follow.

Wally had been a little alarmed when he had arrived here in this place and amongst these men. They were surely emaciated but he could see the spirit which shone from their eyes was not yet dead and gone. So, Wally cooked and cared and cradled. The three C's as he saw it. And he would continue to do so until these men were healed inside and out, and he knew he would. He knew he must.

Wally turned on his side and pulled his blanket up, it was a cold night, and he was glad of the fire. It was a comfort as much as anything. He put his hand under his sugar bag pillow to feel his gun. He was not naive.

The next day Wally got back up into the bulldozer, a job he loved very much. He took pride in his work, and he knew in his heart that if he brought disrespect down on himself, then he brought it down on Dan and Mary. He brought disrespect down on every man woman and child who had loved him unreservedly. It would disgrace is home and family in the long hut.

Wally would do the best job he could at whatever he worked. For Wally loved all these people back just as unreservedly. And Wally found that a day spent doing his best was a very good day indeed and he was happy.

Tonight, he had a bit of a surprise for the men, he had scored steak from a man from one of the farms round about while working the bulldozer down near the road.

CHAPTER 3

Wally had worked at the mine for just over five weeks, and it was pay day this coming Friday. He had just finished work and was off to the laundry to do his washing. He shouldered Matilda and set off to get it done. He walked into the laundry and filled the trough with water and scraped a little soap into it. Wally washed his new shirts and hung them in a tree to dry. He also washed a pair of pants and a singlet. He'd get some new pants when he got to town and keep them for good ones. His pants he had he'd worked in, and they were covered in stains from the grease oil and diesel. He scrubbed at his clothes until his knuckles hurt.

These skills he had learned from the women of the long hut, his mothers, and his sisters. They were clean people who did not take kindly to dirtiness in their midst. And to Wally's horror they did not consider him at any stage, to be too big to get a slap or his ear pulled and in front of the other men. The men watching never laughed at him but looked embarrassed which was worse.

And as a penance you may get sent to do the job again, with 'and do it properly this time Wally' ringing in his ears. He owed them a lot and he knew it for at no stage did any one of them accept his bad arm as an excuse. If he was dirty or smelly, he didn't eat.

He had just finished doing the washing when he heard a commotion coming from the camp. Men's voices, loud and aggressive and argumentative. It wasn't like them to talk this way as he noticed a deal of bad language. Then he realised most of the aggression was coming from a voice he didn't recognise. There were other voices trying to calm the situation that he did recognise. He pulled the plug in the sink and let the water go.

Wally turned to go back to the shelter, he had to see what went on here. It was when he heard Eric's voice trying to reason with the stranger that Wally quickened his step. The stranger was abusing Eric and when Wally came into view, he saw that the man, a big bald man with his back to Wally, was standing over the smaller Eric.

As Wally walked up the men looked hopefully towards him, and he smiled to reassure them. Eric turned his head and looked at Wally and then the stranger did. Wally's blood ran cold, and he stopped dead, he knew that evil face. The last time he'd seen it was when they gave the man a beating for shooting Mary's dog.

He had changed some he'd gone bald, gained weight and his face spoke of all the drinking he did. But it was Rodney sneering at him, and Wally was strangely pleased to see him. His pulse quickened as he realised what an opportunity had just fallen in his lap. How he had hoped for this day.

An unpleasant sneer made its way across Rodney's hostile face. 'I thought it'd be you. I told myself it couldn't be that half-witted, pathetic bloody cripple that has taken my job but here you are.' Rodney took a step towards Wally. 'Are you scared Wally? You fuckin should be, I'm going to kill you stone dead and use that dozer to bury you. I haven't forgotten last time I saw you. Not so many of you today huh?' Rodney slid his eyes from side to side and hissed, 'nope. No Dan to save you today.'

Wally grinned and said softly 'you gunna talk all day you gas bag?'

Some of the men standing around stood now with mouths hanging open. They just hoped Wally would be alright.

Wally took a step forward, his fists clenched at his sides. 'You, big fat ugly bastard of a human being. You're nothing but a cowardly bloody bully and I aint scared of you. Not in this lifetime anyway. You might wanna take it steady though shit head, I'm not a frightened girl, or a poor old trusting horse. I'm gunna bury you with that bulldozer and I'm going to enjoy doing it. You are gunna be sorry you ran into me.' Wally finished on a growl that was a surprise to everyone.

Rodney was taken aback, and he put a foot behind him. For all his big talk Rodney was a bully and a coward. His eyes flicked down to Wally's crooked arm. He grinned maliciously into Wally's face. Every bloke there knew the mistake Rodney had just made regarding Wally's arm.

Rodney was sure he could take the cripple nice and easy; he only had one arm. He'd dreamed of this day, getting a go at this punk with no Dan to back him up. By Christ he had! They'd taken skin off his hide the pair of bastards.

The men watching on realised there was quite a history here and none of them liked the big bully, Rodney. They looked from one to the other, Rodney must have done a terrible thing to make Wally so mad. None of them had ever thought to see Wally so mad, Wally was all heart. And maybe that was part of it.

Rodney had Wally on size and aggression, and they suspected experience to. But they couldn't have been more wrong. But none of them knew that Wally had been with the second eighth battalion before Jack even. Wally was a commando.

Rodney looked mighty impressive as he went into his boxer's crouch and putting his fists up, did a little dance to and fro. Wally saw his chest heave and his step slow.

Wally laughed now and said 'well now you've just gone and buggered yourself. Save your strength old man and maybe I will take it easy on you. But first I will give the boss the final choice.' Wally turned to Eric who looked startled. 'Do I still have the job in the dozer Eric, or do you want this in it? I will abide by anything you say man.'

Eric gave his head a shake. 'You.' This was Eric's duty, and he knew it, but he was shitting himself all the same. Rodney was a frightening bloke and Eric worried along with the rest of them that Wally would get badly hurt.

Rodney was talking again now, 'Oh, you'll abide, will you? You fuckin little turd I'll give you something to abide.'

Rodney rushed at Wally hoping to knock him off his balance. If Rodney could just get his arms around him, he'd break his back. But a split second before he made contact with Wally he wasn't there, and Rodney stumbled forward and measured his length on the hard ground taking skin off his face. He was humiliated and the men were laughing at him. But Rodney wasn't finished, and he got to his feet. Hatred masked his face as he turned back to Wally. 'You got lucky you little fucker, but it won't happen again.'

Wally walked calmly up to him and as Rodney threw a punch at him Wally brushed it aside with his left arm. As he brought his right fist crashing into Rodneys face the men heard him say, 'this one's for Mary you mongrel. And this is for Jim, and this is for Lilly.'

The blood spurted from Rodneys face as Wally punched him again and again. It was Eric's voice that got through to Wally and he stopped swinging. Rodney fell, he was out to it and a cheer went up.

Wally looked desperately at Eric now, 'I've got to get to a phone.'

Eric had his arm around the big man 'why son?'

Wally looked at Rodney who was coming round, 'I need to warn Dan. This bastard is just as likely to seek revenge there. Dan can handle him, but he'll need to be on his guard.' Wallys voice went up a little, 'this mongrel was never supposed to come back.'

The men looked knowingly at each other, so there was a history here.

After they sent Rodney packing, Eric got Wally to a phone up at the office and he spoke to Dan. 'Hello Dan.'

Eric could hear the man on the other end as he said 'Wally! It's good to hear your voice little mate. Is anything wrong buddy?'

'Yes Dan, I'm afraid it is. I just ran into Rodney, you remember Dan?'

After a brief silence Dan's voice came back 'yeah mate. Are you alright?'

'Yeah, I'm okay Dan but I'm afraid I had to give him a bit of a hiding.'

Dan gave a hic of a laugh and went on now, 'well good for you. Is he gunna live Wally?'

'Yes, Dan unfortunately. Anyway, I just wanted to warn you to be on the lookout for him. Please Dan be careful. Watch everyone Dan, especially watch the kids, you remember what he did to Lilly. I got a bad feeling Dan; we haven't seen the last of him.'

'Alright mate you have my word. We'll go back on watch; we've done it before. And I have always trusted your gut feelings mate, you know that.'

'That's good enough Dan. I miss you all and I love you all. I'll be back before you know it Dan and we will watch the grass grow once again.' Eric and Dan both heard the falter in Wally's voice.

Dan's voice was soft as he replied. 'Alright buddy and will you promise me to keep an eye out for him? Do you want me to come up there and get him Wally?'

'No mate I'll just end up coming home with you if you do. And he's gone Dan he's run off.'

'Yeah, okay but you come home if you need to. I'll come and get you buddy. Anytime anywhere, know that, Wally. Just know it.'

'I know. I'm sorry Dan, I'm sorry. I . . . . I'm sorry I made you cry.'

'Don't be sorry little mate and don't be sad. Go on this wonderful journey that has been placed before you and enjoy it. We'll be here when you get home. We love you buddy, I love you. And remember, I'm here if you ever need me. Just call, okay?'

'Thanks. Goodbye for now Dan.'

Wally put the phone down and stood looking at it. Eric could feel the sadness in the man from where he stood. He walked over to him and took his arm. 'We must get back to camp Wally. That bastard could come back.'

Wally nodded at Eric and a tear slid down his face. Eric's heart ached for him, and as he walked him to the car he said 'we'll go into town come Saturday son and we'll get a little drunk hay? Maybe even find us a woman or two hay. Then we'll go home to one of mum's beaut teas. And you can post your letter home. Come on son.'

Wally let go a great sob and got in the car and shut the door. 'Before I forget Eric. Thanks for letting me use the office phone. Will you get in trouble for it?'

Eric shrugged and grinned 'probably not son.' The two men drove back to camp in silence then Eric said. 'Is he that bad Wally? Do you reckon he would hurt kids?'

Wally nodded and a tear slid down his cheek. 'Christ' breathed Eric.

The very next Saturday after the fight, the boys downed tools and went into town. Thanks to young Wally the blokes were cashed up. Wally's ability to feed everyone on very little had saved them from subbing their wages so much. And Wally's cooking they said, was Better than any fancy restaurant. Not that they'd ever eaten in a fancy restaurant Freddy pointed out one night.

The men all laughed, there was a tune to laughter that Wally could pick up. A very beautiful tune he thought, one that always brought joy to his heart. And Wally noticed that these men all laughed a lot now.

And these blokes were already showing signs of better health. Their cheeks had filled out and they had a bit of colour. They worked harder now and enjoyed it, and their arms were bulking up a bit. And Wally had encouraged these men to do some washing on their few hours off on a Sunday. He'd even shared his soap and showed them how best to hang it out to dry.

The other thing that they did was to swim in the river. Every Sunday after they'd washed their clothes they walked to the river and swam using a little soap to get clean. Then donning clean clothes, they sat down to fish. They talked as they fished, and some dozed off. There was an air of peace about them and a newfound trust in each other.

They were cleaned up now, ready to go to town. Wally smiled as he ran his eyes over them, even their hair shone. Most remarkable was the light shining bright from their eyes.

When Wally fronted up for his wage he was flabbergasted. He hadn't seen so much money at once, all in a little brown envelope for him. He started to wonder if the boss had made a mistake. When he counted it there was one hundred and forty-seven pounds and ten shillings.

So that Saturday Wally kept the forty pounds and banked the one hundred. He also put his pension cheques in the bank equalling fifty pounds. Wally smiled to himself; he was a rich man. He had over a hundred and fifty pounds in the bank. He had almost enough for a nice car.

Eric had told Wally that he had gotten paid for operating the dozer not shovelling and then there was overtime and the weekends they'd worked. So, Wally bought stores, enough for a month the men had given him money for this, and went to the pub. But before he did that, he went to post his letter.

The lady in the post office addressed it for him and put a stamp on it. She smiled as she handed it back to him and he slipped it in the post box. Wally thanked her for her kindness, and she smiled at him.

'Your family' she asked? She saw a lot of men come in and send money home in envelopes addressed by her, seven today already. These were still hard times indeed.

Wally nodded and thanked the lady again for her help. He left the post office and headed for the pub. The blokes were all there, some of them already showing signs of their drinking. They all wanted to buy Wally a drink, but Wally smiled and shook his head. Nevertheless, when Wally stood at the bar a drink appeared in front of him. Eric was standing at the bar where he'd sat when Wally had first met him.

The barman hailed Wally and asked how he was. 'Heard you was the new dozer operator out there now son, well done.' He put a drink in front of Wally and leaning over he said softly 'from the blokes, mate' and thumbed over his shoulder. He smiled at Wally and went to serve someone else.

It was a busy Saturday already. Miners, labourers, farm hands, shop workers, railway, and highway workers, mill workers and even the odd businessman and salesmen. All here in the bar, joined together by a common cause. To revel in a little drunkenness. To forget their woes and laugh at nothing in particular. Just for a little while.

Wally looked at Eric who beckoned him over. 'This is the man of the hour' Eric told everybody. 'Took on that bloody Rodney and ran him off. Gave him a bit of a hiding before he left to.' There was much laughter and back slapping, and Wally felt the weight of it. But he kept smiling.

Wally had a few beers and shouldering Matilda, went off to look at the mighty Murray River. He wasn't much of a drinker, and he sat under a tree and watched the animals going about their daily lives and began to regain his serenity. He was a little heavy today; his chest was aching for home. He bit back the tears and looked across the river.

'Why so sad?'

Wally looked about him, could that beautiful woman on the other side of the river be talking to him? He was alone on this side, so he lifted his hand and waved across at her. She was fishing. 'Getting any' he asked as casually as he could? For some reason his heart pounded, and his vision swam momentarily. Wally was shocked.

She grinned at him; 'some' she noted his swag. 'Are you a swaggy?'

'Something like that' replied Wally. Maybe she was just rude.

'And I thought they were all gone. Well good for you.'

Wally didn't answer, he felt awkward yelling back and forth across the wide river. He got up to leave. He'd just leave her in peace to her fishing he told himself.

'Wait on' she sang out as she got to her feet. She picked up her line and bait and came across the bridge. She smiled as she walked up to him, and Wally felt his heart beat a little faster. But Wally had started to feel awkward, and he was getting tongue tied as was his won't. He knew that any moment now words would fail him altogether, and she would walk away. If he had a quid for every woman who had turned and walked away from him while he stood there at a loss for words.

Wally was amazed when she held her hand out to him, 'my name's Melissa, what's yours?' He noticed she had dark brown hair and was quite tall. He looked into her brown eyes and smiled faintly.

Wally took her hand and shook it 'Wally' he said simply. He noticed she looked at his crooked arm and then she smiled up at him. 'You're that bloke who belted Rodney in the kisser a few times and sent him on his way aren't you? I heard about that already.'

Wally blushed scarlet and he put his head down. 'It was unav . . . . it was unavoidable.'

Melissa put her head back and laughed but Wally didn't shrink from it. He knew she meant no offense and he found himself laughing with her. She said now, 'I bet it was. He's a nasty piece of work that one. So, you work out at the mine?'

'Yes' Wally's conversation was drying up fast. He was down to one syllable words and one-word sentences already. He shifted Matilda higher on his back and looked at the river. 'How many did you get?'

'Just got my first.'

The young woman glanced at his kit; 'do you have a line with you? Oh, I'm sorry you've probably got way better things to do.' Melissa put her head down and looked awkward.

'None that I can think of' murmured Wally, 'and I do love fishing the river.' He opened Matilda to get his hand line.

Melissa sat beside him, and they spent a few leisurely hours fishing. At the end of the day, they had six good size fish. They didn't speak much but Wally enjoyed the afternoon and the company. And despite being in the company of the woman he was able to enjoy the peace and the feel of the river.

She fished to and seemed to like the quiet. Wally knew instinctively that she shared his love of the river.

It was almost sundown when Eric tapped Wally on the shoulder and asked if he wanted to come home for tea. Then he noticed Melissa and stood back. 'Of course, if you have better things to do I understand completely. But come and see mum tomorrow, will you?'

Wally stood up blushing, 'of course . . . . of course I will. What time you wanna head off back to the mine?' Wally knew he was too loud. He picked up two fish and handed them to Eric in some newspaper.

Eric smiled at him and then at the young woman. He knew Melissa and he couldn't have placed Wally in better company if he'd tried. Maybe he would fall for the woman and stay. But Eric would refrain from interfering.

'Around lunch time, after lunch Wally,' he said now 'that'll give us time to get out there and get ready for Monday. Anyway, enjoy your fishing, you to Melissa. How's your uncle?'

'Oh, he's in hospital again, his back.'

'That's no-good lass. If you need anything while he's away, you just go along and see Gladys, okay?' He smiled at them both 'well, be seeing you lad, bye Melissa.'

Eric walked away a smile on his face. It was under one such a tree on this very river that he'd had his first encounter with the fairer sex. How he had loved that woman, had fallen for her big time. But alas she had left him for another shortly afterwards.

Eric left the young couple under the big tree with branches that hung clear to the ground, it was like a room. A very big room in one of nature's finest palaces. Eric would go home and tell his mother about Wally and Melissa and maybe give her some hope. He knew how his mother felt about Wally, had seen the bond that had sprung up between the two of them.

Melissa said now, 'you wanna put the billy on Wally? We could cook some of these fish for our tea. Are you sleeping out tonight?'

'Yes, to all of that.' Wally went to get wood and Melissa watched him. Wally knew she was watching him, and it pleased him, she had a glint in her eye. He suddenly straightened and looking at her wide eyed he said 'Why?

'Why what?'

'OH nothing. Yes, I'm sleeping out tonight I do every night.'

'You are so lucky. I have my swag with me, and I am sleeping out tonight to. Do you wanna sleep with me?' Melissa laughed 'I didn't mean it like that. You know.'

'I know' said Wally trying to hide his alarm and appear nonchalant. 'But what if somebody sees us?'

'So what?'

Wally made a fire and put the billy on in a panic, they were a ways from the town here so . . . . His heartbeat faster and faster as he went about scaling the last two fish and filleting them. Thank God he had given Eric scaled and cleaned fish for his mother.

He daren't look at the beautiful girl who had just asked him to sleep out with her. Did he want to? Yes, he bloody wanted to, but he had no idea about any of this. This one hadn't walked away from him. She'd stayed and was watching him intently. His hand shook.

Wally put it aside as he made the tea, poured it, and handed her a cup. When he'd drank his tea, scalding himself in the process he put a pan on and fried the fish along with some potato from Matilda. It was beautiful there on the riverbank and as Wally ate, he began to relax, and his heart began to beat nice and steady. The river had calmed him right when he needed it most.

After they had cleared away Wally sat with his back to a tree. It was a strange night, but he guessed it would seem that way. He got up and stoked the fire and watched the sparks fly into the night sky. He smiled down at her and she got up.

Wally had to get busy quick, he got his swag and rolled it out. 'Do you want me to do yours?'

'No thanks I can do it.' When she threw her swag down, right next to his he was stricken. What should he do? What would Dan do? Oh, to hell with Dan, he knew what Dan would do. He looked at Melissa making her swag up, maybe he should just . . . . He shook his head.

'When you are finished arguing with yourself do you wanna come and sit beside me? I won't hurt you.'

'OH, shit woman.'

'Oh, come on Wally, it'll be lovely.'

Wally sat next to her, and Melissa scooted closer to him. Wally leaned out and grabbing his jacket he placed it over their knees it was getting cold. She started to talk. She talked about the town and how much she hated it and how much she hated her uncle. Wally jumped when she picked up his hand and held it.

But she just carried on talking like it was the most natural thing in the world. Wally relaxed a little. Then she got him to talk a little. He talked mainly about his journey, and he didn't really notice when his fingers had become entwined with hers. But he did know he liked it.

They sat in silence for a while and she said quietly, 'take me with you Wally. Please! Uncle won't care he hates me as much as I hate him. Why do you think I sleep out all the time? He's always drunk. I practically live under this tree Wally, not that I mind.'

'Oh, Jesus, woman I can't. I live in a camp and work at the mine. It's bloody dismal and . . . .

'I don't care. Would you think about it?'

Wally nodded.

When Wally got into his swag that night, he was positively aglow. Melissa, he thought had fallen asleep on her swag. He sat on his swag for a while and stared at her; she was lovely. He sighed. The way the fire light played around on her skin . . . .

'Do you want to kiss me, Wally?' He froze. 'Kiss me, Wally. Please. No one has ever loved me, Wally.' She looked at him now a sadness in her eyes, 'not that I can remember anyway.'

Wally edged stiffly towards her on his hands and knees though he told himself to stop. He was leaning over her wondering what to do when she wrapped her arms around his neck pulling him down on top of her.

As Wally's lips came down on hers, he felt something spring to life. Something that hadn't done any springing for a long time. He kissed her long and deep and she met his need. Melissa undid her blouse and Wally got the idea. The woman moaned softly in the soft perfumed breeze, and Wally had another idea.

Wally lifted her dress and placed himself inside her. He'd never felt anything like it. When she started to moan and thrust her hips to meet his he told himself again to stop. And again, he took not a jot of notice. And to his delight the woman underneath him came to a shuddering orgasm and he let his own orgasm wash over him.

Wally held the lovely Melissa to him almost all night and didn't sleep a wink. He had lost his heart to her, and he knew it. He'd make things right and he would find a way to be with her.

In the wee hours of the morning Melissa stirred and took him in her arms. He made love again to the lovely Melissa. The wind had got up and Wally had decided not to stoke the fire. And when at last he was sated, and his own fire burned low he fell asleep in her arms until daylight.

When Wally woke up it was to see Melissa had the fire going and had made him a coffee. She handed it to him, and he took her chin in his hand and kissed her. 'Thank you very much woman.' He took the coffee.

Wally pulled his shirt on and got out of the swag. He looked at Melissa who was studying him from the other side of the fire. 'Well,' she said?

'Well what woman?' Wally was nonplussed.

'Do you want to be with me?'

'Pretty sure the man is supposed to ask those questions.' Wally lifted his coffee cup to his lips.

'Oh, so because I am just a female I am expected to wait around until you make up your mind whether or not you will discard me. Well go and get fucked Wally.'

Wally scalded his mouth for a second time and stared at her in amazement. 'Well, women aren't supposed to use such language.' He cursed as the hot coffee dripped on to his shirt. He tried to flick the coffee off with his fingers, the damn shirt was clean on.

'It's alright for you to swear though.'

Wally scowled at her now, 'yes well men are allowed to use such language yes, but I shouldn't have done it in front of you. And yes, the man usually makes the decisions about the couple to, because men are able to look at things more objectively than . . . . '

Once again Wally's mouth hung opened in amazement as he ducked her coffee mug. He got covered in hot coffee as it sailed past and cursed afresh. Bloody Dan would likely get him killed with his so-called bloody good advice. Wally decided to scrap it and do his own thing.

Melissa got down on her knees and furiously started to roll up her swag. 'Just a minute woman' Wally said leaning over her to lift her to her feet. Instead, he tripped over her foot and fell on her.

Melissa swung round and punched him on the nose. 'Oh, you think that'll get you out of it do you? Well think again buddy. Bloody typical that is. You're in the shit so you think a Root'll fix it.'

Wally stared wide eyed; she had a bloody good right hook he thought now. He was aghast but he started to laugh. He laughed and laughed until the tears rolled down his cheeks and his face ached. He had never laughed like this before. Melissa was glaring at him, so he needed to explain. But all he could do was shake his head and laugh.

As she went to walk past him, he grabbed her foot and taking her hand he pulled her down into his arms. Holding her he stroked her hair and got his breath. 'Yes.'

'Yes what?'

'Yes, I want to be with you woman. But give me time to work it out, okay? Are you willing to come all the way to Queensland with me that's where I'm going. It's a bloody long way woman.'

'Oh Wally of course I am. I . . . . I love you, Wally.'

'Listen I gotta go back out to work but I'll get back in next weekend if I gotta walk. Be here on Saturday night hay? We'll get it sorted woman. Maybe I should get a car to take you there in, save you walking all the way to bloody Queensland.'

'No Wally I love walking and I want to see the rivers properly. Just like you do. You don't know how many times I've walked along this river and wished I could just keep going. Forever. Just go where the river takes me and never look back at this place.'

Wally gazed at her for a moment and pulled her close. He kissed her and as he got up off the ground to help her up, he knew. 'Shit' he said out loud. He had hold of her hand and was pulling her up onto her feet. He let it go in his shock and she fell back. 'What the hell Wally?'

Wally with a look of amazement and wonder on his face fell to his knees in front of her now, 'I love you to.'

When it was time to go Wally kissed Melissa with all his might. He held her tight and told her he'd see her next Saturday and that he'd try to get a ride in. As a tear slid down her face, he kissed it and wiped it away with his hand. 'Don't cry woman, we'll be together soon enough. By the time we get to the other side of New South Wales you'll be sick of the sight of me.'

'When are you going Wally?'

'Oh, in a couple of months or so. I want to go down the Murray here and back up the Murrumbidgee for a start.' He cupped her chin and lifted her face to look at him. 'You could probably start thinking about what you'll need. Just remember we have to carry it, okay? Now I gotta go; do you want me to walk you home?'

'No thanks Wally, it's in the opposite direction to Eric's house.' She kissed him again and told him she'd be waiting under the tree with her swag. She told him she would wait there until he came and that she'd wait forever if she had to. 'I'll be here.'

Wally smiled and kissed her softly. 'I will probably have to leave halfway through the night to walk all the way back to work. But you are worth it woman.' He kissed her tenderly again and smiled at her as he let her go. How he hated to go, but he'd need money now. He had responsibilities now. He told her this and was rewarded with a soft smile and a tender kiss. And this time he walked away.

Wally turned the corner into Eric's Street and heard her behind him and he turned to face her. Taking his arm she looked beseechingly up at him, 'I'm sorry Wally but isn't there anywhere out there that I could stay?'

'Let me look into it. Do you mean you'd camp with me?'

'Yes Wally, yes. Oh yes, I would.'

'In a tent?' Wally was astounded.

Melissa nodded and reached up and kissed him gently. 'All the way to Queensland darling from this day on.'

Wally promised to look into it and watched as she walked away from him. Only this time he watched with a smile on his face and a song in his heart. What a glorious feeling this was he told himself. At the corner of the street, she turned and blew him a kiss, how he loved her.

Smiling he set off to Erics house where Gladys answered the door. 'Oh, it's lovely to see you again dear. Eric is just getting a ground sheet for his swag; he's staying out there a lot more now. I am assuming because of your cooking; I have heard all about it. And thank you for the fish love, it will be tonight's tea. And I have one in the fridge for tomorrow night to thanks to you. You need a fridge out there to Wally. I keep telling him.'

Wally smiled and said, 'Thank you for the fruit cake it went down a treat. I'm sorry I didn't get to see you last night I got busy fishing. I have some nice ones to take out to camp. The meat safe is fine for this time of year.'

Eric came in with tarp, he handed one to Wally. 'Bit better than that old one of yours mate. Can't have you getting sick.'

Eric smiled at his mum. He had sat and relayed Wally's story as best he could to her over tea last night. He had included Dan and Mary and the long hut. The people they had saved and the extent of Mary's generosity. Her love and compassion and Dan's strength and determination. The love Wally spoke of, and the changes in the men out at the mine. And she had been moved to tears, the first tears Eric had seen her shed since she first got the news of her son's death.

Then Eric had told her of the difference he had brought about in the men out at the mine and how much more work they got done now. 'I'm thinking of getting Wally to do the cooking for them each night at full pay.'

He told her how they had cleaned themselves up and how much healthier they were now. And he told her yes, he would buy the damn fridge himself.

'And a freezer to Eric, it gets hot out there.'

Then Eric got around to telling her how he had handled Rodney. 'He sent him packing but I don't think we've seen the last of him mum. And that phone call Wally made to Dan was just chilling. Especially the fear in Wally for the kids. Who knew he was such a devil?'

And then he had told his mother of Wally's meeting Melissa. Gladys had smiled and replied, 'well, she's a lovely woman and I think we should have done something about that uncle of Her's years ago. I've always said it, but no one listens. I'm glad they found each other. And I sure as heck hope Wally gives the no-good blighter what for.'

'Yes, he's a good man mum. Maybe he can bring about a change there. I dunno how he does it.'

'He is a beautiful soul, Eric. We all lost so much these last years. The depression and the war and now the long road back. Well come on get off to bed Eric.'

'Goodnight mum.'

'Good night son.'

Gladys studied Wally now. Wally took the tarp from Eric and thanked him; with the new blanket he'd found in the shed he'd be nice and snug. Eric and Wally got in the Ute and headed off to pick up the blokes. They had slept the night at the back of the pub on a big lawn there.

'Did you and Melissa stay on the riverbank mate? She's a lovely young woman but her uncle is a brute.'

'What do you mean Eric?'

'He knocks her around and she doesn't deserve any of it. Didn't she tell you?'

'No but she's eager to get away from him.' Wally looked thoughtful and said, 'she asked me to bring her out here, but it's, like I told her I camp with the blokes.'

'Well, you don't have to camp with the blokes. The rivers only about a half mile away if you had a tent. I know how you love to get down there to fish, I mean the amount of time you spend there anyway lad.' Eric cleared his throat, 'you'd be welcome to use the water and laundry at the camp and to bring her to share meals. Up to you, mate, it's not a big walk to the river.' Eric smiled now, 'not for you'. He wanted Wally to have a woman, so he'd stay, but he didn't want to give up his cook.

'I'll have to give it some thought. She says she wants to come with me on my trip but it's a bloody long way to Queensland. I told her this, but she insists she wants to do it and on foot. But I don't know.'

Wally opened his window he needed some air. He missed the woman already and he was guessing she missed him to. It was a glorious thing. And the more he thought about it, the river wasn't a long walk from the camp. And Melissa would need the practice if she was coming with him.

Eric was talking now. 'Well in that case living together would be a good idea. See if you get on alright. Anyway, either way son it sounds like things got really serious really quick. I thought they would, you two are a good match. In fact, I think you are made for each other.' Eric smiled at Wally, unless he was very much mistaken the man was smitten.

The blokes were waiting on the foot path looking the worse for wear. They had all put in before he went to town for Wally to buy stores, he would buy the food for a month. Wally had protested that it was too much, but they told him they knew that. And smiling and nodding Freddy told him that he deserved something for all the work he did for them. Then he'd got rude and told him to shut his trap and take it. Wally had laughed.

Wally looked at them as they got in and was surprised to see some new clothes here and there. A couple of the blokes Freddy included, had new second hand coats. So, they all had good coats now and Wally was pleased, coats were warm at night over your blanket if you could keep it dry throughout the day. He was pleased that all the money he knew he'd been saving them wasn't all going down the back of the men's urinal at the back of the pub. Wally thought he'd seen men ducking out of the pub 'to send a letter home' they said. Wally noted how pleased they looked; they'd sent money home alright he thought.

Wally found that he was even happy for their families. It was a good feeling all round he smiled to himself. He went about throwing swags in the back, helping the older fellows. Most of the blokes hadn't come into town, they sort of took it in turns.

Eric noticed it to and smiled. He also noted the boxes of groceries and hoped that Wally intended to cook it. Eric knew also that he'd have to put at least an hour on Wally's timesheet every day to cover all his work and let him go an hour earlier. Eric had never got so much work out of these men.

Wally had shaken his head when Eric suggested it on the way home. 'I don't need paying for it' he said.

'No, maybe not but I do need to pay you.' When Wally opened his mouth to speak, Eric put in 'men might have died this winter, Wally. Let us thank you for it.' Eric smiled across the car at him, 'I got eyes mate.'

They were at the turn off and Eric turned up the track which needed a bulldozer over it. He said softly 'I have seen the changes you've made, and I can tell you I am grateful. And so incidentally, is that lot up in the back. They've got warm good clothes and strong backs now, and they have laughter in good measure mate. No you take it son you've well and truly earned it.' Eric braced himself for the corrugation, 'and I'll get you to go over this bloody awful road to Wally.'

Wally smiled 'okay then Eric and thanks. I've got a few new responsibilities now Eric.'

'You have that son, you have that.' Eric smiled at Wally, 'and doesn't it suit you young Wally.'

CHAPTER 4

It had got around that Wally had a new girlfriend and the blokes wanted to know all about her. Wally had made a large pot out of a four-gallon water drum which he was using now to deep fry some battered fish. He patiently answered their questions. He looked around the group, he was pretty sure their numbers had swollen.

Wally had had a conversation with Eric who had assured him that Melissa was over twenty-one. 'She's twenty-four I think' he'd said.

Wally didn't know what to do for the best. He had a couple of options as he saw it. He could get a motor bike or car or maybe even a horse to get into town to see her or he could buy a tent. Even if he got a tent, he'd need to get a car of some sort. Then he'd have to teach her to drive it. But Wally knew he had to have a conversation with the woman concerning her uncle.

He was talking to the blokes about this now. Freddy asked, 'what does the young lady want?'

'Well, she wants to be out here with me, but I'd have to leave her all day on her own. And then if she got sick or hurt, I have no way of getting her to hospital or the doctor. I will have to think on it.'

'Lad, I go into town most weekends. I can give you a lift.' Eric was getting hungry. 'And I'd take her to hospital if she was sick of course I would.'

'Yes', said Wally looking around the group obviously distracted. He saw new faces. 'How many for tea gentlemen' he asked smiling? He looked at the dwindling pile of fish and hoped he'd make it.

Eric answered. 'Yeah, there are a few more tonight. So, some of these blokes haven't paid their dues.' It had been decided the week before that the blokes would all put in ten pound each for their month's food. Eric went on 'they will.' He looked about 'I know you new blokes have all bought your groceries lads, but we all need to put in. Otherwise, it doesn't work.'

One of the blokes asked if he could hand over his food and it was decided he could do it that way for now if he wanted. The others did to.

They numbered sixteen in all but tonight they were twenty. 'Okay' said Wally, 'we need some new plates and spoons.'

Wally left a tucker box on the table that doubled as a bench under the tree about a foot from the shelter. In it he had bread and filling of some sort of meat or cheese or leftovers and even some jam for their lunches. They took a sandwich for lunch now a real luxury. And they also had cereal milk and sugar for breakfast. These men were eating three meals a day now.

The fish and chips were a hit with the guys. Wally left them to do the dishes and went to his bed. He had a lot to think about, it was a long way to Queensland. He knew he loved the woman but to take her so far from her home. Well, he didn't want to get halfway there and have to turn around and bring her back because they didn't get on or because she was homesick or footsore. So, living together in the meantime would seem to make sense. Wally smiled to himself, he wanted her with him, and he'd move heaven and earth to make it happen.

When Wally saw Melissa at the weekend he would try and suggest that they leave it another two weeks and then maybe live together. Wally also wanted to see if she would be okay living in a small tent. All the way to North Queensland, it could take a year or more. He smiled here into the darkness as he thought how she did really seem to love him.

Eric had posted a few men around the mine to patrol the perimeters in case Rodney came by. It was another thing that Wally worried about, he knew the disregard Rodney had for women and Melissa would be alone all day. But Wally had started to dream. He dreamed of a good life with Melissa, and he couldn't let anything happen to her.

Wally hadn't had a woman since he first went off to the army. He had always thought it was because he loved Mary but now, he knew that wasn't so. He had always feared rejection, had always expected it. He was a cripple in most folk's eyes.

But Melissa hadn't rejected him in fact she had relished him. He had made love to her, and he had pleased her. He started to wonder if he should marry her before they left or maybe get engaged.

Wally opened his eyes; it was still dark. He looked about; something didn't feel right. He heard a noise and looked off to his left. A shadowy figure was bending over Freddy. 'What's going on' he demanded loudly? The scream which ended abruptly, almost stopped Wally's heart and he leapt out of his bed.

'Freddy' he roared and seeing Eric getting up he ran off after the man who was beating a hasty retreat. Wally thought he knew who it was, but he suspected a robbery was in progress. He was dead wrong about that.

A few hundred feet from the camp Wally caught his man. It was Rodney and Wally knocked him clean out. Dragging him back to camp he noticed Eric wrestling with Freddy. A tall, older man called Colin had lit the lamp and the men milled around Freddy, some had their hands to their mouths.

Wally looked at Freddy and sucked air loudly into his lungs. Freddy's eyes bulged and shone with terror. There was a dagger like knife protruding from Freddy's neck. Wally knew what went on and ran forward and grabbed Freddy's hands. 'Don't pull it out Freddy for Christs sake' he yelled at the frightened man.

'Has to . . . . ' was all Freddy could manage.

Wally put his mouth closer to the very frightened Freddy. 'We'll have to take you into the hospital and let a doctor take that out of there very carefully. Can't be more than a quarter inch from your jugular mate. And if we try, we might cut the inside of your throat and you could choke. No mate no. Please don't touch it.'

'O . . . . okay bud . . . . '

'Good man Freddy. Now lay still for us hay.'

He bandaged Freddy's throat wrapping the bandage around the knife as he did so. Eric leaned over Wally now 'reckon we should put him in the back and you in there with him mate?'

Wally nodded. 'Those bloody corrugations will cause a lot of problems Eric. Could make it a lot bloody worse than . . . . '

'You leave that to me mate we'll take the bush track along the river, goes all the way into town, smooth as a baby's bum. Now what about that bastard. We have to hand him over to the cops.'

'Yeah, I'll get him trussed up like a turkey. You go get the Ute and bring it up.'

'I'll come with you into town in case he gives you any trouble,' said Colin.

Eric nodded grateful. 'Thanks mate.'

'Me to' put in a large youth named Brian and a couple of the others.

And so, they set off to get Freddy to a hospital. The river road was slower but there were no corrugations which probably would have killed Freddy. Wally sat in the back of the Ute with Freddy while Eric raised the alarm. Then the police were called. The river road had been a good idea and the doctor said so later. It seemed to cut miles off the trip. The highway was quicker if you had a vehicle.

A doctor came to look at Freddy nodded at Wally and went off to get a stretcher and a nurse. Wally had crouched over Freddy all the way into town and the old man had clung to him. So Wally was dropped at the hospital with him to be there if he was needed. Though he wanted to be there when they handed that blasted Rodney over to the police.

As he was leaving the back of the Ute he leaned over the now conscious Rodney, 'this one's for Mary and what you did to her you bastard.' He smiled maliciously as the spit Rodney had aimed at out him missed and fell back on himself.

'That's karma' he said now. 'I don't suppose you know much about karma yet, but you will. Some folks might just call it justice.'

Then the police had arrived, and Wally got his wish. He'd stay and watch them handcuff this bastard, for Mary.

Freddy was on a stretcher and on his way to the operating room. A surgeon would take the knife out and they said they thought they had a good chance of a successful outcome. Wally knew the old man only needed a fighting chance.

Eric told Wally to stay in town and look after Freddy for a few days. 'We can do without the dozer for a while mate. And go see that girl of yours and sort that out and I'll be back Thursday. Have you got the money for a tent; I mean a good one?'

'Yeah, I do thanks mate. Now that Rodneys going to jail I guess we can go ahead with plan A.' Wally looked across to where the police were putting Rodney into a car.

The sergeant came over to them. 'I'll need to get statements from you lot. But we'll come out to the mine and do that. Would next Monday see everybody there?'

Eric nodded, 'we'll be there.'

'Will he be staying in jail' asked Wally?

'Yes, these are serious charges and we wanted him for a couple of other incidents he's been involved in. He's a bad character this one and we are pleased to get our hands on him. It'll be a while before this bastard sees daylight again.'

Eric and the others left for the mine; they had work in a couple of hours. Wally sat in the hospital waiting room. He hoped Freddy would be alright he had taken a liking to the old man. He reminded Wally a lot of Ben, Ben had always been good to him.

The doctors took a couple of hours to extract the knife from Freddy's neck. 'Good job that young fellow did what he did mate, it probably saved your life. It was tricky alright. You had a fraction of an inch, and had you touched the jugular with the knife you would have bled out before you got here. And you'd have most likely choked anyway.'

The doctors told Wally that Freddy could probably go home at the weekend depending on how he healed. 'He's lucky you were there and were able to stop him from yanking on that knife. As it turns out his wounds are fairly minor though quite deep and should heal up soon.'

Wally saw Freddy briefly later that day who tried to thank him. Wally told him not to talk too much. He went on to say 'I've been delegated to mind you, Freddy, to babysit you. The other blokes went out to the mine to work. The police have locked Rodney up and they will need statements. Apparently, they wanted him on other charges to. But what I can't bloody work out is, why you? Why did that bastard want to kill you?'

Fredy shook his head and pointed at Wally. He mouthed the words 'he wanted to kill you.'

Wally looked puzzled and gave his head a shake. Freddy took his arm and whispered, 'your spot.'

Wally sucked in air as the truth dawned on him. 'Yes Freddy, I slept there on those really cold nights so you could be near the fire, I remember. He must have been watching the camp, so he did want me. I'm sorry Freddy.'

Freddy shook his head very gingerly and mouthing the words thank you he passed out.

Wally went off to find Melissa, Eric had told him where she lived. On his way to her house, he met her in the street. He was glad to see her, he'd been lost for a while. God, he hated towns hated being lost. He never got lost out in the country. The sooner he got back out on the road the better he told himself for the umpteenth time. He did love the river roads; you always knew where you were.

Wally told Melissa what had happened to Freddy now as he lay in her arms, she held him to her and rubbed his back. It was beautiful thought Wally and some of his fears dissipated. He had cooked tea for them and then they had made love. Now he lay at peace with her. That was until he thought about Melissa's uncle.

As if picking up on his thoughts Melissa spoke. 'Have you thought anymore about me Wally? I want to get out of home.'

Wally got up on one elbow and looked down at her, beautiful in the fire light. 'Why Mel? What does he do to you?'

'Well, he . . . . he. Never mind all that now . . . . '

'No Mel I want to know, what does he do to you?'

'He is cruel Wally. He beats me with whatever he can reach. Mostly he uses his belt.'

'Has he ever touched you, Mel? Has he ever molested you?'

Melissa went to get up, she knew he would read the truth in her eyes. Wally got up now 'lead me back to where you live Mel? Where is he now?'

Melissa told him and said that he would be drunk by now. Wally pulled her to her feet and told her to take him there.

They walked the streets in silence, Wally trying to calm himself, held Melissa's hand. They turned into the house and Melissa got a key from under a pot. She opened the door and Wally pulled her out of the way and entered first. He'd heard a noise inside the door.

Melissa's uncle Gus sprang out from behind the door to land a blow, but his fist fell short when he saw Wally. He stared belligerently at Wally and demanded to know what he was doing there. Then he spotted Melissa, 'there you are you little slut. Where have you... '

He stopped talking, Wally had him by the throat. 'She's been with me, have you any objections? Blink once for no or twice for yes.' Wally turned to Melissa now, 'go and get your things Mel. You can't stay here with this.'

Wally let go of Melissa's uncle and he started. 'Now see here . . . you can't just come in here and take her. She's mine.'

The blow Wally landed on him sent him sprawling the length of the passageway. As he sat there spitting out teeth and blood Melissa went to her room.

'Don't take your eyes off him Wally, he's sly. He'll get you from behind he has knives and guns.' She told Wally as she left.

Wally noticed how afraid she was and said softly 'I'll watch him baby. Go...'

'Oh Wally, what is to become of me?'

'You'll be alright love, you'll be with me, now go get your things.'

When she was gone Wally looked down at the man cowering at his feet. He took his belt off and by the time he was finished he was panting, and Melissa's uncle was all screamed out. 'Who are you' he sobbed?

'You will never see her again. Not while I'm alive.' Wally had a sudden thought, one of those thoughts that were more like an epiphany. His eyes narrowed, 'who owns this house?'

The man on the floor stared defiantly up at him. He remained tight lipped.

'I said who owns this house?'

'None of your damned business.'

Melissa came out as he finished, and she answered him. 'It belonged to my parents, but they left it to him.'

'Have you seen the will?' He flicked his eyes up at Melissa as he waited for an answer. The fear on her face was breaking his heart.

'No. I was ten when they died Wally.'

Wally aimed a kick at Melissa's uncle Gus's midriff that doubled him up. 'You go and get it.'

Gus got his breath back, 'I don't have it any . . . . ' It took a while longer to get his breath after the next kick.

Wally grinned down at him, 'I can keep this up all night man, can you?'

There was a silence and Wally kicked him again. 'I don't mind how long it takes you to talk you bastard, you deserve a good kicking.'

'It's in my bedroom.'

'Fine' said Wally grabbing him by the scruff of the neck and hauling him up, he dragged him to the room Melissa hadn't gone into. He threw the man on the floor and told him to get it.

'Get what?'

This time Wally kicked him in the leg. The steel capped boots were leaving bruises, but Wally didn't care. Gus stayed quiet, cowering on the floor. 'Get it' Wally yelled and kicked him again.

'I'll go to the police.'

'So will I' Wally snarled now.

After two more kicks Gus went to get the papers from his desk. His hands shook so much that Wally had to open the draw. He pulled on it, but it was locked. 'I don't know where the key is . . . . '

'That's fine' said Wally and kicked the desk and stomped on it until it lay in pieces on the floor, and there were papers everywhere. 'Which one.'

Gus leaned over and pointed to some papers clipped together. Wally pounced on them, opening them up.

Wally looked at them for some time, he wasn't good at reading, but he knew what he was looking at. A sneer passed over his handsome features and he kicked Gus once again before he turned to look at the frightened woman. There was a deep sadness in his voice now as he spoke to her. 'The house is yours Mel.' He kicked the cowering man again and waited for him to stop screaming, 'it has been since you were eighteen.'

Wally looked at the man on the floor and bellowed, 'get your things.'

'Why?'

'Because you are leaving. You are leaving this house, and you are leaving this town, and you will never return. I think I have made myself clear.'

'No, I haven't got anywhere to go.'

'Neither did she and yet you set about abusing her, a child. Now we have two choices here. You can leave and never return, or we will go to the police. You'll go to jail for the rest of your life you miserable bastard.' He turned to Melissa. 'What do you want dear? Does he go or do we charge him?'

Melissa looked at Wally, no one had ever stood up for her before. No one, even though they knew what went on. 'I don't want to stay here. I hate this town and everybody in it.'

'Alright my love but he's not staying here either. If you want, you can put this house up for sale. Get rid of it.' He bent over Gus 'and if you ever return here, I will kick you to death. Now get your things and get going.' He leaned down and said softly, 'if she charges you, you will die in jail.'

'I'll need to come back with a truck . . . . ' Gus, who had just made it to his feet, found himself sprawling in the passageway for the second time. He was dazed and he knew he couldn't keep taking this kind of punishment.

'You won't need a truck.' Wally turned to Mel and winked at her, 'I'll stay here and hold him, and you go and get the police. I have a feeling this bastard could be known to them. Go on now my love.'

'I have been assaulted here' Gus whined from the floor. He told himself now to keep his mouth shut and try to get out of this alive.

'Fine I'll go to jail for a few nights, and you will go to jail for quite a lot of years. How well do they know you down at the station hay?' Wally lifted his eyes to Melissa 'we really should charge him love. He's a predator and he's not gunna stop.'

'Are you gunna let him do this to me? Your own flesh and . . . . ' Gus had made it to his feet again, 'I'll go!' He lifted his hands to cover his face which was dripping blood.

Wally pointed to a suitcase. 'Get!'

'I need to get suitcases from the shed if you're not gunna let me back. And I have a tea chest to that . . . .

'Alright, get your damn suitcases but forget the bloody tea chest.' Gus stared defiantly back at him, and Wally started taking his belt off.

'Alright, alright' Gus got his things and left the house.

Wally grabbed his arm as he was leaving 'return here and I will kill you, make no mistake about that. Now give us your keys.' Wally snatched a bunch of keys, from his hand.

'I'll need the car keys' Gus told Wally keeping his eyes down.

'Is it your car?' Wally could tell by the look on the man's face that it was not. 'It belongs to Melissa doesn't it, you mongrel?'

So, Gus left the house on foot. Wally waited a few minutes before he spoke again.

'Are there any more keys to this place Mel?'

She shook her head 'I don't think so Wally anyway you can lock most of them from inside. So, we just used the front door key.' Melissa looked at him now, 'we can still sleep down on the river though, can't we? Please?'

'If that's where you'll feel safe. Do you have any money love?'

Melissa shook her head on her way to the door. Melissa led Wally to the front street and to a telephone box. He dialled and told the operator the number. The phone was picked up and Mary said 'hello'.

'Hello Mary. How are you?'

'OH, Wally how lovely. Are you alright love? Dan told me about Rodney, we haven't seen him at all.'

'No Mary you won't. To cut a long story short he tried to kill me and failed. He is in jail Mary. I wanted you to know. The mongrel is in jail at long last. He will harm nobody ever again.'

There was a silence on the phone and Mary sobbed 'thank you Wally. You are my hero. Thank you. Here is Dan. Please take care Wally and write soon hay. Goodbye love.'

Dan was astounded at the story Wally told him. 'Are you alright Wally?'

'Yes, Dan I am better than alright. I have met someone Dan.' Wally put his arm around Melissa and pulled her close to listen.

After the longest silence Dan said quietly 'you mean you . . . . you . . . . a woman?'

'Yes, old man a very beautiful woman and I love her very much.' Wally paused a moment and went on, 'Dan, Rodney was wanted on other charges and together with the attempted murder charge he will go away for a very long time. I just wanted you to know. Justice is served at long last.'

When Dan said goodbye to Wally he said 'and you love this lady, Wally? I cannot believe it. I am happy for you lad. I hope we will get to meet her someday.'

'You will Dan. There's something about someone loving you Dan. I am the happiest man in the universe. She is coming on my journey with me to. But I will go into that another day, it's been a long one mate and we're just gunna head off to bed now, down at the river.'

'Well good night lad. And again, I couldn't be happier. And I will sleep better now knowing that someone has your back out there. Someone loves you son. Someone loves you.' Dan sobbed and Wally smiled, he knew why Dan was so emotional.

Wally took Melissa to the tree down by the river and laid out their swags. He had taken her for a hamburger which they'd eaten for their tea. They liked them so much they'd got another one each to eat on the way to their camp.

Wally watched now as the police car pulled up just above them on the bank. The sergeant got out and walked down to them. 'Good evening' he said politely.

Wally knew instinctively this wasn't about Rodney and he got to his feet. 'G'day officer, what can I do for you?'

'I have just come from the station. We have in our custody a very bruised and battered Gus Thomson.' He raised his eyebrows, a not unkind expression on his face. He kept his eyes on Wally, he'd seen the boots he wore. He managed to keep the smile from his face.

'Yeah' said Wally nodding. He looked down at Melissa and it hurt him to see how frightened she was. She stood beside him now and Wally knew instinctively that her fear was for him. He put his arm around her.

The sergeant was speaking again, he said softly, 'can we possibly come up with a reason to keep him there?' He slanted his eyes at Melissa. She nodded and Wally held her tight.

The sergeant whose name was Ike smiled and said 'very well. Can we get started on a statement I don't want to let him go. He is, what shall we say, known to us and with your statement we'll get him to cough for some of these other charges and get him behind bars. I cannot say as to whether or not we will need you in court at this stage but is it something you could see your way clear to do?'

Melissa looked up at Wally and he nodded and smiled. 'Do you need time to think about this Mel? If he gets out, he could do this to someone else, likely will. These people get worse baby, not better.' Wally turned to the sergeant now and shrugging he said 'we were about to have this conversation when you pulled up. Mel?'

Melissa nodded and said 'we might as well get it done Wally. It's just that it's embarrassing.'

The policeman smiled kindly 'we'll get it done as quickly, and as painlessly as we possibly can. As long as we've got something on paper to throw at him.' He opened the back door for them to get in.

Their night wasn't over yet thought Wally tiredly as they got into the police car. He hoped this wouldn't be too hard on Melissa, he put his arm around her. In the back of the police car Melissa put her head on Wally's shoulder. She looked up at him and smiled sadly and gave her head a shake, 'thank God for you Wally.'

Wally kissed her gently 'I'm here baby. Now and forever I'm here. You will never be alone again.'

The policeman in the front heard it and he decided he liked the young man. And it was high time somebody kicked the shit out of that little prick back at the cells.

'Come on woman, let's get started then. If you still want to come out to the mine to live with me, we'll need a tent. Are you sure you don't want to stay in your lovely little house now?' It was morning and they'd eaten a small breakfast. 'That bastard's not coming back for some time.'

Melissa shook her head 'I want to be with you.'

'But out there, you'll be on your own all day long. There is a nice little place down by the river where we could make camp. But the river is almost half a mile from the mine. Now I also cook at the camp so you will have to come up there for meals. The blokes have all said they are okay with that.' Wally paused and went on, 'now that you have a car we can cut down on that walk. For the sake of time.'

'I can't drive Wally.'

'Well, I can. Now is this what you want? I only have until tomorrow night then I'm back out there for work. And we have to go and see Freddy.'

The two unlikely people went shopping. They picked the car up and took it with them and got a tent and a double bed blanket. Wally insisted that they get suitable clothing for Melissa and had to go to the men's wear shop to get her trousers and shoes for walking long distances.

Melissa got jeans that she could make into short pants that came down just past her knees, and she got men's singlets for the Queensland weather. She also got good socks and tennis shoes for walking to and from the river if she had to.

Wally got the tent the swag and a couple of back packs from the army disposals shop. He also bought another waterbag.

He went to the supermarket and got supplies for her for while he was at work. She would need breakfasts and lunches. Wally told Melissa he would teach her to drive also in case she needed to. This way, he'd said she could drop him to work and have the car all day.

The car was a light blue, FJ Holden Ute and Wally loved it and Melissa suspected they would be keeping it. The next day they loaded the Ute with their purchases and headed for home on the banks of the great Murray River.

When Wally got the camp set up on the riverbank, complete with fold up chairs and fishing lines Melissa jumped into his arms. 'It's beautiful Wally, my first home. My first real home. How I love you Wally and thank you for standing up for me.'

'Just doing my job woman' he said pulling her closer. Wally had dared to dream, and this was it. And Dan was happy for him, and Wally was happy for Dan.

Happy that he was no longer a source of guilt and misery for the man he loved above all others.

Melissa looked thoughtful; something was worrying her. 'Out with-it woman, a problem shared is a problem halved.'

Melissa avoided his gaze, 'it's just that I see how much you love that car. So, is it in Gus's name or mine? Why would he put it in my name Wally?'

'Well, he did. And he did that because he had to trade your car in on it, I'm supposing. It'll come in handy for now Mel and later we'll consider our options.'

'Okay Wally, as long as it's yours.'

Wally was touched, he lifted Melissa into his arms and kissed her. 'You wanna try her out baby' he asked nodding towards the tent?

'Oh yes Wally. I can't wait until bedtime. Do you want me to take my jeans off or will you do it.'

'No that's my job woman. I know me duty.' Later as he lay in her arms, he said softly 'our first home baby' and gave vent to a sob. She held him and sobbed with him. Then they fell asleep exhausted.

Tomorrow was another day, a very big day. It was the first day of the rest of their lives together. They slept easy, all night long like babies do, and the moon shone down on their tent.

Wally had to start early so he rose before the sun. After a coffee he took Mel for her first driving lesson. After she had been through the gears a couple of times, he told her he probably should do the driving for a couple of days. She smiled and kissed him passionately as he was leaving.

He sat in the driver's seat his arm resting on the door window. 'I'll come and get you as soon as I knock off and you can come up while

I cook tea hay? We'll have some tea and come back here. Be careful at least while I have the car and you are here by yourself. And if you are frightened by someone produce that bloody gun. They'll soon clear off.' He looked thoughtfully down towards the river 'and be careful walking about in the tall grass, there could be snakes.'

'Yes, Wally I'll be fine for Christs sake, I've been looking after myself for a long time. Off you go and you take care on that awful bloody monstrosity you drive. Jesus Wally.'

'You cuss like a . . . . a navvy woman.' Wally had trouble finishing the little saying Dan used on Mary when she let fly. He smiled at Melissa, 'the comics and your book are in your backpack. I love you.' He looked seriously at her now 'and when we get home, we'll work on these gears okay?'

'I didn't do too good did I wally?'

'I wouldn't say that baby. You did extremely bad.'

Wally sped off as Melissa tried to punch his arm. He looked in the rear-view mirror as he waved back to her, and she was standing watching him go. He had something a bit special for the tea tonight, he'd scored a large piece of roasting beef, and he had a small sack of potatoes from two weeks ago that he had to use.

He got to the shelter in time for a coffee with the blokes. Everybody stood around while somebody asked him if he was finished setting up camp. Wally nodded good naturedly and waited for it.

'You mean making a nest don't you' laughed one of the youngsters. His name was Mike, and he would have been about fourteen. The youngest of them Wally thought. He lived with his mother and provided for her.

He smiled kindly at the young man now and said 'That's what he means Mike. And yes, we are all set up. I hate her being down there by herself though.'

'Can't wait to meet her' a bloke called Geoff put in.

'I know her' said Mike, 'she's friends with my sister.' He looked wide eyed at Geoff now, 'she's a bit of a looker mate. For an.......' Mike stopped abruptly his eyes widening and his face reddening.

'For a what' asked Wally thumping Mike on the back? Mikes face was scarlet, and the blokes all gathered round 'go on Mickey for a what?'

'You know . . . . somebody a bit older like . . . . '

'Are you calling my beautiful young lady a senior citizen there, Mike?' Wally laughed loudly and the blokes laughed with him.

Mike coughed and his face went an even deeper red. Wally hugged the kid to him and smiled 'I suppose we seem a bit elderly to your generation mate but don't ever say that to her face. Here's a bit of advice from an old fulla to a young pup. If you ever feel safe enough to talk to a lady about her age refer to it as mature.' The men all laughed and walked off to work.

As Wally walked beside Eric to work the older man said quietly. 'I heard that somebody beat the living daylights out of Melissa's uncle Gus. Said he was bruised up all over and had some hide taken off with a belt. Sure, would like to buy that bastard a beer Wally. You coming into town this week mate?'

The two men laughed, and Wally said, 'yeah I got a bit of a thirst worked up mate.' Wally went off to get on the dozer. Eric walked off shaking his head, he was glad Melissa had Wally now. And vice versa.

Wally was nervous he hoped Mel would get on alright with these blokes at least for a time. It had become important to Wally to have some money for the trip. He hoped to have a tidy nest egg in case they needed it. But he was torn, he wanted to take the car and have somewhere a bit safe for Mel, yet he had looked forward to walking it. He'd wanted to take the steamers along the way to and maybe work on them.

Wally would need to think very seriously about it. He took his responsibilities very seriously. He had an idea forming in his head that if they stayed put for six months and got a good bit of money behind them, they could take the car and ride the rivers or walk them at their leisure anyway. Wally had started to dream about how he could make the Ute into a home on wheels.

Wally climbed up in the dozer he loved this job anyway, for now. He hoped Melissa would be alright by herself. He was pretty sure she would be she'd camped on the river for most of her life. At least now, he told himself, she could go home without fear.

It all but broke Wally's heart when he had sat by her side as she made her statement at the police station. The policeman had coughed and sniffed a couple of times. Wally knew one thing for sure if Gus got out of jail, he'd have to teach him to swim. Wally would let the river take care of the piece of human garbage. The fish would get a feed off him.

Then just when he thought things couldn't get any worse the police man indicated to Melissa that he would need to photograph her back. Wally realised he'd never actually seen it and his face burned. And when he did, he was horror stricken, the scarring was awful. 'Oh Mel' he choked and held her in his arms. The policeman sat back in his chair white in the face. He sat swallowing for a few seconds before he went on.

Wally could also see why Melissa wanted out of the town. Somebody should have gone to her aid, but no one had. Wally shook his head and tried to put it out of his mind, he had work to do.

When Dan had said goodbye to Wally and hung up the phone he turned to Mary. 'Well, it is done Mary, the boy has achieved what I could not.' Dan sat heavily in a chair picking up his coffee cup. 'The bastard is in jail where he should be.'

Mary sat next to the man who had stolen her heart the very first time she'd seen him. The man who had always made her feel loved and happy and she picked up his hand and held it to her. When he lifted his eyes to hers, she spoke gently. 'It is all my fault Dan. You didn't make a fuss because you didn't want to embarrass me farther and I love you for that. And he never came back here Dan, nor would he have. I have felt safe all these years Dan, thanks to you.'

'Oh Mary, there isn't a day goes by that I don't think of our little girl down there on the riverbank with your parents. How I loved her Mary.' Dan lowered his head and gave a cough, 'I go there sometimes with flowers, and I sit with her for a while.'

'I know Dan, I see the flowers when I go there.' Mary lifted her hand and wiped the tears from his eyes.

Dan leaned forward and taking her in his arms he kissed her gently. After that long and lingering kiss with no thought for the people around them he lifted his head and spoke in a whisper, 'do you still love me woman?'

'Oh yes Dan, still crazy about you.'

Dan stood up and taking her hand he led her to the door, 'come my love, I need to hold you.'

CHAPTER 5

Life went along smoothly for Wally for some time and he and Melissa found a joy in one another they hadn't thought was possible. Not for them. Rodney and Uncle Gus in the same bloody jail. Perfect thought Wally almost daily as he gave thanks for the new day.

He and Melissa got the house sorted out and up for sale. All the blokes loved Melissa and welcomed her amongst them. They thought she was beautiful even though she dressed a little strange. His Mel had taken a liking to jeans and shirts.

Freddy had stayed an extra week at the hospital, he'd gotten pneumonia. When he got home, he was delighted to have somebody to sit and talk to him. Eric had decided to let Freddy go home early with Wally to help him with the tea. Freddy had met Melissa at the hospital when she had come with Wally to see him. She had brought him sweets and some fruit.

Wally had nourished and nurtured these men to the point they were all fit and healthy and they looked it. They laughed a lot and had money which they sent mostly to loved ones at home. Most of these men had cut back severely on their drinking to, in fact some of them didn't bother with it at all now. They were well turned out, clean, and bright eyed that night for tea with Melissa. Wally was proud of them, and they could see that on his face.

They had some new clothes and most of them had bought laundry soap. And to a man they had a pride shining from them. Had an air of confidence now, life was no longer hopeless. And three of the young blokes had girlfriends in the town. And Eric had begun organising an acre near the river for them to build a permanent home if they wished. He had cleared it with the company of which unbeknownst to anyone he was a part of. Eric often smiled to himself and knew it was Mary's story that did it.

One such bloke was talking about pitching a tent not too far from Wally and Melissa, 'That way they wouldn't be so alone down there,' said Ray. 'And Melissa and Sue might become friends.' He smiled at Wally now, 'and she drives.' Ray had actually seen Melissa's attempts. He hoped she'd get the hang of it before they did the gearbox in, and it became necessary for he and Wally to change it out.

Ray smiled now as Wally nodded and heaved a sigh. 'That could only be a good thing, Ray.'

Their number had swollen to nineteen living in the camp, that was almost everyone. Only a few of the blokes who had families in town went home each night now. Wally and the blokes had been given the go ahead to build the new wall and the chimney. The blokes slept warmer and drier and Wally had a kitchen when it was nasty out. And Mel had somewhere warm to sit as he cooked the food. Time marched on and the weeks went by. Wally had saved most of his wage and his bank account grew.

Melissa usually sat and did the vegetables and such and Wally loved having her there. Wally had been given permission to knock off an hour or so early at full pay with an extra hour besides, to get his cooking job done. Eric had seen the advantage of a well-fed crew and had told Freddy to knock off and help him. Freddy was a little weak since his hospitalisation and Wally mostly ordered him to sit.

Wally always jumped in the car to drive to the river and get Melissa, but she liked to walk and always met him about halfway. Her driving was coming along slowly. Wally suspected his couple of days would stretch into a couple of months. Wally wasn't sure how much more crunching and kangaroo hopping the bloody car would take.

Ray and his girlfriend had pitched their tent with Wally's help and had gone down river far enough to still have their privacy. And whether by necessity or mutual affinity the two girls had become friends and were a lot less lonely during the day. And Steven and his girlfriend Linda, were buying a tent to and they would pitch theirs a bit farther along. It was a beautiful life and Wally was happy. He and Melissa had been camped down there for almost five weeks now.

Mel was a lot happier this last week as on their last shopping trip Wally had taken her to a couple of shops. One was the jewellery shop for an engagement ring. After she had tried it on, and Wally paid for it she had practically run from the shop and got in the car to cry. Wally had sat next to her and held her hand. 'I'm sorry Mel, I didn't mean to make you cry. I should have asked you first. I know it love. But I love you, Mel.'

She had leaned over and kissed him 'and the answer would have been yes, and you know that to,' she grinned at her ring 'it is beautiful Wally can I wear it?'

'Oh Mel, of course you can my love' he kissed her tenderly. 'We have one more stop. I just want to look at something.' Wally drove to a shop that sold electrical goods. He took her in to look at radios. You could get much smaller ones than Dans now that you could carry around, and

Mel soon found the one she wanted. the man in the shop assured him he would get a good reception on it, but he may need to use an aerial.

Wally paid thirty pounds for it. 'If it doesn't work bring it back and go up to a bigger one or I will give you your money back. I can't do any fairer than that mate.'

Wally connected the aerial up to it put the battery in it and it worked a treat. And that night they sat in their chairs listening to it. As Wally sat listening to a soft love song by the Ames Brothers he got to his feet. He took Melissa's hand and, pulling her to her feet he took her in his arms and danced with her there on the bank of the Murray River under the big ghost gums. He sang to her, and she held him tight. 'Oh Wally. My Wally, how I love you.'

And as the band played on the radio Wally sang 'you you you, I'm in love with you you you . . . .' The gentle breeze that sprung up as if on que gave Wally a shiver that went through him and thrilled him to the bone as he danced with his lady love. He finished 'you, you, you, there's no one like you, you, you, you could make my dreams come true, if you loved me to.'

Best of all in Wally's life now was the fact that he slept with Melissa every night. He had well over three hundred pounds in the bank, he'd kept forty back for the ring for Melissa. He would propose to her properly and take her to dinner somewhere nice. Soon.

Over a month after his call to Mary and Dan Wally received a letter from them. Eric had gone into town and had brought the mail home. Wally sat and read it.

29/6/54

Dear Wally,

It was good to get your letter mate and learn of your achievements. I am proud of you; we are all very proud of you Wally. Number one man as Ben still calls you. He sends his love by the way. Everyone sends their love lad.

And your phone calls, though alarming were most welcome. To hear your voice, Wally. I am glad to hear that mongrel is in jail, you did that Wally and thanks. How is Freddy doing? Most pleasing was your news about your young lady. Mary was ecstatic and wants to know where you are having the wedding. I told her on a riverbank somewhere. Am I right Wally?

I am glad you love the rivers, and I am glad I taught you some good things. Thank you Wally I cherish the time I had with you. I will be here waiting and just watching the grass grow and fishing the river. Waiting for your return son.

Now Wally, while you are close by, some of us would like to come and see you. Could you give us a couple of days to work with when it would be convenient. I know you are busy so we would be brief. But just to see you Wally, an hour would do. We need this. We could have lost you because I refrained from doing the job properly when I had the chance. I'm sorry mate.

Josh and Kath are expecting another and if they have a boy, they are going to name him Walter. Walter Daniel Vance no less mate. Of course, that won't interfere with you calling your first-born son Dan, will it? Ha-ha.

We sent a letter off to Jack and let him know you are trying a bit of a tour around about and he wishes you the best. He says to remind you that he is on the phone and that you can reverse the charges now if coins are a problem. And he'd know all about that wouldn't he Wally? ha-ha.

Well, I gotta go and I'll post this in town. Love you mate, get back to me with some days and times hay and we'll catch up a little. We want to meet Melissa to of course and welcome her to the family. Okay bye for now son,

Love Dan

After he'd finished reading, Wally sat quietly for a time wiping his eyes occasionally and Melissa sat and waited. They were both sitting down by the water. Melissa slipped her arm around his shoulders, and he turned and buried his face in her neck. Melissa felt his hot tears and stroked his face.

Wally sat up and looked at her. 'They want to meet you, Mel. They are coming here to meet you. Dan did a lot of fine talk about needing to see me and that may be true but it's you girl.' He handed Melissa the letter.

He took his hanky out which was always clean that day and wiped his eyes then blew his nose. Dan was coming, he couldn't believe it. Wally would have to write a letter soon. Tomorrow, and then they could slip into town at the weekend to send it and Mel could come with him. He'd talk tomorrow to Eric and try to settle on a day.

Eric looked excited 'good on him son, bloody good on him. Bring him up to meet us and have a meal. We'll cook it. Well anyway there's this weekend or there's three weeks' time. That'd be best so they can get

your letter and get themselves organised to. After that Wally anytime, you just let me know hay and we'll make sure you have a couple of days off. Would that be long enough Wally? Anyway, two or three days we'll work around you Wally. Have you told them you are engaged son?'

'No not yet, when they get here, I think. Thanks Eric thanks very much.' Wally's face broke into a grin he couldn't help. 'If they get here Saturday afternoon, they will probably go home that day or next. Anyway, I'll put these days to them and see what they come up with and then as soon as I know you'll know. I can't thankyou enough Eric.'

'Wally, you don't have to thank me at all. I am looking forward to meeting them we all are, I think. Go on son, go write your letter.'

Wally took Melissa home and from a box under the bed he broke out his candle, pencil, and paper.

Melissa helped him word it and Wally sharpened his pencil with his gutting knife. He began to write.

1/7/1954

Dear Dan and Mary,

I hope this letter finds you all well as we are here. I was overjoyed to hear you will come to see us and Melissa is excited like you wouldn't believe. She told me not to say that.

I had a word with Eric, and we have this weekend which is not really suitable I know. But then there is two weekends time after that. And we can have the Saturday and Sunday depending on what you can do. After that he says anytime but could I give him a weeks' notice. And at that time, you could stay for three days. You can stay as long or as short as you wish Dan it will be good to see you. Even for only an hour just to see you.

But I will only get these days off work.

Everyone at the mine wants to meet you I have done a certain amount of boasting I'm afraid. You know me Dan, I can't help myself I am so proud of you all. I love you all and I know Melissa will to. She has no family. I told her she has now, Haha. We have a plan to dig in here for a while, I thought about six months, but we will pull out as soon as the weather is good again. I don't want to travel too far in the hot months. So that will be more like eight months. I would like to have a good bit of money behind us now that I have this new responsibility. But I do love it Dan.

I have a new duty at work now Dan I am camp cook. You have been invited to dinner on the Saturday night if you can stay so you can sample my culinary delights as Eric calls it. Yes, Dan I am mighty glad that bloody Rodney is in jail. The cops came out to the mine, and we all gave statements. If he pleads not guilty at the hearing, I may have to stay for the trial anyway.

Don't forget if you have time for a spot of fishing to bring your gear. I remember our long talks we used to have while fishing and I miss them. We bought a radio the other day Dan a little beauty. I developed a thirst for knowledge from you and that radio of yours. Anyway, gotta go, early start tomorrow mate, Bye for now,

All my Love

Me and Matilda and Melissa

Wally folded the letter carefully and put it in the envelope which Melissa had addressed for him. She sealed it down and smiled at him. 'You write very well Wally.'

He smiled softly at her; his mind had strayed a little as it was wont to do when he looked at her.

The weeks flew past and all three couples down on the riverbank in their tents got along famously. Saturday nights they all sat around the fire talking. They did this mostly at Wally and Melissa's tent because Wally had rigged up a tarp to sit under out of the rain. Sometimes some of the blokes from the camp came down with Eric in the rover.

They came to see Wally and his little community by the river and to tell stories. They also came for the radio, they all loved to listen to the hit parade. Sometimes one or other of these two blokes who lived nearby would come and sit with Wally and listen to the news. Wally's thirst for knowledge was as infectious as Dans had been.

Wally still fished the river, set his three traps that he had now, and took his gun hunting to supplement their food supply. There were wild pigs and feral goats to be had all along the river. Only now Melissa went with him and sometimes in fine weather they took their old swags and camped out. Wally couldn't believe his luck finding such a woman.

Wally knew he would marry Melissa before they left, he wanted it all to be right. He had never felt anything like this love for her. He had never experienced anything like her love for him.

Wally was excited about Dan coming and found himself looking forward to it. He also looked forward to the camp people meeting the Murrumbidgee people. He knew they'd get along.

Wally was also busy clearing a patch of scrub in readiness for his visitors to pitch their tents in.

Two weeks after his letter to Dan Wally got a note in the mail.

14/7/1954

Dear Wally,

Sorry, this has to be so short. Hope you are well and happy as we are here. Thanks for the dates lad and we have at last formulated a plan. We have settled on two weeks from this date. That will be Friday the 27th of July. Dennis and Noreen want to come to, you see and those are the days they could get off work. Ben is coming and Josh and Kath. They are bringing their kids and Bryce and our Libby etc are coming. Not sure how many kids are coming.

So, we will bring the Ute and the truck and the old tent Wally. And we will camp there with you Friday and Saturday night and come home on Sunday. And yes, I will definitely bring my fishing gear and we will find somewhere quiet to do some fishing. I look forward to that lad, as we all look forward to meeting our newest member.

Not sure yet who else is coming. We will bring both vehicles because some have to come back on Saturday, for work. I know Kath has to be back and I think Noreen as well. So, we will see you around about five o'clock on Friday the 27th hay. I can't wait. So, bye for now little buddy

Love from Dan and the Family

PS. Give my love to Matilda.

Wally handed the letter to Melissa who read it and grinned at Wally. 'I have got a family now.'

'You have baby. And may I say that I think you are ready to drive your car yourself now my love.'

'Oh Wally, could life be more perfect?' She smiled softly at him.

Wally smiled, 'I can't see how can you? And I reckon you are ready to go get your licence. You just have to remember your hand signals.'

'I know Wally, I remember them. Here I'll show you.'

It was Friday the 27th at last. Wally was up on the dozer; he was grading the road through to the highway to get rid of the corrugation, he was almost finished he reckoned he had about a quarter of a mile to go. At four thirty it was almost knock off time, so he turned the dozer around to head back to the camp.

He was excited to see everyone and for them to meet Melissa. He had been excused from camp duties tonight so he could spend more time with his family. Wally had organised their tea and he had made a nice smooth road for their vehicles.

As he was about to turn off the road and park the dozer, a truck came up beside him followed by a Ute. Dennis and Bryce and the boys were in the back of the truck with Dan and Mary and Libby in the front. The Ute came along behind with Josh and Kath and their baby Jack. Noreen rode up in the back with the children, Noreen loved to ride up in the back. Wally smiled; she was a big kid at heart was Noreen.

Wally stopped the dozer and jumped down, right into Dans arms. The two men gave vent to their deep feelings loudly as they hugged each other. They laughed and cried at the same time in equal measure.

Wally hugged them all and wiped his eyes and nose. After a while Wally said 'I just need to park this up Dan and then we can knock off. Just follow me up to the camp up there.' Wally lifted his eyes to the camp and noticed the nineteen blokes including Eric waiting there to meet Dan and his family. Wally smiled inwardly.

'Righto' said Dan and he looked the bulldozer over. 'Jesus Wally, you are doing a bloody amazing job mate and you did that road? And to think how I used to treat you. But I listened see Wally. I listened to Tom talk about his wife, and I knew I was guilty of babying you.' He glanced at Mary now and smiled back at Wally, 'so I took no notice of Mary who thought I was too hard on you, and I pushed you. And not a day goes by now that you don't amaze me.'

Wally stared at the man he had loved and admired above all others and grinned, 'and not a day goes by now that I don't give thanks for it.'

There in full view of the men at the camp and Melissa who was driving up in the FJ Dan put his arms out to Wally who stepped into them. 'Thanks Dan. I am what I am and have what I have because of you. You and Mary.' Dan smiled; the significance of Wally's mentioning Mary here was not lost on him. He was well pleased that Wally was happy, he could see it in his face.

He patted Wally on the back. 'Now let's meet the lady who has captured your heart, Wally.'

Melissa pulled up and found herself smothered in hugs and a tight knit throng of people who surrounded her. But Melissa felt the love and it did her heart good. Wally came to her rescue telling her of the plan to park the dozer.

Ben sidled up to Melissa, 'I have always wanted one of these FJ's, mind if I ride with you?'

Melissa smiled and nodded eagerly, 'please do. Wally taught me how to drive, it took me ages to get the gears right.' She laughed with Ben and Wally. Dan who stood a little to the side saw it all. He saw what a beautiful human being she was, and he was happy that Wally had found someone so special.

Ben smiled at the young woman, she was lovely, and he was most happy for Wally. Ben had always loved Wally and wished that he brought better news.

Wally smiled at Ben who grinned from ear to ear, 'she is a little beauty son, and I don't mean the FJ.'

They all laughed and got back in their vehicles, and did the last few hundred yards to the camp.

Eric and the boys watched as the crew from the Murrumbidgee pulled up and got out. They noted the stamp of the man driving the truck who they had realised was Dan. He was much younger than they had imagined. He wore a hat, but his hair was dark, and he was tall, straight backed, and well built. Though Dan was almost in his early fifties he maintained a youthful appearance.

Everyone was surprised when a very ancient looking Samuel bounced out of the back of the truck with about a dozen kids. And then, he picked up the baby Jack, and carted him around on his hip. When he spoke, he left people in no doubt that he was as sharp as a tack. Wally loved the old man and hugged him joyfully. 'Wally' said Samuel, 'it is most lovely to see you.'

Sarah, who had been engaged to Mathew, was with them. She practically lived out at the long hut now. Wally noticed how Bryce stayed close to her. The young man was obviously smitten. And unless he was wrong the young lady felt the same.

And Mavis alighted from the Ute to stand by Ben. Wally recalled how close this pair had been especially since the debacle over the engagement ring. But they had all moved on from that, these people didn't hold grudges they couldn't afford to. Dan always said, 'you stay together by forgiveness not by punishment, nor banishment' and he was right.

Eric was introduced to them all and he found them to be among the nicest and most polite people he had ever met. They were proud but humble and they laughed a lot. They were clean and happy and healthy, and Eric was able to see where the changes in his own camp had come from. He found he was proud of his men also, and knew he had these people to thank. These people and Wally.

Mary and Dan were treated with a kind of reverence. The men were looking at the legend of Dan and Mary, and they were impressive people, both tall and strong. A beautiful pair indeed. And the men milled around them wanting only to stand in their presence for a short while. Everyone shook hands and Eric invited them to sit for a while. Dan graciously accepted for the family. He could see the love that went on here and he knew it had Wally's stamp all over it.

Even the smallest child in Dan's group was presented to the men of the camp with a glowing pride. And the youngest member was Jack Junior or JJ as they called him. Wally took him from Samuel and held him for a while.

Dan sidled up to Eric and commented on the size of his operation. Eric smiled back. 'We are lucky to have Wally. As I think you know we lost our dozer operator and Wally was able to take that on for us. We were horrified at what could have happened here to Wally. And we could have lost Freddy. But I didn't think Rodney was that bad. You just don't know sometimes. Of course, he'd only been here a couple of months. He was a quiet cove sort of sullen and stand offish. But Wally has been a Godsend all round.' Eric took a deep breath 'I should have known Rodney was evil.'

'Don't beat yourself up Eric' advised Dan softly, 'I have found that the worst of people are the very best at disguising it.' Eric smiled gratefully at him; he liked the man.

The Murrumbidgee gang were taken into the shelter and given hot tea or coffee. The men noticed how Dan's people sat round him. And they saw that the man was a safe haven for all of them and they for him. And how the children ran to him and jumped about on him with never an unkind word. Yet when Dan told them to get down, they didn't hesitate to do it. All with no offence taken.

The strange thing was the pride the men of the camp felt about their home now. It was well built, well-kept and clean. A good place to live. And they noticed how the Murrumbidgee people relaxed. The ladies were invited to sit on the rolled-up swags and drums and whatever else while the men of the camp sat on the ground.

Bryce stuck close to Wally he had always felt a close kinship with Wally. Bryce felt closer to Wally than he did to Kane. It was obvious to anyone with eyes that the young man idolized him. And Bryce was harbouring a burning desire to go with Wally on his journey.

Mary walked up to Melissa a smile on her face as she took Melissa's left hand in hers lifting it towards her for a better look. 'What's this I see young lady? How have I missed this? Look Dan, look.' Mary did her little hop that she was wont to do when she was excited.

Dan looked and a grin spreading across his face made him appear even younger. 'Wally!' He said and took Melissa's hand in his own. 'This is what I think it is Wally' he said turning towards him?

The grin on Wally's face said it all and Dan felt his heart right itself in his chest as he embraced Wally and stood aside for Bryce. In fact, stood aside for everyone who wanted to hug the young man again. Dan was euphoric. Wally, his favourite son was happy.

The men of the camp milled around smiling and wanting to be a part of the happiness. They loved Wally and Dan saw it was so as people clamoured around him.

This was a place not unsimilar to the long hut Dan realised now. And some of the building methods looked suspiciously like Wally's. They had a good roof a southern wall and an easterly wall and a fireplace made of old drums. They were serviceable though and were put together similarly to the fireplace they first built in the long hut. Dan smiled inwardly, Wally again.

He smiled and sighed deeply. Mary put her arm around the man she loved and said, 'thank God Dan. Thank God. Some good news here some bad news there. The best we can hope for is just that.'

Dan took this woman of his in his arms and cried, he sobbed unashamedly and told Mary, 'Yes indeed thank God.' He looked across the top of her head where Wally was being hugged by Ben and Melissa, 'thank God' he murmured. Eric who watched this from the other side felt tears spring to his own eyes.

Dan stepped back from Mary and Wally was there with Melissa standing in front of him. He took the young woman in his arms and kissed her gently. When he rocked her gently to and fro in his arms, Melissa broke down and cried. She wept over a decade of grief into Dan's shoulder, and he was wet with tears. But he held her and rocked her as he did all his people when they needed it.

He would not ask what was wrong in front of all these people, but he did realise that something was indeed wrong. The young woman had so much pain welled up in her; how glad he was that she had found Wally.

And Melissa knew she loved these people, and she also knew she was loved by them. For the first time Melissa had a family of her own. Her arms went around Dan, and she hung on tightly to him. There was something so familiar about that embrace.

It was while Wally and Dan were fishing and talking quietly at the river that Wally told Dan about Melissa's uncle Gus. 'Jesus Wally, what sort of a bloody world is it?' he put his hand on Wally's arm. 'Well at least I taught you how to skelp the hide off these bastards, it's what they fuckin deserve. And that bloody Rodney, attempting to kill you son.' Dan shook his head as he looked at Wally a tear in his eyes, 'do you think Uncle Gus will get his come-up pence Wally? From the law?'

Wally nodded, 'I think they both will and . . . . well, Gus has been at it before an' all. Copper reckons those two will be keeping each other company for years, even decades to come.'

'Bloody good o' breathed Dan leaning back against a tree. He looked at Wally now 'I enjoyed sleeping in the old tent last night Wally. It brought back memories that I don't want to forget. And you wanna know something? I slept like a baby.' The three men laughed amicably together.

Ben was with them, and his heart broke for the young woman, Melissa. But Ben had to talk to Wally. He broke in gently now and asked Wally if he could speak to him. Dan went to get up, 'no Dan, best you sit with him. Sit with us Dan.'

Dan sat back against the tree and braced himself; this would hurt. Again, it would hurt. As many times as he heard it, it would hurt.

Wally sat stunned as Ben told him he was dying. 'The doctors tell me I have cancer.'

Wally shook his head 'no Ben, no. No.' Wally felt something break inside him, something he would be trying to heal for a long time. He sat in silence.

'Come on you two' said Dan gently, 'we will go on and as usual, we will look after each other to the best of our ability.' He put a hand on each of them now, 'and we will all meet again in that great long hut in the sky.'

Ben smiled gratefully at Dan, 'here, here Dan. On the banks of a river as beautiful as this.'

Dan smiled and nodding at Ben he added, 'where the fish jump, already scaled onto your line.' Ben laughed softly.

'I'll come home,' said Wally after a silence.

'You'll do no such thing' said Ben now. 'You will go on with your journey and I will wait here for you to return. I may have a few years left in me yet young Wally. It's a slow growing cancer they tell me. I have Dan and Mary and all these other beautiful people around me and I am happy lad. And I have found love Wally. I am getting married to Mavis.'

Wally leaned to the side and put his arm around Ben. Ben had been one of their mainstays. He had been Dans shoulder to lean on and the significance of this, just now hit Wally. Ben would leave deep cracks in the foundations when he departed.

Ben hugged Wally tight and let him go. Smiling now he said 'be happy for me Wally. I am in love lad and to a wonderful woman. And I have had a letter from my daughter who is coming to see me soon, she is married with another child. Think on it Wally, a grandchild. Yeah mate, just be happy for me.'

Wally looked into Ben's face, and he knew he looked into true greatness, true goodness. 'I'm glad for you Ben and I'm glad for Mavis to. Maybe Ben, if me and Mel get married before we go, we could have a double ceremony. Around Christmas time and we will come home for it. What do you say Ben?'

A tear slid down Bens' face accompanied by a bright smile. Wally was flabbergasted, Ben really was happy. Wally smiled back and Dan got a bight.

Ray came by about an hour before sundown on Saturday and brought his girlfriend to meet the people from the Murrumbidgee. He was informed of the wedding plans of the two couples and was formally invited. All these people would be invited Wally knew. Dan caught the young man look at his girlfriend Sue.

He sat forward in his chair, 'why not make it three indeed. If you are thinking of getting married, then why not make it a triple wedding. What do you think Mary?'

Mary was already smiling indulgently at Dan. 'It's a wonderful idea Dan but you should let these young people make their minds up.' Mary smiled at them in turn, 'It's a wonderful idea though.'

And so, it was decided on that weekend that it would indeed be a triple wedding. Sue and Ray were happy and all they needed to do was iron out the details. Mary and Dan assured them that they would take care of the reception and that the priest could marry the three, as easily as he could marry the one couple.

And Dan and Mary talked about the procedures and how to get it all started. Wally knew that Mary and Dan meant well, and he also knew this was all his fault. But he hoped that Melissa would be on board with all this. It was her wedding to. He stole a look across at her and she was grinning from ear to ear and talking excitedly to Sue. It was good to see her so happy he thought now, and he was glad. His heart fairly soared when she smiled across at him.

So, the people from down by the river went up to join the people from the camp for dinner. And as Wally had predicted the invitations went out. And everyone there was delighted.

Then dinner was served with gusto and pride. 'Hells' bells' exclaimed Dan, 'Wally, you really can cook mate.'

There was much laughter at the fire that night and the legend that was Dan and Mary was witnessed and confirmed.

Dan and his people settled back wherever they could find space. They were all familiar with this style of eating, they had done their fair share of it during their time on the road. The food was good, and Dan said so now. Most of the people there nodded their agreement.

Wally served everybody and then he served himself. He looked around at these people as they talked excitedly about the wedding and Christmas. Yes, they'd make it a grand feast celebrating both occasions in the one. Christmas and three marriages.

Wally found himself looking forward to Christmas this year, more than he had ever done.

Most of the men in the camp did to. Some of them couldn't remember a Christmas when they hadn't got blind drunk to try and forget it was Christmas. Some of the blokes would go home for Christmas and most of them knew very well they'd be happy when it was over.

As the night wore on stories were told, the fire was stoked, and kids dropped off to sleep. They had laid a couple of swags out on the back of the Ute and the kids snuggled up in them. They went to sleep to the sound of voices and laughter. The adults would leave them there under Wallys tarp with Samuel.

The people of the long hut settled down to listen and to talk and to laugh. It felt good and a great peace and tranquillity settled on each of them. Eric thanked everyone for coming and said that they would come to the long hut for the wedding and for Christmas.

Melissa went to sleep with her head on Wally's shoulder and he put his arms around her and cuddled her. His heart sang, his fiancé loved his family, and they loved her.

CHAPTER 6

I t had rained solidly for two weeks, and the ground was waterlogged even up at the mine. It had started at the end of August and now it was halfway through September. Eric stood with Wally under the shelter waiting for the rain to let up just so they could go out in it.

Wally and Melissa and the other couples had moved their camps to higher ground. Though Eric had never seen the water come up that far, he thought it was probably a good idea. There was a flood plain upriver that usually took up any excess water.

Work all over the mine had slowed to a trickle and Eric said now that he wished the bloody rain would go away. Eric went on to Wally, 'I was talking to that mate of mine on the Murrumbidgee Princess in the pub last night. He's going down the Murray to the Murrumbidgee. Anyway, he is going past here tomorrow, and he will go up the Murrumbidgee and then back down to the Murray here. He is doing the round trip for a while. So why don't you hop on board mate there's not a lot going on here? I told him last night to keep an eye out for your tent and to call and see you. He says if you are willing to work, then you can travel for free and you can take Melissa. Of course, you will have to make do in a tiny cabin. What do you say son you'll only be gone not even a couple of weeks I think.'

Wally stood with his mouth open as Eric stood grinning, waiting for a reply. 'Do you mean it Eric?'

'Of course, son, go on. Do you good.'

'Thanks Eric. I don't know what to say.'

'You just said it mate. Anyway, you have worked bloody hard here Wally and I appreciate everything you've done here.'

'Well, I'd love to if you are sure Eric.'

'Yeah, look mate, even when it stops raining it'll take another week to dry out enough to put the dozer in. And cooking for themselves will keep this lot occupied.'

'I'm bloody stoked Eric.'

When Eric had left Wally went home and ran to the tent to tell Melissa the news.

Wally watched the steamer glide majestically through the waters of the Murray with an excitement in his belly. She pulled right up to the bank near their tent and the older man hailed him with a big grin. 'You must be Wally.' He said throwing a sort of gang plank over the side. 'Are you coming?'

'Hell yeah' replied Wally who had his old swag on his back. He turned and took Melissa's hand to help her up on board and then came up himself. He shook hands with the man whose name was Clyde. Then he turned around and pulled the gang plank up on board after him.

Wally looked apologetically at Melissa when he saw their cabin. She smiled at him and shrugged. 'It's fine Wally' she said.

Wally was trying desperately to get his heartbeat under control. He was here at last on a paddle steamer on the great Murray River. And once again he hoped to see his family as they began their trek up the Murrumbidgee for, he had told them he'd be on board the Princess today. Eric had let him use the phone in the office and Dan told him he'd be there, and Dan never reneged on his word.

Over the next two days Clyde taught Wally all about the steamer and how to drive her and how to look after her. He explained everything to Wally and made sure he was driving as they waved to Wally's large family near Balranald.

Everyone on the steamer waved, and Wally knew a homesickness that almost overwhelmed him. But Dan was there grinning from the bank and running alongside them. Wally could see the pride in his face and his own eyes shone with the same thing.

At the wharf Wally brought the steamer gently in to rest. They had some unloading to do, and a few passengers were getting off. Clyde came up the front of the boat, he wanted to say hello to Wally's rather large family. Clyde had heard all about them in the pub the night before. Clyde found himself amazed at how ordinary these people looked, because he knew they were anything but ordinary.

Clyde left Mack to unload the goods they had for the Balranald general store and the post office, there wasn't much. Two passengers alighted and one of them said hello to Wally. Dan was introduced to Clyde, and he was very interested in the paddle steamer. Clyde was interested in these people of the Murrumbidgee. He had been a swaggie himself during the great depression and he was pretty sure he'd always found something to eat along here.

Clyde was also pretty sure that most of the kids they had with them probably should have been at school. Clyde invited Dan to bring the kids on board while they were docked. At the end of the meeting when it was time for the steamer to go, Dan told them they'd had their lesson for the day. An honest to goodness working paddle steamer he said with a light in his eyes.

When it was time to say goodbye to Wally however, the man had a tear in his eyes. 'Enjoy your trip, Wally. Does this mean that you've abandoned the dozer for the steamer?'

'It means only that it is too wet for the dozer but not for this.'

Clyde laughed and said, 'lucky for us, he's a natural and a one man show.'

Dan said softly as he stood eyeing the vessel, 'damn shame these ladies are leaving the river if you ask me.' He went on as if to himself, 'these and the drovers and the stockmen and their horses. Bloody shame.' He took a deep breath a faraway look on his face, 'progress they call it.'

Clyde nodded; he understood every word of it. Knew the heart ache only too well.

After an hour at Balranald the Murrumbidgee Princess set forth along the Murrumbidgee River. Wally was home, he was back on the Murrumbidgee. Dan and Mary with Ben and the others waved and called out their love and their goodbyes. Wally called back that he would see them on the twenty-fourth of December.

The couples would be married at three o'clock in the afternoon of the twenty- fifth. Wally wondered how much Dan had paid the priest to do it. But he had told Wally it was all arranged. All the couples had to do was show up with a heart full of love and a desire to be married.

Dan watched from the bank as this son of his, as he'd always considered Wally, set sail on the steamer for parts unknown. How his heart swelled with pride as he told someone next to him, that was his boy on the steamer, the one driving it. But lurking in his heart was the pain of watching him leave.

Mary smiled at him; he had never given up. Had never taken a day off from all the caring. Not in all the time she had known him. And these boys of his as he called them, they got hurt, they got scared and insecure at times and he felt it all. If she had a quid for every time, she'd held him in the night as he cried for one or the other of them . . . .

Mary had never known anyone with such a capacity to love, and his love was strong and enduring. How she loved him this man called Dan. And his love for her had never wavered, never slowed over the years. His loyalty was the stuff of legend indeed.

When Dan had come home from visiting Jack, he had been distraught and so had Wally. Dan had informed her that Jack's face was broken. Then Dan had pulled himself together and told her that Jack was broken no more. Jack was strong and happy and a man to be admired. And he told her that Jack wore his face as a badge of courage and so he bloody well ought. That face had nearly cost him his life.

Mary sighed, Dan would go ahead and make all the plans for the triple wedding. Mary had playfully asked him if there were any others in the districts who were getting married around now. But Dan had taken her seriously and given it some thought.

She watched the steamer as it rounded a bend and was gone from sight. She felt it to. Why must love be the thing which hurt you the most she wondered? But then it was love that put your heart back together, wasn't it? In fact, she thought now, you could count on it. The happiest and deepest love could, and would at some stage, bring you undone, she sighed deeply. She slipped her hand into Dan's, and he held on to it. He would turn any moment now and smile at her and put her heart back together.

Wally loved driving the paddle steamer and he even loved shovelling coal into her furnace. Her heart as Wally thought of it. Wally liked everyone on board, Clyde the captain, Huan the cook and Mack the driver come fireman. Mack was busy doing some repairs and painting along the way while he had some time free.

The passengers and spectators alike flocked to Wally asking him questions about the boat. He answered them as best he could, admitting that he hadn't had much to do with them.

Wally felt inside him a deep sadness that this would all soon be gone. Gone, these majestic ladies, gone from the river leaving ghosts in their wake. And Wally to would be gone from the banks and he would eventually leave a ghost behind.

He looked at Melissa now, he couldn't wait to be married to her. then her ghost would walk beside his as they traversed these rivers for eternity. Shit, he told himself now, he had a job to do. He had to get to Jack's. He picked up the shovel and opened the furnace door.

Their next stop would be Hay, they had some parcels for Hay. Wally looked up at the rain, would it never stop. Good for the gardens for the market he thought now with a pang. He remembered how Dan had started taking him to market teaching him that side of it.

'You need to make your money here Wally unless you want to do all those months of work for nothing. Even during the worst of it' he'd said, 'we have to make money. We can't keep going if we don't.' Dan was better at that side of it than anyone, Wally had always thought. Not the least because he was a charming and charismatic man. Wally knew Dan could charm the birds out of the trees if needs be. Hell, the flowers lost their appeal to the bees when Dan showed up.

A voice beside him brought him out of his reverie. 'You are a natural young Wally. Shame she won't be around long enough for you to take over from me hay. I know a river man when I see one,' Clyde smiled sadly. 'They are lovely people; your family Wally.' He looked down at his boots, 'I have no family, none at all.'

'Yeah, thanks mate there was a time I didn't have one either, so I know how it feels. They are market gardeners besides the farming, and they will be glad of this rain.'

Clyde sucked in air; how could he forget them, the large family of the long hut? He said, 'yes, now I've got them. They are Mary and Dan of course. I remember they fed me a few times. Didn't Mary used to leave food on a table near the highway?'

'Yeah, that was Mary. She made me go down and replenish it a few times. I grumbled once and she asked me if I'd forgotten what the hunger was like.'

Wally laughed at the memory. 'And she stood there and waited for me to answer. Of course, I said no I hadn't and went off with the bread and tomatoes to the highway.'

Clyde laughed with Wally, 'well we were mighty glad of it Wally. Mighty glad indeed.' He looked down stroking his beard thoughtfully, 'I remember those tomatoes young un. They were bloody beautiful. And I heard the stories about how they fed the town during the worst of it.'

Wally smiled and nodded. 'When do we get to Hay' he asked now? 'Tomorrow.'

Wally felt the excitement in his belly, he was just as excited to arrive at a place as he was to leave it. The mark of a true wanderer.

Wally pulled into the jetty at Hay; The Murrumbidgee Princess glided in smoothly. She knew how to attract a crowd thought Wally. Their last two passengers got off and some parcels. They took on some more parcels and some boxes.

The rain continued to fall, and the river went on and on. Sometimes Wally was conflicted as to who it was that followed and who led. He usually conceded that he followed the river. He stood at the wheel and straightened his back, how he loved it. He knew some anxiety when the river got less and less, and someone had to stand at the bow and direct him through the sand bars and obstructions. They got through and Wally relaxed again.

Wally watched the sunrise over the red gums which bound the river. Beyond the gums and the natural vegetation, he ran a practiced eye over the farmland. The rain had slowed up here and they just got the odd shower. Wally was waiting for Melissa to come see him. He smiled to himself, she had started with cleaning their cabin and had now cleaned just about the whole boat.

At Narrandera Wally pulled into the jetty. A truck waited with tea chest bound for Gundagai. Wally gave a hand to load them on to the steamer. 'Are you the new driver' asked a bloke handing him tea chests.

'No' said Wally, 'just giving a hand this trip. I work on a mine down near Swan Hill.'

'Oh, on the Murray. So, you are a Murray man.'

'Not really' said Wally 'my family farms down near Balranald.'

An older man off to the side chimed in 'I know Eric, he's a good bloke. What do you do there, Wally?"

'I operate the bulldozer.'

The loading done Wally took his place up at the front and added coal to the fire. Wally quite enjoyed shovelling coal, and he soon had a good blaze going in the furnace.

And the old steamer took once more to the river bound for Wagga Wagga with Wally at the helm. Melissa stood beside him waving to the crowds as did Wally. He was overjoyed at how much Melissa loved the trip on the boat. 'Here we go Mel' he said softly, 'following the river to who knows where hay.' He smiled, 'do you think those people wish they were following the river out.'

'Maybe Wally'

'I think most of them are here to see the old girl here' exclaimed Wally with a huge grin. Most of those on the bank of the river answered that grin and Wally waved.

'We should get ourselves one of these when we retire hay.' Wally was laughing as he said it.

Melissa felt tears spill down her cheeks 'Oh Wally do you think we could?' Wally's arm went around her 'of course we can my love. When we come back, we shall start saving and I'll work every day.'

It was teatime and Mack came out to relieve Wally while he went to eat. Wally sat with Melissa and Clyde who was looking tired. 'How are you going Wally, up there? Not sick of it yet?'

Wally smiled back mischievously and said as he sat down 'what sort of question is that?'

'A petty silly one lad.' Clyde took a swig from his mug 'I heard your conversation out there this afty, Wally. You serious about buying a houseboat when you return from Queensland?'

Wally grinned 'we certainly are. Only way for us to end up really. Melissa shares my love of the rivers and these boats.'

'Good thing lad. I will hang on to the Murrumbidgee Princess as long as I can. And when you come back, she is yours. Tell no one of course we can't have anyone getting jealous.' Clyde smiled and rose to his feet.

Wally was on his feet, 'the Murrumbidgee Princess?'

'That'll be her son yes. The Murrumbidgee Princess.'

'Jesus Clyde, I don't know what to say. We'll pay you for . . . . '

Clyde put his hand on Wally's arm and shook his head, 'I shall retire soon, and I will live on her as long as I can manage. After that she is yours, and no more talk of money. You are already a part of this boat.' Clyde held out his finger and tapped Wally in the chest with it, 'and she, Wally is part of you. She is in here Wally.' Clyde smiled now and said, 'I am tired son' and walked away leaving Wally with nothing to say for once.

That night Wally sat at the helm of this most majestic of vessels and began to dream. He would keep her running if he had to work full time to fund it. Wally knew this boat was in his heart, knew she was part of him. And Wally knew he loved her.

Wally looked up at the stars and let the breeze cool his face. He realised it had stopped raining and he got up and stepped out from the wheel room. It was a beautiful night with the smell of the river, the water, and the eucalypt. A kookaburra laughed somewhere up ahead, and Wally smiled.

As they approached Gundagai, Wally noticed how many men were fishing on the banks. They had quite a load of flour bound for Gundagai. On the way back they would unload bread at all stops along the way.

When Wally brought the Princess into the bank at Gundagai it was three o'clock in the afternoon and the sun was shining. When the goods had been unloaded Clyde told Wally to cut the motors and take the rest of the day off and that he was headed for the pub. Wally grinned and said he'd be breaking out the fishing gear. Clyde smiled and walked off up the gang plank with Mack.

With the Princess put to bed Wally and Melissa shouldered their swags and went off upriver to find a patch of worms. They told Huan that they'd be back first thing in the morning.

Wally and Melissa sat side by side and threw their lines in. It was quiet and Wally felt at peace. He loved the river, and he loved the steamer. He was looking forward to sleeping on solid ground though.

At teatime he and Melissa went to a café and bought hamburgers and chips. 'These are good' Wally stated as he took out a quarter of his burger in one bight. They'd gotten two each, but Wally usually finished off half of one of Melissas'.

Wally found a grand tree for them to use for a bedroom that night and he slept like a baby beside Melissa.

The next day they set off back towards Wagga Wagga. They were on the return journey down the river. How Wally loved it, and he knew Melissa did to. Wally turned the boat, and they began their journey down the Murrumbidgee. They had unloaded and loaded, and they turned and headed back for Balranald and the Murray.

They got as far back as Narrandera and found it was still raining there. After Hay they got into the winding narrow parts of the river where navigation was tricky. This always brought Wally out in a sweat. They got through. The trip on the Murrumbidgee would be over in just nine days from its beginning.

Back once more at Balranald Wally got the chance to have a word with Dan and Mary. They told him and Melissa that they had everyone's birth certificates, and the priest would be sending off for the marriage certificates this week.

They asked Wally to ring them sometime in late November and they could iron out some of the wedding details and to have the other couple with them. 'They need to have their input,' said Mary. 'The reception, Wally will just be the usual you know like our Christmas feasts. You could ask them if they would be happy with that.'

It was time to say goodbye again and Mary and Dan and the murrumbidgee people hugged Wally and Melissa. Wally and Melissa got back on the boat and Wally fired up the motor and they pulled out of Balranald. Dan and Mary and the others waved goodbye. Dan looked at Mary now, 'I miss him' he said softly, his heart breaking.

'So do I love.' Mary's arm went around Dan. Ben wiped his eyes and Mavis put her arm around him.

It rained all the way back down the Murray to the camp. As they drew near to the camp Clyde suggested they slow up in case. And there at the site where the tents were was Eric. He was grinning from ear to ear as he came on board.

'I'm sorry to have to do this to you Wally but we have need of the dozer at the mine mate. We have had one hell of a mud slide at the North face, and it will take days to clear it away.' Eric slid his eyes to Clyde who was grinning, 'we could do with our cook back to.' Eric shrugged, 'I'm sorry mate to drag you off like this.'

'You don't have anything to apologise for Eric. I appreciate this time that you have given me. Sure, I'll just grab the gear, we have it ready I'll just be a moment. And thanks again Eric, and it's good to be back.'

Clyde told Eric what a good worker he thought Wally was and said 'if it wasn't for you, I'd be trying to poach him. I met his family they are good people. I remembered as Wally was talking about them how they fed me and some others during the depression. Yeah mate, good people. None better.'

'Yeah, I'll be sad to see him go he's one of the best dozer operators I've ever seen.'

'You are gunna feel it alright mate. He is coming back though, isn't he?'

Eric nodded and smiled now at Wally who was coming up the gang plank. Wally shook hands with Clyde and promised to keep in touch. 'As soon as we can we'll come and see you and I have the address. And thank you for the privilege of driving this old lady, Clyde.'

'And thank you Wally, for everything.' Said Clyde.

Wally walked up the gang plank with heavy tread. 'Do you want to start now Eric on the clean up?'

'No mate tomorrow is soon enough. We have been back at work for a few days but it's slow. The rain has slowed up a good deal, but we are still getting showers.'

Wally trudged on up to the tent holding Melissa's hand. He had had the most amazing ten days, and he told Eric this now.

'I'm glad son I really am. By the way lad, mum has invited you to dinner next weekend. That's the weekend we'll be in town. You and Melissa, she wants to see Melissa.' Eric dropped the swag he was carrying just inside their tent. 'You knew where to camp Wally it's pretty dry under the tree here. And these trees aren't prone to falling down like some are. And that trench you've dug to divert the water has saved you a flooded tent by golly.'

Wally smiled 'thanks again Eric for this last ten days. I enjoyed it immensely.'

'I thought you might.' He walked to his land rover and turning he smiled 'it's good to have you back son.'

'It's good to be back Eric.'

CHAPTER 7

It was the twenty third of December and the people of the long hut were hard at it. They had cleaned the place from top to bottom and had freshly painted the kitchen and eating area. Most of the men had been busy outside in the yard and the garden. The clothes were all washed and pressed and ready to don.

The most experienced of the women were busy now making food. They had made three small wedding cakes and three Christmas cakes. They had prepared four turkeys and eight chickens, they were stuffed and, in the fridge, ready to cook. The long hut had two fridges now. They had two hams ready and two legs of lamb that they would roast and have cold. And lastly, they would cook forty chops and serve them as well.

They had turned one hundred potatoes and a dozen onions into salad along with tomatoes onion lettuce and cheese salads. There would be beetroot and steamed vegies as well.

The girls had made sixty loaves of bread and dozens of buns and rolls. There were cakes and patty cakes as well. And then they had made rice, potato and pasta salads.

All up there would be over eighty people there for dinner so they would need to make enough. They had collected all the tables they had even bringing three from Mary's place. They had topped up with tables and chairs they'd borrowed from the hall. Dan had protested but Mary told him she had no idea whether half the town was coming or all of it.

Next the women got to work preparing several large pots of lamb and vegetable stew and a ton of potatoes for the Christmas eve dinner for when the guests from the mine arrived.

'Are you getting excited Ben' Mary asked now?

'Yes, I am. I'm glad Wally will be here for Christmas to.'

Ben went off to check the smoker they were smoking ten rabbits, ten chickens, and two dozen fish, also for the feast. Dan smiled at Mary, 'could this day get any better Mary?'

Bryce's voice behind them brought them about to look at him. By his side was Sarah. 'Dad, Mary can we talk to you?'

Dan and Mary nodded keeping a straight face. 'Go on son,' said Dan softly.

Bryce shuffled his feet and ran his hand down his face. 'Well see, we . . . . that is me and Sarah, are tired of keeping a secret . . . . '

Dan cut in with a grin, 'Oh you think this is a secret' he smiled indicating the two of them with his hand.

'Oh' said Bryce while Sarah grinned at him. 'Well anyway, we want to get engaged.'

'You got a ring son' asked Dan and Mary looked sharply at him? Bryce nodded.

There was a silence while they looked at each other. 'Well, I think that's bloody marvellous you two.' Dan held his arms out to them, and they stepped into his embrace.

Mary got into the embrace and then stepped back. 'Why don't you get engaged and announce it at the wedding?'

'Well, we wouldn't want to steel anybody's thunder . . . . '

'And what have I told you about these old wives' tales Bryce' answered Dan? 'You won't be stealing anyone's thunder you'll be adding to it. Three weddings and an engagement on Christmas day is a lot of damn thunder. Why I bet you could hear it clear down to Melbourne. And clear up to heaven Bryce my lovely boy.' Bryce squirmed inwardly at being called a lovely boy, but he was sure his father had to do it.

It was decided to announce their engagement at the wedding. Bryce went off to help put the tents up near the long hut for the men from the mine to sleep in. They would lift the sides and tie them out high to make more room, and also to let the breeze through.

Dan looked at Mary and she said, 'yep, it just got better my love.'

Dan pulled her into his arms and held her. 'You know Mary, this just gets better and better to. It feels just as thrilling to hold you now as it did that day down by the river, more in fact. Do you think we should have a rest, Mary? Have a little lay down for a bit?'

'No Dan, your rests are just not restful. Come now we have work to do.'

Dan kissed her and went off to help rearranging the furniture to fit eighty. They'd had nearly that many before but not quite. There were townspeople coming as well. Mary had asked Dan how many he'd invited. Dan had looked down at his feet. 'You don't know do you' she said?

Dan looked up 'well you didn't keep count either did you?'

Mary smiled now as she watched him go. No, she hadn't kept count had she?

More than half the people slept outside of the long hut now in small dwellings and so they had room for another large table and more stools. Everything was washed and polished and aired. There were curtains now at the three windows and flyscreens. They had put another window in at the family end and the two windows in the kitchen all had shutters. And all the windows had sills now and the women grew herbs in them.

The whole place had been painted a creamy colour, except for the woodwork. Floors and rafters were polished wood. The slate in the kitchen was polished and the tables and chairs were polished wood. And they still used the beautiful wooden dishes the older men had made. Mary suspected half the town still used them they were beautiful. And they were all you could afford in the dark years before and during the war. But people still used them.

There was a Christmas tree in the kitchen area which had been decorated by the older kids. And as usual every child there had a present of like value to come. Dan looked about him now, how he loved this time of year, how he loved these children. And how he loved the looks on their faces when they opened their presents. He sighed contentedly and how he loved his wife.

On the twenty fourth of December the two couples, Wally and Melissa with Ray and Sue set off for Balranald. They left early at four in the morning, so as to give a hand with the preparations. They would return home on boxing day and go back to work the next day.

The girls wanted to get there and make sure their clothes and hair and everything else would be looking its best. Wally and Ray sat up in the back while melissa and Sue sat in the front. Melissa had her licence now and could handle the car just fine.

They arrived in time for lunch. There were two land rovers at the mine and the boys, along with Steven and Linda and Eric would arrive before teatime. Eric found himself looking forward to it and he had a bit of a surprise for Wally. He had already cleared it with Dan who said they would be happy for him to bring his mother for the wedding. Gladys and Linda sat in the front with Eric.

Some of the men had stayed back at the mine to look after the place. But fifteen men had come to see Wally and Ray get married. And these fifteen men looked forward to Christmas for the first time in many years. Their excitement was palpable, and Gladys commented on it to Eric. 'It's a shame' she said sadly.

'Come on, cheer up mum' said Eric, 'didn't you see the new fridge I got them. And next Christmas mum we'll make sure they have a good one hay.'

'Yes Eric, thank you. I will hold you to that son.' She leaned across and patted his cheek.

Some of the men in the back of the rovers couldn't remember a Christmas they hadn't got blind drunk to forget. Forget it was Christmas. Some of them had never had a happy Christmas, to them Christmas was a time of year the old man got drunk and belted everybody, so you stayed away from home.

Some of the blokes were going home for Christmas and knowing full well that they'd be glad when it was over. They'd try and get through it without losing their temper. Then there were fewer still going home to their wives and children who were happy about it. A bit of a mixed bag, Christmas thought Eric.

Yet there wasn't a man climbing into those vehicles who wasn't looking forward to meeting the people of the long hut and seeing it for themselves. And they were not disappointed. As they drove into the compound the people spilled out to meet them. They were greeted like long lost relatives.

The men were directed to the tents where they would be sleeping, to stash their gear, they had all brought their Matilda. Dan assured them that their belongings would be safe and none of these people of the long hut would steal from them. He also assured them that if they were uneasy about it and wanted to cart their Matilda with them no offence would be taken. That was when the men from the mine knew they were at home at the long hut. And they realised that Dan was a very decent bloke. Dan in turn knew that their Matilda was more often than not, all they had in the world.

The ladies had a sleeping area inside where Gladys and anyone of the ladies could sleep. Most of the partitioned family areas had been taken down as more and more of their number moved their sleeping area out of the long hut. They never moved very far maybe a few feet; they mostly needed the comfort of it. A veranda ran around three sides of the hut, and the smaller huts were off that. So now the family area was a line of beds round the wall partitioned by curtains for some privacy. Noreen had brought that idea home from the hospital.

Wally was pleased to see Gladys he hadn't thought she would come. She hugged him and kissed his cheek. 'I wouldn't have missed it for anything' she told him.

A great stew was served that night with a side table consisting of mashed potatoes, and some pies, pasties, and salads. There were also loaves and rolls and buns with home-made butter and jams. Everything homemade and delicious. Eric nodded to Ray, 'see where Wally learned to cook hay.' Ray nodded his mouth was crammed full of bread, butter, jam, and cream.

Then after they'd eaten, they were treated to the children singing carols and the children of the camp put on quite a show. They had candles lit and placed around the area and they sang beautifully. They had done every year since that first year and Dan sat next to Mary for it. On que the moon peaked over the horizon in all its orange splendour.

Dan as usual got teary eyed, he couldn't help it he did every year. And the men from the camp and the people of the long hut all sat quietly and listened. Some began to sing along softly to the ones they knew, and Dan's heart was gladdened. He nodded to them and smiled to show his appreciation clapping loudly to them all at the end of each carol. Alas Dan had never learned to sing them.

Mary sang along and so then everyone joined in. Soon the Christmas carols rang out across the land and disturbed some cockies trying to sleep high in the gum trees along the river. They objected loudly and added their voices to Christmas. Dan thought it was a beautiful thing, a little bit of magic, and his heart was at peace.

There followed an evening of talking together like old friends and Gladys was astounded at what these people had achieved here. They all were, some had doubted and thought that Wally may have exaggerated. He hadn't.

Dan stood up at one point and told them they were all invited back next Christmas. He got quite a round of applause. Eric looked hard at his mum; she was teary eyed.

Gladys found that she envied them. Yes, they may live on top of one another a bit, but they would never find themselves alone with their problems. Alone and isolated with their burdens. And she watched the effect that the children had on them and was surprised to realise that this was what kept them all so young. Young and happy.

Mary sat down beside Gladys and said softly, 'we are here Gladys should you ever need us.'

And the tears that had been threatening, spilled down her face as Mary took her hand and held it.

'Thank you,' said Gladys.

Dan cut in, 'we are neighbours now, we will keep in touch.'

That night after the kids had all gone exhausted to their beds, Santa clause came. Dan was as always front and centre laying the presents under the tree. He took such care, sometimes trying one present in a few places before he put it down.

When it was done, he looked at Mary and as the others watched on he spoke softly to her. 'So many Christmases we had nothing to give them Mary. Not even a decent feed. I give thanks for this as always.' He looked down and with his head bowed and his hands hanging at his side he said, 'and I give thanks daily for you Mary.'

Arms reached for the man, not just Mary's arms but also many of the other people. Wally said in a clear voice 'and we give thanks for you, mate.'

Yeah, this is where it comes from thought Eric, this attitude that Wally carried. And wasn't he glad of it, they all were.

Christmas morning was the usual bedlam as the kids lined up at the tree eyeing the presents underneath it. They all still got just one present. If they couldn't give them all two presents, then not one of them got two. Never one above the other, a good policy Dan thought. And it was bedlam as they jittered about waiting. So much so that they didn't hear the car pull up outside. No one knew anything about it until a familiar voice rang out 'Merry Christmas.'

'Jack' the shout went up 'Jack'.

There was a moments silence when all eyes were on Jack standing beside a strange woman smiling at them, and then a stampede. Even the kids dragged themselves away from the presents to greet their beloved Jack.

Jack was engulfed in a sea of people, some crying some laughing and some shouting, yes and some he didn't know. It was just moments before it suddenly seemed to hit them there was something different about Jack.

Mary's hands flew to her mouth, and she stared at Jacks' face. It was a terrible scar and everybody there was on the verge of tears. But Jack was different in another way. He was tanned and strong looking so much so that he appeared taller. Jack dressed different to, and the scar made him look bigger. And it made him look tougher. In a strange way the scar completed the man, and stranger still it suited him.

There was an air about him that bespoke his peace and his newfound confidence. Yes, Jack had changed in just about every way. Like Dan had told them he was no longer broken. And he had a beautiful woman with him who had a baby in her arms. And Jack was grinning from ear to ear.

They all knew Jack now had a son called Billy Walter. Somebody did ask Jack once in the Mataranka pub, why he called his son Billy and not William. Jack had smiled at this and said, 'what Willy Wally?' Fred had choked on his beer. The drovers had all laughed and Jimmy had said 'well, I think it's a good name Jack.' And everyone laughed louder. The laughter died on Jack's face, what had he done? He had shrugged and got another beer. By the end of the night, it was funny again.

Dan and Wally approached the three people as if they might disappear. Jack smiled at Dan and Wally and embraced them. 'Just in time to watch these little ruggers open their pressies.' Jack looked at Mary who stood beside Dan and smiled. He went on, 'I always loved this day, loved watching them tear that paper off. We got on the road at three o'clock so we could be here for this. This Christmas morning chaos is among my happiest memories.' He looked at Dan now, 'all those letters I write home are done with the pen I got from you.'

Mary walked towards Jack a tear in her eye. 'Your poor face Jack. It must have almost killed you.'

Jack was astounded, he still loved this woman, but it no longer hurt. He hugged her to him and then turning to his beautiful wife, 'Mary, I would like you to meet my wife, Mary.'

Dan saw the look of confusion on Jack's face and his heart lurched in his chest. Maybe Jack wasn't as over Mary as he had hoped. Poor bloody Jack.

The two women shook hands shyly and then they hugged, and the paper tearing ceremony got underway. Kids squealed with delight as they unwrapped their shiny new toys. Dan reached behind him and produced a little present and handed it to Jack's son.

'You knew,' cried Mary.

There was the usual stampede for the doorway as the kids needed to get outside with their toys. They had cap guns, bows and arrows, trucks, dolls, and all manner of treasure. And best of all, these kids knew how to share, Dan had insisted on it quite strongly.

Jack was taken outside and introduced to the men from the mine, it was Eric who commented on his face. 'What happened to your face Jack? You wouldn't be the ball breaker we've all heard about, would you? The bull ball breaker?'

'No' exclaimed Jack loudly, 'Dan? Or was it you Wally?' Jack looked back at Eric now.

Eric shook his head 'wasn't anybody in this camp Jack. I heard about you in the bloody pub.' Everyone was laughing. Eric went on, 'well that's where everybody heard it, Jack. In the pub. And now people talk, all up and down the Murray and the Muurmbidgee about the bloke who thought to kick a bull in the balls.' All the men laughed, and Jack stood grinning.

Jack looked doubtful for a bit and then suddenly he sucked in air, 'Wally. You were in the pub with Wally. Come here big guy' Jack put his arm around Wally in a head lock and rubbed the top of his head with his knuckles. 'I bloody miss you.' He swung his other arm around Wally and planted a kiss on his cheek.

Wally proudly introduced Melissa to Jack and Jack held his arms out to her. And Melissa found that old familiar feeling in his embrace. They were such nice men these men of the Murrumbidgee. They were gentle and loving, Melissa had never known anything like it. She had never before known such gentle natured people.

Jack stood with his arm around Melissa now and said to Wally 'so did you know that me and Mary are renewing our vows today?'

Wally was delighted and Dan stepped forward 'and me and my Mary to.' He grinned and hoped he hadn't hurt Jack.

Just then a car pulled up, it was the local taxi. Dan turned and grinned when he recognised Fred getting out. On the other side was Tom. Dan and Wally with Jack made for the taxi. Tom walked around and took Wally in his arms and then Fred did.

Wally wiped his eyes 'what are you blokes doing here?'

'Well, you are getting married aren't you, Wally' asked Tom?

'Did you think we'd miss it, Wally' said Fred? 'So, this is your long hut Dan' he said as he shook hands with Dan. 'Pretty bloody impressive man. And are you gunna introduce us to all these people? What a wonderful place. Christ almighty man and all out of cast offs.' Fred couldn't seem to drag his eyes away from the building.

Dan smiled and nodded, Fred was excited, and it was good to see them. Wally stepped forward now and said, 'this is Mary, Dan's wife.'

'Ah, Mary' said Fred as he took her hand in his. 'I have looked forward to this day dear lady.' He smiled his most dazzling at her and she fell under his spell. Like so many before her.

Jack stood by studying the big man. He wondered again if Fred even noticed. Fred turned as Wally introduced him to Melissa, he took her hand and said, 'such beautiful women down here must be something to do with the Murrumbidgee.'

After that the people were introduced to Fred and Tom. Tom looked at Wally a soft smile played round his lips. 'Congratulations man she is lovely. And Jack and Dan have been keeping me informed of your accomplishments. I am proud of you mate. Emily couldn't come I'm afraid, but she sends her very best. And she says she'd be happy to dance with you Wally.'

Fred clapped Wally on the back, 'well I hear you are coming up to Queensland to have a go at the bulls hay. Heard you were getting a bit jealous of Jacks looks huh.' Wally laughed and nodded.

And so it was that three couples got married and two couples renewed their vows and one couple got engaged. And the kids played until they dropped. And everyone ate until they could eat no more. All the people from town and the camp and the long hut were very taken with Tom and Fred. It did seem that they were the entertainment, and they lapped it up.

The priest stayed for some refreshments and then had to get back for mass. He had come to love and respect these people and he enjoyed their company. He had liked the two men from the top end also. He had been horrified to see Jacks face now, but strangely he'd never known the man to be so happy and at peace. And didn't the lord work in mysterious ways?

The men of the mine ate their fill of the best food they'd ever eaten. They had been impressed by all of these people and Eric had promised that they would not be strangers. Mary had suggested bringing Gladys for extended stays sometimes when Eric was away. This had brought a huge smile from the old lady. In all the years that followed she visited the people of the long hut and remained firm friends with them until her death in sixty-seven. And they spent Christmas together these people from the mine and the long hut from then on.

Tom said he and Fred had to get on the way home the next day they had flown down but were needed back home. Tom had stood aside with Jack and Wally and Dan and said, 'what a lovely place to grow up' as they watched the kids play. He turned to Dan 'I had to see it for myself man. This is nothing short of amazing. You were right Jack.'

Dan turned to Ben and extending his arm in a grand yet humble gesture he announced, 'this is Ben, our master builder.' Tom shook hands with Ben eagerly.

Fred strode up with Mary and joined in. 'Well, I'm glad we came.' He looked across at Wally 'bull catching starts in around five months, will be in full swing in about seven months. Think you'll make it Wally?'

Wally shrugged 'maybe next year Fred, I'm not sure.'

'Well let us know when you get a bit nearer hay?'

A bit later Fred strode into the long hut with Mary and stood looking about. 'This is magnificent, and you did this with materials from the dump? We live in a similar structure, but it was a large shed and we built bedrooms away from it. Jack and them, live in a similar structure to. Well, I take my hat off to you people.' He smiled down at Mary.

She asked him about droving and Fred gladly told her about it. 'Our team has been together for a lot of years' he finished. 'Yeah, we are family now much the same as you are here.'

Mary smiled and looked at Jack, no wonder she thought, no wonder he loves where he is. These people were amazing and so was Jack now. Mary looked hard at him; his scar made him look more mature more . . . . she wasn't sure. He just looked better for it. And Fred and Tom had come a long way for him and Wally. Mary thought they might lose Wally and she felt saddened.

That night around the campfire while the moon rose and shone down on them; the drovers from the Katherine River in the Northern Territory, the miners of the Murray and the farmers of the Murrumbidgee and a bull catcher from the top end sat around and talked. A peace settled on these people which was euphoric. The children went off to sleep to the hum of voices talking and the intermittent rumble of laughter.

Mary sat with Gladys and Eric and Bryce got talking to Eric. Dan sat beside Mary and held her hand, he was happy. The distances involved in this country coupled with the very bad roads meant that no one knew if or when they would sit like this again.

Dan listened to the talk, how he wished Jack and Wally weren't leaving. He also listened to Bryce land the job of driving the dozer. Dan sighed he supposed he'd have to let him go to. Libby sat at Dans feet and eased his heart some.

The next morning everyone packed up and got into their vehicles and left for the mine. Jack promised that he would come by on their way back to the top end. He said to Wally, 'we'll stay for a few days hay. Do some fishing like the old days man. I need to talk to you Wally it has been so long.' Jack slapped Wally on the shoulder 'I hear you are a dozer operator Wally, and you are a paddle boat driver to.'

Fred and Tom were about to leave, and Tom said 'Emily would be proud of you Wally. Is it alright if I tell her all about it?'

'Of course, Tom and thank you for your talk that day.' He turned to Jack, 'Yeah of course Jack, it'll be good to sit and fish with you again I have missed it to.' He turned to them all. 'It was Dan, he taught me to drive the truck and the tractor, and I've got my licences now. He also taught me to ride and look after a horse. Yeah, Jack come by and stay a while if you can mate. We'd love that wouldn't we Mel?'

Fred smiled at Wally, 'so you will come droving with us then. I mean now you can ride hay?'

Mel smiled and nodded and Jack and Wally both knew she was overwhelmed. They also knew she was happy, Jack had heard the story, the awful story of her uncle. But he knew she'd be alright now she had his brother looking out for her. Jack was overjoyed for Wally.

Though Jack did wonder at himself. What on earth had possessed him to put his bloody arms around Mary of the shanty?

Jack and Wally sat by the fire and watched Jacks little boy dart about, he was like Jack. 'He falls over a lot, Jack' Wally said with concern.

Jack smiled and nodded 'he hasn't been walking all that long they tell me it's normal. Doesn't seem to hurt him all that much.' Jack spoke softly now, 'so when are you coming up to Queensland Wally?'

'Soon Jack we'll probably leave here in March. Mel is looking forward to coming to; she loves the rivers same as me.'

'It's a bloody long way mate.'

'Yeah, I thought about that Jack, and I think we might be better off driving. We can stop and walk the rivers and fish and maybe work if I need to. It's a long way for Mel to walk and a car would be somewhere a bit safer.'

'Are you thinking about this car Wally? The FJ there? It is a bloody nice car mate.'

'Well, I considered getting a newish land rover. A long wheelbase like yours and I can make a bit of a home in the back of it. You know stick a canopy on it with sides you can roll up or down like you've done with yours. Well, they've got a bit more room and there's the four-wheel drive if you wanna head bush.'

Jack took Wally to his rover and showed him how he'd set it up. 'And under the bed here it has a kitchen you can pull out like a drawer look. It has two draws and a small two burner stove in it. And on the other side we have another drawer for clothes and stuff.'

Jack walked to a large trailer with a stock crate on it for more room. 'In the trailer there we carry stuff like a bush shower, a thunder bucket and fuel and water. We even carry a tent in case we need to stop for longer periods. I've got two spare tyres to and some odds and ends. We also have a large tucker box, our fishing gear, and an esky. We carry a toolbox and a shovel' Jack pulled the shovel out, 'and that makes her into a five-wheel drive.' The two men laughed amicably. Jack pulled out three rabbit traps 'in case we need them. I haven't forgotten Wally.' Jack smiled and reached on top of the load 'a couple of chairs and a fold up table.'

'Hell yeah' said Wally 'this will do just fine. I have got something to work on now Jack.'

Jack looked back at Wally's tent and said 'that's a pretty big tent Wally you might be better off with a smaller one hay.'

All too soon Jack was gone leaving Wally with a lump in his throat. He was glad to be alone with Melissa and he talked excitedly now. He told her of his plan to get a land rover and deck it out for them. 'The same as Jack's, that's if you agree Mel, we'd have to trade the FJ in on it, that's gunna hurt. I'd like to get a trailer to carry the tent and so forth, we should carry as much water and fuel as we can. What do you think Mel?'

Melissa smiled and nodded, 'when can we get going Wally?'

Wally chuckled and pulled her closer. 'I've got a week end off in a few weeks Mel so we could go and get the rover and everything I'd need. We are halfway through January so if we look at end of March. That'll give us time to save a bit more money . . . . '

Wally thought he heard a car. He put his finger to his lips and got up and pulled his pants on, then his shirt. Melissa did the same. Wally didn't have the faith in the police and the judicial system that most people had, and he worried about Rodney. He'd bought ammo and had taught Melissa to shoot.

Wally stepped out of the tent his gun in his pocket. He relaxed when Erics land rover came into sight.

Eric pulled up and got out he had a funny expression on his face that Wally was unable to read. He was smiling as he walked up to Wally 'hope you weren't in bed mate. I wouldn't come this late, but I had a phone call today. It was Jim at the real estate agency they have a buyer for Melissa's house.'

Melissa walked over and stood beside Wally now. 'Thank God Wally. I just want to be rid of it.'

'Okay then' said Eric, 'the offer was for six thousand pounds. A bloody good offer Melissa, you probably won't do any better. Tomorrow lunchtime I will take you to the phone and you can talk to him. If you want to come Melissa, be where Wally's dozer is at around midday. Maybe you can work it out Wally. You could get over to the camp and meet her there and bring her to the phone.

Well congratulations you two and I'll see you in the morning.'

'Yeah, thanks Eric,' said Wally. Melissa joined in 'yes, thank you.'

Eric smiled at them 'you're welcome young lady.'

Eric coughed and looked down at his feet, not making any move to get in his car. Studying the ground he said, 'now I have a wedding present for you Wally at last, you and Melissa. Only if you want mind, but Clyde is coming by this week on his way down to Albury Wodonga and I know you wanted to go there. He'll be gone about six days. You be on it if you wish, he'll call some time Thursday.'

Wally stood looking at Eric then grinned 'I'll be on it Eric and thank you very bloody much.' He turned to Melissa who grinned back at him, 'what a bloody honeymoon, hay woman.'

The house was sold, and Melissa asked the real estate agent to put the money in Wally's account. It was Wally who turned and said, 'why Mel?'

Jim smiled as she answered 'well I don't have an account. You know at the bank.' Melissa flushed bright red.

Jim said, 'Well if you sign a paper to that effect that will be fine. You two are married now.'

Wally turned to look at no one, 'we should have your name on my account Mel. We should make it a joint account.' Wally sounded surprised, surprised at himself.

Wally and Melissa went off on their weeklong boat trip. They went down the river to Echuca and they had some time to kill there. 'Be back in two hours' said Clyde. Wally and Melissa headed straight for the car yard and found their land rover. Wally paid a deposit on it and the man told him they'd hold it for him. It was a year old, and Wally paid just under a thousand pounds. The manager of the car yard had offered them four hundred trade in on their FJ if it was as good as they said.

'We could even slip down after work if we have to Mel,' said Wally on the way back to the boat.

Melissa threw her arms around Wally and kissed him there in the street. 'Like I said thank God for you Wally.' She clasped her hands in front of her and jumped around, 'oh Wally I can't wait.'

At Albury Wally was amazed at how busy it was there. It was five o'clock and Clyde went off to the pub. Wally and Melissa went to find a tree. Once they had set up camp, they sat down to catch a fish for their dinner. But the fish weren't bighting.

Wally went off to a nearby café to buy some fish and chips for dinner. He paid for the fish and chips and left the shop. Wally heard a strange sort of scream and his heart lurched in his chest. It was Melissa. He ran to their camp and there under the two trees were two blokes attacking his Mel. They were dragging her about.

Wally dropped the parcel he was carrying and pulled one of the men off and punched him. The second man tried to run but Wally caught him. He turned and Wally saw that his face was scratched quite badly. The man lifted his arms in front of his face and began to whine, 'please . . . . I . . . . I didn't want to do it . . . . he made me.'

'Fuckin rubbish' said Wally and belting him in the face he knocked him senseless.

He ran to Melissa and held her, she wasn't crying. He held her at arm's length, 'are you okay sweetheart' he asked softly?

To his surprise she smiled and said 'yes Wally. I knew you would save me; I knew it.'

'Do you want to go to the police Mel?'

'No baby, but I'd like to go back to the boat.'

The first man was getting to his feet, so Wally grabbed him and punched him to the ground. Then he stuck the boots in. After that the man crawled away as fast as he could.

The next morning Wally was glad to be leaving. Mel stood beside him as they pulled out. 'I'm sorry Wally' she said softly.

He looked up a little surprised 'for what my love?'

'I have been such a lot of trouble to you.'

'Well see, now you're just talking rubbish woman. I bloody love you and you make me happy. Right?' He took her hand 'I never dreamed I would ever be this happy Mel.' He squeezed her hand and she smiled. He let go of her hand and went on shovelling coal. 'Let's get out of here' he said.

That trip Wally was glad to get home. He said goodbye to Clyde and promised the old man that he would be back. 'I belong here Clyde' he said, 'I belong to these rivers. But I just want to see those far off rivers in those far off places. To catch the fish, they house. But I will never belong out there, I belong here.'

'Good son, that makes me feel better. Now here son, hang on to these.' He handed Wally some papers. 'The deeds to the old girl here. You own her now son, but I still need to live here for a bit.' Clyde looked squarely at Wally, 'it is in my will, though nobody will contest it there isn't anybody.'

Wally looked at the papers and looked at Mel where she stood on the bank. He drew the old river captain into his arms and hugged him gently and heard him sob. When he felt the old man's arms go round him a tear made its way down his own face. Wally straightened up and sniffed, 'I do not look forward to taking possession of this boat. I can't even think about it. I love you old fulla.'

Clyde smiled and said goodbye. 'I'll see you when you get back' he said over his shoulder. Wally watched him go.

And he was gone. Wally hung his head; he didn't think he'd get home in time. 'Do you promise Clyde' he whispered, and he felt Melissa's arms go round him.

The next week Melissa and Wally brought home the land rover and Wally set about making it a home on wheels. They also ordered a trailer which they would pick up in four weeks.

And by the end of March, they were ready. He promised Eric he would be back in no more than two years. Wally had trained young Bryce to operate the dozer and he was almost as good as Wally. Eric was happy with this arrangement; the young bloke was very similar to Wally.

Bryce and Sarah took over Wally's camp minus the radio, the tent was a bit big to throw on the trailer, so they'd got a smaller one. But Wally wasn't parting with his radio.

'Ooh' said Bryce 'you've got a radio in your rover. I'll give you five pounds for it.'

'Bloody cheek,' said Wally. 'Are you hearing this Mel?'

Sarah laughed, she was a good cook and the men had arranged to pay her to do the cooking. Wally knew Bryce would be okay, he had a knack for the bulldozer, and he enjoyed the work. He told Wally one day he might get himself an earth moving plant someday.

Wally said he'd probably want to get a job on his dozer one day. Bryce smiled and said, 'I'm gunna get a land rover and do it out just like yours one day. Then I'm gunna drive that heap of shit I've got right into the river.'

Then Bryce told Wally how he wanted to go to Queensland, but he had responsibilities now. 'I'll get up there someday' he said, 'after hearing you and Jack and Dad talk about it and meeting Fred and Tom. Hey, Jacks Missus is nice, isn't she? She's quiet but nice, I'm glad for Jack. He spent so long in love with dad's Mary' Bryce gave a hic of a laugh, 'and don't I know what that's like.'

'You Bryce' Wally smiled. 'Not you to?'

'Yep Wally, me to. I moved on a bit quicker than you and Jack though.' Wally was dumbfounded. Bryce went on quietly, 'now I know you are over it thanks be to the Gods, but Jack?' Bryce shook his head, 'and with the looker he's got an' all.'

It broke Wally's heart, so Jack had not gotten over her. Bryce was a very astute young man, and he was very understanding. Bryce was a lot like his dad. Poor bloody Jack, still Jack seemed happy enough.

Wally changed the subject now, 'it's a shame Kane didn't get home for Christmas.'

'Kane's only concern is Kane. You know Wally I know it's awful, but I never actually liked him. I love you and Jack and everyone else but not him. Dad struggles with it and so does Mary. But he's changed since he went away. He doesn't have a girlfriend because he fancies himself a ladies' man. No Wally, there's no love lost between me and him.'

'Well, you are nothing like him Bryce.'

'Are you going bull catching to Wally? What's it like did you see any of it when you were up there?'

Wally nodded. 'I am Bryce, and the drover Tom has offered to take me droving to. Don't know as I will, I'd be away from Mel.' Wally looked down at his feet, 'I think I'd try it Bryce, think I'd give it a go. And look how happy they are Bryce; I mean they enjoy life.'

'Yeah, they seem to be a pretty happy, laid-back lot alright. By the look of Jacks face this bull catching is bloody dangerous. You will be extra careful won't you Wal?'

Wally heard the falter in Bryce's voice and slinging an arm around the young bloke he promised he would.

Bryce said now, 'how exciting is it?'

'It's bloody amazing and I haven't even caught one yet. But I will Bryce.'

'Well just don't go kicking one of them bastards in the balls Wally. What the hell would possess him to do that?'

The two men laughed and then Wally realised that Bryce didn't know the story, and Wally decided to tell him. 'The bull he kicked was squashing his mate Alby against the side of the vehicle Bryce. If he hadn't done what he did that bull would have killed him.'

'Shit, I didn't know Wally. So, Jack's a bit of a hero. What's this Alby like?'

'He's a bloody nice bloke, they were mates in the war in New Guinea and they look out for each other now. Well anyway Jack saved Alby and the bull knocked Jack down and was all set to stomp him into the ground apparently. Well, when Jack went down Alby ran back in and dragged him out. So, they saved each other that day.'

Bryce shook his head, 'I'd like to meet him one day.' Wally smiled at the young man he loved like a brother. They were all brothers these men and who knew, maybe one day Alby would be counted amongst them. Wally found he hoped so and went on to tell Bryce about the rest of them, the rest of the men from the top end. Bryce listened intently.

Sarah went off to give Melissa a hand at the fire, the two girls got along well, and Wally was glad. He turned to Bryce now, 'I'll be back Bryce in a year or two. I belong here on the banks of these rivers. Grand as those other rivers maybe I will come back home to the rivers I love. To the people I love and who love me.'

'Your job will be here for you Wally.'

'Nah. I will go back to the Murrumbidgee mate, always the Murrumbidgee.' Bryce looked intently at the fire as if he were studying the flames. 'Yeah Wally, but it's a good thing to travel about a bit before you settle down. I like Melissa man she's a good sort and I'm happy you found her. And she is well suited to you to.'

'You're still not getting the radio.'

CHAPTER 8

Finally on the twentieth of March, Wally and Melissa were ready to go. They had their home in the rover and a tent and a trailer. They were set, and they had almost seven thousand pounds in the bank. A fortune, but one that Wally wanted to hang on to. Though in his gear in the lock up box were the deeds to the boat. He planned to give them to Dan to keep for him while he was away. He knew two things; Dan would keep them safe and would be comforted.

They would call in and say goodbye to the people of the long hut. Wally hugged Bryce, Ray, Sarah, and Susan. Luckily Susan and Sarah got along well and also Linda. Bryce and Sarah would move into Wally's tent, everyone seemed to really like the young man. Wally knew that Bryce was a good bloke, one of the best like his father. So, like his father.

They called in to the mine and Wally shook hands with the men and promised he'd be back before they knew it. Eric looked Wally's rig over and nodded his approval. 'Well, I wish I was going with you young Wally. And don't forget to drop us a line sometimes. Even if you just say hello, I'd hate to cause you any stress.' He smiled.

Freddy walked up and embraced Wally, he started to speak but couldn't go on. Wally took his hanky out of his pocket and wiped the old man's eyes and nose then handed it to him. Freddy tried to speak, and Wally pulled him into his arms. 'I know old friend I know. I'll come back I'll be back before you know it. Brycie will look after you he's a good man.'

Freddy smiled through the tears 'I know he is Wally I know he is. He's like you and he loves you. It's breaking his heart you're leaving.' Freddy shook his head now, 'go on son get in your car. We'll be here when you get back. And thanks for everything you've done for us.'

Wally had a heavy heart as he drove away. Melissa saw it and slid across the seat and put her arms around him. Wally put his arm around her and held her close. He stopped the car a few miles along the river road. 'Do you realise that we're doing it Mel? We are on the river trip starting with the mighty Murray River.' He took her in his arms 'do you think we should try all the gear out?'

'Gear?'

'Yeah . . . . You know. We should probably try the bed out.'

'It's too early . . . .'

'Why is it?'

'Wally it's not lunch time yet.' She smiled now, 'I suppose the bed is made up so we could have a lay down.'

Afterwards as Wally lay in her arms he sighed, 'what do you think of the bed?'

'It's comfy Wally and plenty of room. I can see us sleeping every night in this for the next few years. Oh, Wally, I love you.'

'And I love you Mrs Wally. Now do you wanna do some fishing? Because we can.' Wally grinned 'for the time being we can do what we want when we want.'

'It's wonderful.'

'Of course, I'll have to get work in a few weeks or months, but for now . . . . ' He rolled over and kissed this woman who had stollen his heart. 'Fishing for our dinner. Well shortly anyway.'

They fell asleep there on the riverbank, it was so peaceful, and Melissa felt safe in Wally's arms in her new home. Wally had made a bedroom out of the back of the land rover. He'd put up a four-poster frame a little higher than the cabin and had put a canopy over the top. He'd put tarpaulin curtains on the back and sides that you could roll down and tie them to give them absolute privacy. It would keep them dry when it rained to. Or you could roll them up and tie them up.

Wally had also taken out the back window of the rover and so they could access the cabin through it if they needed to. He'd put a roof rack on the cabin which had a low box attached to it with all their fishing gear, a rifle, and spare shoes. The box was securely fitted to the vehicle and had a sturdy padlock on it.

Wally had also made a sturdy box where the glove box was and that had a sturdy padlock on it to. They kept their valuables in it, Wally was not naïve. When they were away from the vehicles Wally had his handgun in his pocket. Melissa had put studs on the pockets of his pants for him.

On the back of the frame covering the rover Wally had made an awning so they could stand or sit at the side of the rover without getting wet. Wally carried a tyre pump in case they got bogged in the sand and had to let the tyres down.

Wally had also had a tarp fitted across the back of the land rover which covered the tray and their bed. It had a rope fitted to it so could be tied down securely to the sides of the vehicle to keep the dust out of their bedding. Melissa put a mat at the back of the car to wipe their feet on before getting in. This kept their bed and their belongings dust free.

When they woke up the two lovers sat and fished the Murray for their dinner. The galahs and corellas screeched and called to each other in the treetops. Wally listened to it all and smiled. 'I wonder how much of that is about us Mel.'

Melissa smiled and said 'most of it I guess Wally. They are probably wondering why we just sit and stare at the water instead of feeding.'

'I think you might be right honey. Listen Mel, do you wanna live in the houseboat when we get back?'

'Well of course I do but we can't do that until Clyde . . . . well until . . . . '

'Clyde will be dead Mel.' Wally stifled a sob but let the tear fall. 'He gave me the deeds to the boat Mel. I do hope I'm wrong.'

Wally got a bight and hauled in a large Murray cod. 'I have big plans to make a beautiful home out of if Mel. I will honour him and keep that old girl on the water.'

It broke Wally's heart once more to say goodbye to Dan and Mary and his family on the Murrumbidgee. Dan told Wally once again what a marvellous job he'd done making a home out of the land rover. 'I am thinking now that I would like to do this with Mary in a few years.' And Wally told him he could have this land rover when he was ready to go.

'I will bloody take you up on that Wally. I'd like to show Mary around up the top end.' Dan hugged Wally to him, 'always a place here for you Wally.'

Mary stepped forward with a gift from the long hut and handed it to Melissa. It was wrapped in newspaper and tied with string. Mel asked if she could open it and Mary said of course.

Melissa gaped at the blanket; it was beautiful. It was a double bed quilt and Mary said that everyone had made a patch for it. 'This blue line that runs through it from here to here is the Murrumbidgee. And this lovely yellow sunflower here, is home.'

Melissa held it to her, and tears rolled down her face. Mary embraced her and then everyone else did. Last was Dan, he smiled, 'goodbyes take forever around here young un.' He took her gently in his arms and kissed her.

'If you need me, I'm there, okay?' He turned and embraced Wally, then he leaned across and took a parcel wrapped in brown paper from a log. 'Something for your Journey my son. Go on now you two and stay in touch. You can open that later.'

'I'll be back Dan you know. I have given you my home to look after. And thanks for agreeing to take care of those deeds Dan, I appreciate it.'

'My pleasure son, I will guard them with my life. And don't forget your home here.'

Wally let go of a great sob and got in the rover. How could he do it, he looked at Mel? She smiled and said, 'I'll understand Wally. If you can't go, we can just stay.'

He shook his head, started the car, and put it in gear. Slowly he drove away while Melissa waved out the window.

Later when they stopped to camp on the outskirts of Milduraon the banks of the Murray River once again, Wally opened his package. In it was a beautiful writing set complete with a pencil a fountain pen and ink and a little box with a dozen stamps in it. There was a writing pad and envelopes. Also in the package was a journal, an honest to goodness, leather bound journal. Wally let the tears flow and Melissa held him.

'I told Dan about the boat Mel' Wally smiled through the tears. 'He is going to get busy and build us a jetty near the long hut. Is that alright with you Mel?'

Mel nodded and held him. 'Him and Ben. We can take the family on a weekend away on it Mel.'

Mel smiled at him, 'some at a time Wally?'

Wally smiled back 'yes, definitely my love, some at a time.'

The next day Wally turned right, and they headed off up the Darling River, also a tributary of the Murray. But Wally was excited to be on the Darling basin now. They would follow the Darling River for a few weeks. It was intermittent the farther north they got and by the time they arrived in Bourk it was a string of waterholes in places. So, Wally and Melissa wandered from water hole to water hole. The townspeople said that they hadn't had any rain for a long time.

They fished whenever they were near water but only caught some now and again. Wally was glad they had a vehicle now and he was also glad to have fresh water with them. Every night they lit a big fire and tuned into the radio. Wally always set his traps and found he had more luck with those than the fishing. They took their time and enjoyed the river the waterholes and the different landscape. They were getting into the outback with its wide-open spaces and they both loved it.

The landscape had turned into sparsely vegetated almost treeless plains, with most of the vegetation being salt bush. They drove past large flocks of sheep grazing the plains. 'You can see for miles Wally' Melissa exclaimed one day.

Every time they went passed a town Wally got fuel and water. At Wilcannia he bought another four-gallon jerrycan of water, and another of fuel, Wally now had some idea of the distances involved out here.

And people gave Wally advice along the way and told him from here on he should definitely call into the hotels if not the police stations to let them know where he was going if they were to head into the bush off the beaten track. 'That way' a barman had told him back in a pub called Little Topar, 'if you don't turn up where you say you will someone will come looking for you.'

Wally had ventured 'but we were planning to take as long as we like on this journey. We can't be tied to a time limit.'

'Well then' said the publican, 'you tell them about a month longer than you think. It's just a backup plan mate. Water is gunna get a bit scarce now for a while.'

'We have a radio on us' said Wally starting to feel a bit hemmed in.

'Well tell someone just to be on the safe side mate. The policeman will know how to guide you.'

'Thanks' Wally had said and left the pub with Melissa to get some sleep.

One night when they were camped on the outskirts of Wilcannia they had woken in the night to a horrible sound. Wally had put his hand under his pillow and took hold of his gun. There was no moon and Wally couldn't see what all the noise was. He could hear his heart beating in his chest, and he told Melissa it would be alright, and to be as quiet as she could.

A pig gave off a great squeal and Wally relaxed and got back into bed. But after that he kept his gun loaded and the rifle to. He kept both guns beside him all night and mostly the tarp pulled down and tied securely.

Wally told Melissa that if he had his rifle nearby, he would have got that pig. 'That's why I need this beside me Mel, so I don't miss another opportunity. A bit of pork would go down a treat, wouldn't it?'

Mel nodded, 'and I will feel safer Wally. A lot safer.' Melissa had said what Wally could not.

It wasn't long after that that Wally got his first wombat. He had three traps with him and when they caught a couple of rabbits, they made stew out of them. 'We practically lived on this when we first got to the Murrumbidgee Mel. This and fish and we were bloody glad to have it. We had full bellies Mel for the first time since I couldn't remember. And we ate a lot of fruit and veg, and I think we were the healthiest we'd ever been.'

'Me to Wally, I had to live on fish and rabbits and a little cleaning job I had that Gus knew nothing about. And no one told him Wally. It was an old swaggy who sold me the rabbits and sometimes I gave him some tea and sugar that I pinched from Gus' Wally felt his heart break at this beautiful woman's' plight. She looked down and said with pride, 'I got that job when I was fourteen and still had it when I met you.'

At night on the riverbank Wally and Mel fell asleep to the tune of birds having their last gossip, screeching to one another down the line. The trees were full of them. The crickets were just getting up and added their voice to the night, and then there was the beautiful warbling of the magpies as they sang one last song of peace. Mel loved it, and she loved Wally. Wally pulled her closer and held her gently.

As the two people travelled the dusty tracks through the out back of Australia they fell in love. They both fell in love with the country, the vastness of it, the strange beauty of it.

Though it was nothing like what Melissa was used to, she felt she was a part of it. She felt like she belonged to it. Back at Wilcannia Mel had bought a notebook and she started her own journal. This was an epic journey that they were on she thought, and she never wanted to forget it. It was not just a physical journey but a spiritual awakening, a shifting of attitudes. She felt the country was teaching her, gently making her mature.

At night she wrote parts of her day into the book. She had trouble with it at times, not knowing how to express how she felt. So, most of her entries were more factual than anything.

Mel was frustrated because this was a most spiritual land, and she was unable to do it justice. Wally often watched from the other side of the fire and knew what she struggled with. He struggled with the same thing. So, they started talking about it and found it helped enormously.

Four weeks from home after they'd been fishing one night Wally decided it was time to write home. He had been feeling that he missed home and family all day long. 'Just a note' he told Melissa and extracted his writing set from under the bed. He sat down with his candle and a piece of cardboard on his knee and wrote to Dan. He wrote with his new fountain pen.

15/4/1955

Dear Dan,

I hope this letter finds you all well and happy. Once again it broke my heart to leave you. I am excited to be on this trip Dan, but I am excited to come back home to. Thank you very much for the writing set it is beautiful.

Every night after tea I write a little something about our day. I will write about our successes and out pitfalls so it might be some use to you should you decide to go on your journey.

The nights are getting colder Mary, and the quilt has been a wonderful addition. It is handy to be able to just throw it over us when we go to bed. Thank you, Mary and Mel says thank you to. She sends her love.

We are not too far from Bourke, and we plan to stay a little while there. I need to do some repairs and check the land rover for problems. We are very comfortable in it, and we now consider it to be home. When we strap the sides down at night, we do feel safe, and our belongings are safe. The half door I made from the back window is handy if we need to get going in a hurry or if it's pelting with rain.

Dan, we will be in Cunnamulla in probably four to six weeks, maybe a bit more. So, if you wish you could write to us care of the post office there and I will call there to check.

The country around here is so very different to back home. We have passed through seemingly endless plains of salt bush which are almost treeless, sheep country mostly. Getting into the semi desert country of the outback and it's so exciting. Fishing is not so good but catching plenty of rabbits. We got a wombat the other day and it was good.

Okay Dan, I just wanted to drop you a line to let you know we are alright and loving the trip. I will post this when we get to Bourke in a day or so. We will give you a call when we get to Cunnamulla in Queensland. We intend to switch across to the Warrego River soon.

Well goodbye for now, we miss you all very much. Please give my love to everybody. All my love

Me and Matilda and Melissa

Wally and Melissa took their time as they travelled to Bourke. They'd make camp on the edge of towns they passed through and visit the local pub for tea though mostly the towns were days between. They found they liked most of the people they met. They often stayed talking in the pub until throw out. And they often stayed in a town for days or weeks. They'd often camp on the banks of a river and walk for miles down that river, exploring sometimes taking a swag.

At Wilcannia Wally got a fish and three rabbits. They ate them over the next few days. The weather was still warm during the day and though they got ice for their esky it was melted in a few days.

They deviated a bit and made their way along the Paroo. At Wanaaring they stopped and spent a night in the hotel and Melissa and Wally did their washing and soaked in a bathtub. They soaked in a tub of lovely clear water that you could see the bottom of the tub when it was full. And Melissa felt that she came out clean and it felt so good. They mostly got clean in river water and Melissa's hair was a mess.

After a few days there, getting to know the locals, doing some repairs, and getting everything clean they headed off to Bourke where they would stock up on tinned and dried food. They would buy a certain amount of fresh food but the bulk of it would be tins.

They were camped at a billabong near Bourke when a team of four builders drove past. They spotted the two camping there and called in. Wally and Melissa asked them to have a cupper which they sat and drank with them. Then Wally asked them what they were building.

'An outstation,' said the foreman. 'We are supposed to build a damn with a tank as well, but we have no bulldozer.'

They talked into the night and Wally mentioned he'd operated a bulldozer back at the mine.

Andy the foreman sat up, 'you any good' he asked?

Wally grinned and said he was. 'You got a dozer' he asked now?

'Yeah, we got a dozer but no operator. Not a lot of blokes wanna do it. You wouldn't wanna do a few weeks would you mate? Pay's good.'

'How good' Wally smiled.

So, Wally pitched the tent under some trees and he and Melissa dug in there for a few weeks which turned into over a month. Wally finished the dam and then helped with the build. He learned a lot about building and plumbing from these men.

They were camped about half a mile from town. For the first couple of weeks of their trip, they'd had a bit of trouble with mozzies, but they got less and less as the cooler weather approached. And Wally bought a bottle of bug off.

The team of builders lived in Bourke, and they went home every night. Wally and Mell were invited to someone's place every Sunday, so they went into town Saturday night for tea and camped in someone's back yard. They enjoyed their stay in Bourk greatly but all too soon it was time to move on.

It was nearing the end of May and Wally and Melissa both had itchy feet. They packed up their belongings and said goodbye to everyone. Wally was pleased that they left town six weeks later a hundred and fifty pounds better off.

Wally and Melissa headed off up to the Queensland border and the dingo proof fence. They crossed into Queensland through the dingo proof fence at a place called Barringun.

'We have got about two hours of sunlight left,' said Wally. 'Do you want to camp here in town Mel?'

'That would be good Wally, there's a camping site over there see.'

They set up camp and walked off to the pub. Wally booked in for tea and sat enjoying a beer with Mel. The barman was a very chatty bloke and Wally soon learned that the man had some work he wanted done around the place. 'You interested' he finished?

Wally agreed to help out for a few weeks. The pay wasn't good, but he felt like staying for a while. He could do some repairs and Melissa could get some washing done. The publican had told her she could use the washing machine.

So, Wally and Melissa dug in once again to do some work in Barringun. They were itching to move on, but Wally knew it would be foolish to pass up some quick money. So, they stayed. Melissa made friends with the publican's wife and spent a lot of time with her. Melissa helped out in the pub on the Saturday night and was soon pulling a beer like a pro. Wally was proud of her.

Wally and Melissa were both amazed at how the pub filled up with people. 'Where did they all come from' wondered Melissa?

CHAPTER 9

Wally and another bloke called Percy Melic finished building the publicans garage complete with a concrete floor. Wally learned a lot about building and concreting from the man. Percy had come out to their camp and camped a few feet from them. Melissa made extra food and they invited him for tea every night. Every weekend Percy returned to camp with a few supplies and gave them to Melissa.

The weather was beautiful, and Melissa got all their bedding washed and cleaned the rover as well. They had put the tent up, but they slept in the rover because they liked it and so that Percy could sleep in the tent.

As they built Percy explained to Wally all the finer points of building. He instructed Wally how to cut the timbers and Wally knew that the experience would come in handy when he did out the paddle steamer. The older man Percy was also excited by the idea of making a steamer into a home.

'I worked on one of those for a year back in twenty-nine. Back when a steamer was a steamer you know, a work horse. Bloody beautiful piece of work the old steamer. Shame they have about had their day. But it would be a mighty fine thing to live on one. A mighty fine thing indeed. I come from down at Echuca, I go down there from time to time. Next time I go down there I'll swing by Balranald hay? See if you need any help and to see what you've done with her. The Murrumbidgee Princess you say. Are you going to leave her with that name?'

'Yes, we will' said Wally enthusiastically. 'She'll always have sentimental value. She had been left to us in a will.'

'Well anyway good luck to you both. How long will you be up in Queensland?'

'I think about a year give or take. I am going to try a bit of droving and some bull catching while I'm up there.'

'Wow, an action-packed holiday indeed' Percy looked at Melissa now. 'And are you going droving and bull catching to?'

'Well of course, if I am allowed to.'

Wally smiled at her 'of course you will come if you want. I won't be going if you are not allowed Mel.'

'Why Balranald Wally' Percy asked? 'Do you have family there?

'I have a family there; they have a farm not too far from there on the banks of the Murrumbidgee River right about where she meets up with the Murray. When I say they are my family we were a group of people thrown together during the great depression, and we stayed together.'

'Ah yes, the great depression. People brought together through necessity. But you stayed together Wally, was that also through need?'

'Dunno Percy, we stay together now for love. We love each other and we can count on each other. Dan kept us all together. That man has the greatest capacity to love that I have ever seen. Most of us have nobody else. My brother Jack, from the same family, went to Queensland and he has found a family up there. They stay together and love each other out of a sense of belonging. Tom is the leader of the drovers; he's a good man is Tom. Wayne is the bloke who leads the bull catchers, they live together in a long hut. And the camp where I stayed at the mine became a family to, it's amazing. Their leader is a man named Eric, a good man, and a good leader.'

Yes, thought Percy as he sipped his coffee, and this man across the fire belonged to all these families. He was the common denominator, and yet he hands the credit for them off to others. He had never met anybody like Wally. Wally and his lovely wife Melissa. 'So, they all live close by like to each other Wally? These people you left behind on the Murrumbidgee. These people you talk about are your only family. Are there relatives or are they all people you met along the way?'

Wally drew a deep breath and started to talk.

'I was alone on the road, on my last legs when Dan and his large group of people came by. He picked me up Dan did and took me with him. When we arrived there at the Murrumbidgee, we were hungry and cold, and the winter was approaching. We had become starving, and we had lost people and we had lost hope. We lived hand to mouth suffering the elements and children and old people died. We were in a bad way until we met Mary.'

Wally fell silent for a while, then 'She was a local farmer and she fed us, there were about thirty adults and ten or so children. Then she helped us to grow our own food on an acre she let us use. She gave us seeds and taught us about market gardening. They still do it, market gardening, and what they don't need they take to market, it's a lucrative little sideline and brings in a lot of money. Some of the blokes work and share their wages with the household. They also take milk eggs and sheep to market. Dan and Mary bought a tractor and the rest of the equipment and now they farm wheat as well.'

Percy looked at Wally in wonder, 'a real rags to riches story Wally. And what a wonderful soul this Mary must be.'

'Yes, well like I said winter was approaching and the council decided to kick us off the commons, some of us would have surely died. Anyway, Mary gave over another acre and helped us build a home on it. We call it the long hut because it was built in the style of the long huts the Vikings built. By the time the winter hit, and it was a harsh winter that year, we were all inside safe and warm. We didn't lose any more people to cold and hunger after we ran into Mary. And all of this long hut was built from materials we got from the dump. Nevertheless, it was a beautiful and happy home.'

Percy stared at the fire his expression unreadable. A look of profound sadness passed across his face and then he smiled. 'Thank God for Mary then Wally. Are they still on her land.'

'Not exactly Percy, she gave them the four acres we lived on so we would feel secure. Most people who live there have built bedrooms away a little bit, mostly just across the veranda. But they all sit down together still for their meals and the company of each other.' Wally took a deep breath 'and Dan married Mary and now Mary lives there to. We all love Dan; he is a fair and loving man. He saved every penny back in thirty-seven to send all the kids to school.'

Wally turned to Melissa she had a tear roll down her face, he'd forgotten that she hadn't heard the story. He reached over and picked up her hand and held it.

'How'd you get that arm Wally?'

'Moving too slow mate. Got a bullet in New Guinea.'

Percy shook his head 'Hasn't bloody stopped you has it mate. I wish I'd found a Dan and Mary that's for sure. I was in the big one Wally, the first world war. The war to end all war they bloody told us. Men are so gullible Wally. Anyway, bedtime for me.' Percy rose to his feet and looked down at Wally 'thanks for telling me your wonderful story Wally and thanks for the service you did for your country. Goodnight, all.'

Wally and Melissa said goodbye to Barringun pub and headed for the Warrego River. They followed the Warrego River to Cunnamulla and stopped for fuel and supplies. They had a tea of hamburger and chips and ate them down on the riverbank where they were camped. Wally had gone to the post office and picked up a letter from Dan. It was burning a hole in his pocket. Next time they settled for a while he'd need to ring home. Needed to hear Dan's voice and talk a while.

There was about an hour of daylight left so he and Melissa threw a line in. 'We are fishing the Warrego River Mel' said Wally with a delighted grin. They didn't get a bite and Dan wondered if they would have to change the bait they used. 'Maybe different fish different taste Mel.'

Mel smiled back at him, 'do you think the cockies up here have a different accent, Wally?'

'I think they might be speaking a different lingo all together Mel.' Wally laughed 'probably still on about us sitting around staring at the river.'

'I wonder if that kookaburra is having any more luck than us.'

'I'd say that's what all the laughing is about.'

'Looks like it's off to the café for tea. Do you fancy chicken and chips love?'

'Sure.'

When they'd eaten and were sat at the fire drinking a cup of tea, Wally smiled and got his letter out, he read aloud.

7/5/55

Dear Wally,

    We were so glad to get your letter Wally and to hear how much you are loving your trip. You would be getting into the desert areas now and I'm glad you like it. I was thrilled to hear that you have been able to walk some of these amazing far-off rivers for a bit to Wally. I'll bet you are glad you took the three traps mate and the guns. I am very proud of you Wally, the job you did on that land rover is nothing short of fantastic. Please be careful to carry plenty of water out there. I tune in to the news every night to see if someone has been reported missing out there. I keep telling myself that you managed to get through the war without me but well . . . .

    We got a letter from Jack. He, as you probably know, went straight up through the middle to Katherine and they planned to see Tom and the boys over there and then go home. I think he said in his letter that he arrived back at home on the seventh of January and didn't get bogged at all. He says they are getting fencing and other jobs done before it's bull catching time. If you want to try it Wally, please be careful mate. I suppose you get sick of listening to a silly old worry wart like me, but I love you son.

    We have sunk two of the posts we will need for your jetty, four to go. We did the farthest out in the water first as they are the main ones and we had help from Sarahs dad as he has done it before. We will get them done hopefully before the winter rains set in, in earnest. Just to be sure we will make the boardwalk a floatable and attach it to the posts so that if the posts give out you will remain above water.

    The crops are in Wally, and we have another harvest soon for the market. The gardens are doing well. I stand outside in the early morning watching the paddocks for the green hue and I miss you lad, miss our long talks.

Libby is going away next year to uni in Melbourne. She will study medicine. Our boy Maynard is almost twelve and he says he's going to stay right here and teach me how to farm. I don't know if we told you, but we bought forty acres from the farm next door, so we now have about a hundred and twenty acres to plough. And we have about an acre of market garden for each market, and also the milk and the sheep. Keeps us busy.

I must go now; give our love to Melissa she is a sweet girl. I am happy for you both lad. Bye for now Wally.

All our love,

Dan and family

When Wally finished reading the letter, he felt a contentment settle on him. He looked at Melissa who looked a bit misty eyed and he got to his feet. 'Come on love, I need to take you to bed and make sweet love to you. Don't I Mel?'

Mel smiled and got to her feet. 'That would be wonderful Wally.'

Wally put the sides up and the moon light washed over them as they made love to the backdrop of the Warrego River. A kookaburra laughed downstream, and Wally's heart soared. How he loved this woman. A magpie warbled its content to the moonlit river and Wally's heart settled in his chest.

Wally got up at sunrise trying not to waken Melissa. He got the fire going and put the billy on. He decided to spoil her this morning with bacon and eggs and toast and coffee. Melissa came out and sat at the fire 'yummy'.

'Yes, indeed yummy' said Wally taking her chin in his hand he bent and kissed her gently. 'All this because I love you Missus Wally.'

Melissa sat and gazed at him. He did things to her, just the sight of him. 'I love you to Mister Wally.' He looked up and smiled at her, and she suddenly wished he hadn't got up so early.

He caught the look and smiled 'we'll eat first hay.'

And after they'd eaten, they cleared away and got back into bed with the sides down. Afterwards Wally said softly, 'do you wanna get going Mel? Get on the way to Thargomindah? And the Bulloo River?'

'Yes, Wally I do.'

They drove for two days to Thargomindah on the Bulloo. 'How much the country has changed Wally. We have gone from lush green farmland through treeless plains of salt bush and red desert and rolling sand hills and now to these amazing woodlands.'

'It has changed a lot, Mel, and even the wildlife is everywhere, and cattle just roam across the roads.'

'And the waterways are teaming with wildlife, especially the birds. Some of them I have never seen nor heard about Wally.'

'I never realised how big the country is. When me and Dan came up here, we flew over it. Doesn't seem all that big when you fly.'

'Do you ever find yourself wishing you'd walked Wally?'

'It would have been a big undertaking, and I would have loved it. But I love that we are doing it together Mel. Much better together, and I love that we have this little home here with us.'

They made camp for a few days on the banks of the Bulloo and the next day they walked for miles along that river. 'You know Mel, nothing comes even close to the Murrumbidgee. It's just because I am biased, isn't it?'

Melissa smiled at him 'these rivers have such a harsh country to live in Wally. They don't get the rain that the Murrumbidgee and the Murray get. These rivers are more tough I think than the Murray.'

Wally smiled and put his arm around her. 'This looks like a good place Mel' he said taking off his backpack and fishing gear.

Wally and Melissa stayed a week in Thargomindah, they liked the locals and the camping spot. Melissa did some washing and cleaned out the land rover again.

They stocked up at the shops and at the service station and set off up the Bulloo towards Quilpie. They took four days to get there and so the two travellers decided to stay put a few weeks. Wally got a job on the highways operating the grader which he did for a month while they saved up. Melissa got a job cleaning at the pub to save her from being alone all day.

On his afternoons and days off Wally and Melissa fished the Bulloo for perch and for the first time Wally had a go at catching yabbies. He cooked them and he and Melissa found they liked them alright but wouldn't want to eat them all the time. The water there was very muddy, and the yabbies had a muddy taste to them.

While they were there, Wally and Melissa went off to find a phone box. Wally rang and Dan answered 'hello' he said.

'Hello Dan.'

'Wally it's you how wonderful. So good to hear your voice how, are you?'

'We are fine thanks Dan, we're in Quilpie now. I've got a job on the highways driving a grader and Mel's working at the pub cleaning. We'll probably leave here in about two weeks and head off to the Diamantina. We'll follow that up to the top. How are things at home Dan?'

'Good mate everyone's good. I thought you'd be about Quilpie by now. Have you heard from Jack?'

'No, we'll ring him when we get a bit closer. We're just taking our time. We tried some yabbies the other day. They are not that easy to catch.'

Wally talked to Dan for a bit and then to Mary and he put Melissa on to talk to Mary. All too soon they got the beeps and had to say goodbye. 'Love you all' said Wally and Dan said to stay safe. The line went dead, and Wally slowly hung up the phone. There in the street Wally held Melissa for a bit and they turned and headed for the rover.

Wally worked another two weeks on the highways, and they stocked up on food, water, and fuel for the next leg of their trip.

Their last night in Quilpie they bought tea and headed back to the riverbank. 'Are you sorry to leave here Mel?'

'Hell no.' Mel smiled 'I've got the urge to go Wally.'

'At least I learned how to operate a grader properly' said Wally as they ate their hamburgers and listened to music on the radio. Wally looked at his hamburger for a while and smiled at Melissa. 'Do you think we're hooked on these Mel?'

Mel smiled 'hell yeah Wally. I love the chips to.'

Wally nodded wondering if he and Mel would be off back to the café to get more of these.

They set off for Wintabarah and they would go about a hundred miles farther on to the Diamantina River. They took their time and got to Wintabarah at sunset on the fifth day.

Wally and Mel decided on two days at Wintabarah. They went to the pub for tea on the second night they were there and one of the locals who had had too much to drink tried to bait Wally into an argument.

Wally tried to take no notice and then the man whose name was Rudy went too far. 'Does your Missus have to drive you everywhere you go big guy? Does she have to get on top as . . . . '

Wally leapt from his stool and grabbing the man by the scruff of the neck he hauled him outside. After a scuffle and Wally hit him a couple of times, he got Rudy down and sat on him. He said, 'I should make you apologise to my wife, but I will let you go home as long as you don't say another word.'

'Yeah, well I know where you're camped.'

Wally let him up he'd have to fight. Rudy swung a haymaker at him that missed, and Wally punched him in the face. Rudy went down and stayed down he never really knew what hit him. Wally's right jab was like a sledgehammer.

Mel ran up to Wally a look of fear on her face, 'Wally we need to go, they are talking about you and its awful. And the barman rang the police. These people are not nice Wally.'

'Come on Mel.'

They ran back to the rover, threw some of the things that had been unpacked back in and left town. Before they left Wally got the rifle out of the box and lay it across his lap, he had his handgun in his pocket. As he sped through the town, he took Mel's hand 'don't be afraid my love, they are just drunks.' He smiled at her 'good job we fuelled up today baby.'

'Thank God.'

There were a few blokes carrying Rudy back in the pub, but no one took any notice of the land rover leaving town in a cloud of dust.

'Hate running off' Wally grumbled.

'Wally there were too many of them and I was scared stiff.'

Wally reached across and touched her hand, 'I know but I should have given him a damn good hiding talking that way.'

'Well, I'm glad we left. And I think you did give him a dam good hiding. That place gives me the creeps. Even the women in the bar were whispering and looking at me. That's when I decided to get going in a hurry and came out to you.'

'Really! Jesus Mel.'

'Let's just get as far away from that place as we can tonight, please Wally.'

A loud bang on Melissa's window brought a scream from the already frightened Mel and she slid away from the window and close to Wally.

'It was a dog' she sobbed. 'Oh, Wally it looked terrible. It looked like a . . . . a demon . . . . ' The dog had come out of nowhere and leapt through the air crashing into the window right beside Melissa. Melissa had just got a glimpse of a terrifying looking animal with wide eyes and a snarling mouth.

'I saw it, Mel. Jesus!' Wally could see Melissa was shaking all over and he worried for her. As they sped along the highway into the dark night leaving the town with its mad dogs and monstrous people behind them Wally held on to her hand.

As they passed through the town limits and a sign asked them to come again another dog came at them. It ran at the car and Wally's mind was on not hitting the animal. Suddenly right in front of them was a very tall man with his mouth wide open and his eyes bulging. Wally slowed up not being able to tell if the man was alright or maybe in some kind of trouble. The man produced a knife, which was more like a machete and waved it about. He was screaming at them, using foul language and Wally made up his mind to get going.

Wally put his foot down and kept it to the floor until they had gone about a mile, and he slowed down a little. He was shaken by the site of the dogs and the man. He looked at Mel who was trembling and white in the face.

'Jesus, why Wally?' '

I dunno love,'

CHAPTER 10

Wally and Melissa drove all night, Wally turned the radio on, and they sang along to the songs that they knew. Melissa felt herself calm and in the early afternoon the next day they had reached the Diamantina. Wally turned right, along a dirt track which they knew would bring them out on the highway at Kynuna. They would then take the Landsborough highway to Cloncurry then Mount Isa and on to Camooweal.'

At Mount Isa they would spend a little time on the Leichhardt River and do a bit of fishing. Wally had come to Mount Isa with Dan.

About five miles along the dirt track beside the Diamantina, Wally stopped the rover. He got out and refuelled using one of the jerry cans. Then with the rifle slung over his shoulder he lit a fire just long enough to make a coffee. He took some bread and butter and put slices of ham in them, and he and Melissa ate a cold meal. As soon as they finished their sandwiches, Wally checked the motor and radiator.

Then he opened Melissa's door and kissed her as she got in. 'I'm sorry Mel.'

'For what Wally?'

'That those mongrels frightened you. I'd like to go back there today and give em all a bloody good hiding, but I will never take you there again. That is a promise Mel, from me to you. Come on love let's get back to our trip.' Wally slipped his arms around her and felt her tremble. He got in and they headed off up the Diamantina. Melissa slipped across the seat next to Wally and he put his arm around her. Singing once more he felt her relax beside him.

'This is like the Nile Wally' said Melissa excitedly. 'You know, all barren desert lands with colourless grasses with little else growing on it. And then when you get to the river it is green with lots of trees and all sorts of wildlife. It's wonderful Wally. Are we safe now do you think? Thanks for getting me out of there, I haven't been that frightened since we left Gus behind.'

He smiled at her and nodded 'we are safe now baby.'

Melissa rested her head on his shoulder and said softly, 'I couldn't bear it if anything happened to you, I couldn't Wally.'

'Nothing's gunna happen to me. I'm glad Gus and Rodney decided to plead guilty Mel. We could've been stuck there for months.'

'I don't think eight years was enough for Gus.'

'Me neither.' Wally took a deep breath 'he does have to behave himself to get out in eight. What are the chances Mel?'

'Not bad unfortunately, he's basically a slimy coward Wally. He'll behave himself alright. I'm glad we sold the house though.'

'Dan said he'd let us know what Rodney gets. He raped Mary you know Mel and Mary was pregnant from it. Well, any way she ended up losing the baby and Dan was real upset about it he had fallen in love with her. It was a little girl and they buried her on the riverbank. Then the bastard came back, took Lilly, Mary's beautiful horse, and tied her in the river to drown and they shot her dog. He was going to shoot it again, but I gave him a biffin. Dan found Lilly and saved her so that is

Jim and Lilly that you met. How could anyone hurt them? Of course, that is a closely guarded secret Mel.'

'Oh Wally. How awful for Mary, she doesn't deserve that. Gus never went that far with me Wally. Just beating me was enough to get him off.'

Wally took Melissa's hand and drove on in silence for a while.

As the sun dipped towards the horizon Wally looked for an elevated position to make camp. He stopped on a hilltop near to the river; they could still do some fishing. And Wally could see the track both ways for miles.

They fished for a little while, Wally had his gun in his pocket and his rifle beside him. He always took his rifle when he walked the rivers in case he spotted something that was good eating. He picked a spot with plenty of big trees they could get behind. After about an hour Wally started to relax himself. The river had a calming effect on him as usual. The bird song brought him peace and Wally nearly fell asleep. It had been a long night, he let himself doze for half an hour. He wanted to be alert tonight.

After a tea of tinned meat and boiled potatoes with sauce they packed everything away ready to leave and Wally topped up the fuel and rechecked the oil and water ready for the next day. They climbed into bed they were both exhausted. When Melissa was asleep Wally sat up and leaning against the cabin, he let himself doze.

Wally woke up with a start, the sun was coming up. He grabbed up his rifle, there was a vehicle coming. He shook Mel awake 'get in the cabin Mel, quickly now.' Wally watched the dust cloud and the vehicle making it get bigger and bigger.

It was an old truck coming and Wally stood at the driver's side door of the rover, the rifle armed and ready to make some noise leaning up against the back of the seat. Wally's hand was around the pistol in his pocket. He turned as the vehicle got near and smiled at Mel. 'I dunno but I reckon these blokes are out carting water. Probably from a station but stay where you are my love. Just until, we're sure.'

The truck pulled up and in it were a boy and an old man, they grinned at Wally. 'G'day' said the old man as he got out. 'My names Bob' he said holding out his hand.

Wally shook his hand 'Wally.'

The rifle in the front seat caught his eye and he grinned 'run into some trouble back in Wintabarah did you?'

The smile slid from Wally's face and his hand went back in his pocket. 'Yeah, a bit.'

'No, it's alright son, we see a lot of it. People on the run from that bloody place. We never go there ourselves, and the copper's as bent as a dog's hind leg.' He smiled at Melissa 'Hello Missus.' Looking back at Wally he said 'you'll be safe from here on, they won't come after you. Gutless lot, bullies. Where you headed lad?'

'We are going up north of Camooweal, my brother works on a station north of there.'

'Oh yeah which station?'

'Mable Downs.'

'Oh, right I know the place a mate of mine used to run it, Wayne Strawbridge. He left it to go catching bulls.'

'Yeah, my brother Jack is with him. Jack and one of his mates Alby.'

'Oh, Christ I know Jack and Alby to. I bought some bulls from them last year.' Suddenly the old man cackled 'don't tell me your brother's the bloody bull ball breaker.' He tapped the side of his face and laughed heartily and so did his son. 'Anyway, I'm real pleased to meet you mate. This is my son Mike. You interested in boiling the billy and we'll have a bit of a yarn? You can keep a hold of that gun in your pocket son; we mean you no harm. Your missus can hang on to that rifle to mate we understand.'

Wally got a fire going and put the billy on. When they were sat down Wally ventured 'we are from down on the Murrumbidgee ourselves.'

'A long way from home then, we live just back up a track that goes out that way' he pointed to the East. 'There's some good fishing along here and teaming with yabbies.'

'Yeah, we might just give it a go. Jack got a job up here and I came up by plane and saw him a few years ago. I met some drovers to, one of them was Tom and then there was Fred and Jimmy . . . . '

'Yeah, I've met them damn; fine bunch, they done a couple of jobs for me. You know moved some cattle for me. Well, you'll be in good company son. You plan on staying up here now?'

Wally smiled and shook his head 'my home is the Murrumbidgee. We have a houseboat back there and we are planning to live on it. She'll need some work, but it'll be nice when we're finished.'

Bob reacted with enthusiasm to the idea of the houseboat. 'You mean a paddle steamer Wally? I saw a couple of them down the Darling one time when I was a young lad down there, they don't come up very far now. I'd love to do it myself.' They talked for a while and then Bob said they had to move on. 'Thanks for the cupper mate and I'm sorry you had to run into that lot. I think they just drink all day every day. In the horrors mostly.'

'It's been a beautiful trip up until Wintabarah. And I do know that they're not typical of the people up here. In fact, I was well and truly shocked.'

As the two people in the truck were leaving the old man shook hands with Wally and waved to Melissa, 'I hope you enjoy the rest of your trip mate and steer clear of Wintabarah. Give my regards to all up there at Mable Downs. Bob Rankin is my name Wayne will remember me.'

The truck left in a cloud of dust. Wally threw their things in the rover, and they got in and carried on their way. Greatly comforted by the niceness of the two people they had just ran into.

Wally and Melissa spent a few more days on the Diamantina, it was rough country and they had to travel very slowly. When they had got to the top almost to the highway, Melissa spotted their first dingo. Wally stopped to get a good look. 'Oh, Wally they are beautiful. Look at them. And these are what the dingo proof fence was built to keep out?'

'That's them Mel, they are more ferocious than they look. The fence is to keep them out of the sheep in New South Wales, they eat them.'

'Look there are more of them Wally. Wally what are you doing?!'

Wally was looking down the sights of his rifle, 'there's a bounty on them Mel.'

'No Wally . . . . no!' Melissa shook him and Wally put down the rifle.

'What is it, Mel?'

'We are not killing them. Alright to kill something you want to eat but this . . . . ? No.'

'Okay Mel.'

Mel let out a screech as she spotted a flock of pelicans, they had found several of them on the banks of the Munawerra, one of the Diamantina's big water holes. Melissa loved pelicans. She had a lovely memory of seeing some a long time ago with her mother. She had looked down at Mel a smile on her face and told her; 'the lovely pelican, his beak holds more than his belly can.' She told Wally this now and he laughed.

On the fourth day they reached the highway and turned left to head a couple of km's for Kynuna. Wally stopped at the pub 'let's get a coldie Mel.' Mel nodded but Wally made no move to get out, he just sat looking about. 'You know we are in the heart of Waltzing Matilda country Mel. This is about where Banjo Paterson wrote it, I reckon. I'm bloody excited Mel.'

'I can see that Wally,' Mel smiled.

Wally was grinning from ear to ear. He turned to her a serious expression on his face 'if I have to punch somebody in the face here, I'll be devastated Mel.'

Mel laughed and gave him a push to get out 'I'm dry Wally.'

Wally turned his back and swung his legs out, looking over his shoulder he nodded and said, 'try not to cause any trouble hay Mel.'

Mel laughed and got out of his door behind him, 'I'll try bloody hard Wally.'

'You swear like . . . . '

'A navvy.' Mel took Wally's hat off his head and threw it back in the car. She lifted her hand and stroked his hair down flat with her fingers 'you need a damn haircut.'

Wally laughed 'after we've had a couple, we can go across there and get tea. Bugger cooking tonight.'

They walked along the veranda of the pub to the door, 'see that's where I learned it, Wally. The swearing.'

They did their washing and some other jobs at the township. With that done, Wally and Melissa went off to find a phone. Wally called Jacks number and Wayne said 'hello.'

'Hello Wayne, it's me Wally.'

'Wally! Hell, it's good to hear your voice little mate. Where are you, Wally?'

'We're at Kynuna, Wayne.'

'Oh, good nearly here. Listen Wally, Jacks not here at the moment I'm sorry.'

'Okay Wayne.'

'Can you call tonight around seven, mate. He'll be finished his tea and waiting for your call. Okay?'

When Wally called back that night, he told Jack that he would call him when they got to Mount Isa. 'And I'll head down that way and meet you. Be bloody good to see you Wally.' Jack talked excitedly for a while and then. 'It's a week before August now so we'll be bull catching for another month or two at least. Hope you get here for that Wally. You were a bit lucky to catch us, we are between jobs, so thank goodness.'

'Don't worry we'll be there, Jack. I reckon about another two weeks. Listen mate, don't worry about coming to meet us we'll see you there. Can I get in touch with you if you're not home.'

'If we are all going to be away anytime I'll leave a note with where we are and how to get there buddy. We won't be on Mable Downs we've done there. Have you got a radio with you Wally?'

Wally said he had, and Jack told him to get in touch with Wayne on that and instructed him how.

Melissa had heard it all and smiled when Wally hung up the phone. 'We gunna make a dash for it then Wally?'

'You know it, Mel.'

The travellers stopped and spent the night at Cloncurry. Wally wanted to sleep on the banks of the Cloncurry River and do a spot of fishing there. The fishing got much better the farther north they came from about Quilpie.

After about an hour Wally landed a huge barramundi. A tear rolled down his cheek and Mel sat down beside him and hugged him. 'Oh, Wally barramundi for tea love.'

'I have dreamed about this day Mel.'

The fish Wally caught for tea was the best thing he'd ever tasted. Even though he'd had barramundi when he was up here before with Jack. But he'd caught this one himself.

Wally and Mel stopped a day in Mount Isa to do some shopping and fuel up. Afterwards they went to a café for some lunch. 'You want a hamburger Mel' Wally asked?

'No, I think I'll try a hot dog Wally and a milkshake.'

'I'll have the same' he said turning to the lady behind the counter. 'Both with tomato sauce I reckon, and could I get a five shillings chips thanks.'

'What flavour milkshakes sir?'

'Vanilla' said Mel and Wally nodded to the lady. He paid her the money and they sat at a table to wait.

'I'll have to go to the post office soon Mel, to get some money out. We've just about gone through that hundred I got back at Quilpie. We've been going through a bit of fuel love. And we'll need to get a bit of shopping before we leave here. It'll be a bit cheaper here see so we might as well stock up.'

'Do we have enough to get to Jack Wally, you know without touching what you wanted to keep?'

Wally grinned at the woman he loved so very much 'yeah, we do love. I think we've got another five hundred before we touch that.'

They ate their hotdogs and chips, 'I love these, Wally.'

'Me to.' They got another one each and left the shop.

Wally pulled the rover up to the riverbank under a red gum. He got out and grabbed the fishing gear and the guns, he kept them loaded now with the safety on. He took the waterbag and then went off with Melissa to the banks of the Leichhardt River. Wally had bought a yabby net at the service station and some bait, and he wanted to try it out. He baited it and the fishing line and threw them into the water of the Lovely Leichhardt River. He sat with Mel, both of them content in each other's company and to quietly fish the afternoon away in the shade of a huge river gum. Wally dozed a little.

Wally froze, a voice he would never forget hailed him dripping with sarcasm 'if it isn't my old mate, Wally.'

Wally turned and got to his feet almost in the one motion. 'What is it you want Rudy? That fight was fair and square except for the fact that you started it. I really don't want . . . . '

'Neither do I' a smile broke out on Rudy's face 'Yeah, I know, no hard feelings. Hell, I only just made it out of that bloody town alive myself. Won't catch me going back there again in a hurry. Yeah, I'm a bloody idiot when I drink but those people are all insane.'

Rudy offered his hand to Wally who let go of his gun to take his hand out of his pocket and shake it. He didn't say a word but put his hand back in his pocket.

Rudy turned to look at the river 'I thought it was you back in the main street, so I followed you. Just wanted to apologise to your wife Wally.'

'Well, there she is.'

Rudy went to walk towards her but found a gun pointed at him. 'You can do it from there. I'd like it better if you did it from there.'

'Fair enough. I'm sorry Missus. I suppose you got quite a fright. So did I when I woke up in jail with a noose hanging above my bunk and I was trussed up like a bloody turkey. But I talked . . . . or should I say paid my way out of it.'

He shook his head 'What a nightmare of a place. They tried to tell me I'd killed you. Well, I said where's his body and they said they'd covered it up. Buried you out in the sticks and if I paid them enough, you'd stay there. I should have bloody known. I had about ten pounds left when they'd finished fleecing me, I'll just make it back to the station. I asked them what happened to your wife, and they told me it was a need to know.' Rudy shuffled his feet, 'I knew I didn't do it Wally, but they weren't gunna let me go unless I paid.'

Wally's mouth hung open but his hand relaxed around the gun. 'Well thanks it was decent of you to apologise. I won't be going near that place again.'

'Me neither mate, if I have to it'll be a hundred mile an hour straight through it. Hay, are you catching anything?'

'Well put it this way' said Wally 'I think we are going out for dinner.'

Rudy laughed 'Well anyway I gotta be in Camooweal by tomorrow morning so I'm gunna head off. I just wanted to say I am sorry, and I hope there's no hard feelings.'

'No, none mate,' said Wally.

'Hay listen Wally, try putting your net a bit closer to the bank if you wanna catch red claw mate. Alright be seeing ya. All the best to ya both.'

'Same to you mate.'

They watched him go and Wally turned to Mel, 'I think he was being sincere love.'

'Yeah, me to Wally. Hamburger for tea' Mel grinned.

'Yeah, we're hooked Mel.' Wally sat back down 'still it's been a delight as usual fishing the lovely Leichhardt River.'

Wally sat listening to the birds, it was a comfort he thought the fact that the birds sounded the same the whole country over. He was about to doze when Mel frightened the life out of him.

'Hay Wally' she hissed and jumped to her feet the colour draining from her face. Wally's heart raced as he looked about. 'Are we getting close to croc country yet?' Mel grabbed the rifle.

Wally laughed and relaxed 'no Mel.' The laughter died 'least ways I don't think so. Well, we'd be getting close, but I don't think we're in it.'

Mel sat down with the rifle, 'how will we know?'

'I think they put signs up. Anyway, what the hell are red claw?'

'I think they are yabbies Wally. Are you going to shift your net?'

Wally got up and shifted it. Within the hour he pulled it up. 'Look Mel, four yabbies . . . . or red claws or . . . . four of em anyway.' He started getting them out 'our entrée woman.' They had forgotten Rudy and Wintabarah. Though Wally had been somewhat disturbed at the tale Rudy told. He thought not going through Wintabarah at all was a better idea than going through it at a thousand miles an hour.

Wally thought that that was yet another sign they ought to put up next to the welcome to town sign. "DON'T STOP HERE; MANIACS ON THE LOOSE."

Wally and Mel got no fish, so they were off to the café to get tea. Wally was quite pleased he was looking forward to hamburgers and chips.

Before they went for their tea Wally suggested they go and get more tea and sugar. They headed back to the rover to eat their hamburgers and chips and got in to bed.

Mel lay in Wally's arms, 'these rivers have a different feel about them now, don't they?'

'I noticed that, Mel. When we go for fuel in the morning, I'll ask about crocs hay, that might be why. Imagine being too afraid to hang out on the river fishing and sleeping there. I'm going back to the Murrumbidgee one day Mel. Nice and safe and you can fish all you like and sleep the day away.'

'Me to.'

CHAPTER 11

Wally and Mel arrived in Camooweal, and Wally drove to a pub. 'This is where Jack and the boys would come to get drunk. We're only an hour or so away now Mel. You wanna get there or have one more night on our own?'

'I don't mind baby. Another night on our own would-be lovely Wally but then I know how anxious you are to see Jack.'

'Why don't we go in there for a coldie first and maybe a bite to eat?'

'Okay. You're an Alco frolic Wally.'

'Well, you've been going round for round with me all the way woman. Maybe I should cut down. It's just so stinkin hot up here, I think it helps me sleep. I don't think I could live here. Though Jack seems to like it.'

'Wally, you have two drinks, that's not a lot. I was joking dearest. I could go on something to eat.'

Wally got out 'hay Mel, isn't that Jacks land rover there?'

'I think it is, let's go in.'

In the bar they looked along the length of it and Jack stood at the very end. He noticed Wally and came to him with his arms out. Wally was sometimes a little embarrassed by all this hugging in certain places, the front bar in particular, but not Jack. Wally stepped into his arms and hugged him back.

'It's good to see you, Wally. You look tired mate it's a long journey isn't it.'

Jack put his arms out to Melissa and as she stepped into them, he kissed her gently, the same as Dan always did.

Wally looked at the barman 'could you give us a schooner and a middy thanks mate. What are you drinking Jack?'

'No, I'm right mate I got a drink down here.' Jack led the way back to his stool. They sat down and Jack said, 'what sort of a trip did you have up here Wally?'

'It was bloody marvellous mate; we fished a lot of rivers on the way up. We fished the Murray the Murrumbidgee, The Darling, the Paroo, and the Bulloo. Then we fished the Warrego and the Diamantina and the Cloncurry and the Leichhardt. And we have not yet finished.'

'Sounds like a good sort of trip, and how about you Melissa how did you enjoy tour trip?'

'It was amazing Jack; I can't wait to see where you live and catch bulls.'

'You'll be sick of it soon enough love.'

Wally studied Jacks face 'you have another scar, Jack. Are you never gunna be satisfied with how your face looks.'

When Wally had had a few beers, Jack said they needed to go, to be home in time for tea. 'Hilda does a good feed Wally do you remember?'

'Sure, do Jack.'

Jack had a look at Wally's rover, 'you did a good job on her Wally. That's quite a build. If you come out to the camps you have your home with you. That's what Mary and I do.'

Wayne, Alby, Eddy, and Mike sat at the table waiting for tea to be ready. They turned as they heard the two land rovers leave the road and come into the yard. 'That'll be them now,' said Eddy. Wayne called out to Hilda. Hilda was looking forward to seeing Wally, she'd get the chance to feed him.

They rose from the table to go and meet Wally's new bride Melissa. Wayne had been pleased to hear of Wally's nuptials. He had been farther impressed to hear of Wally's other accomplishments. Wayne found he was eager to see them.

He shook hands with Wally now, 'good to see you again son, and congratulations on your marriage.' Waynes eyes flicked to Melissa, and he was struck by the woman's beauty. He turned and held his arms out to her and hugged her briefly, he could see that she was very shy. 'It is lovely to meet you, Melissa.' Wayne turned to Wally 'I am sorry I didn't make it down for your wedding . . . . I would . . . . I should've . . . . '

'No mate, it is one hell of a long way. As it was, we had to pack em into the long hut like sardines' said Wally and grinned at the awkward man.

Wayne laughed and clapped Wally on the shoulder, 'good on ya Wally.'

Everyone was introduced and the little company of bull catchers moved to their outdoor eating area where they sat at the table.

Wayne came straight to the point 'are you looking for work young Wally?'

'Of course,' Wally said with a huge grin. He flicked his eyes at Jack, 'I've seen the improvements to Jack's face, and I thought to myself, well . . . . '

Jack slapped Wally on the shoulder exclaiming loudly, 'I knew you were jealous.' Everyone laughed but Melissa was staring at Jack's face. It must have hurt she thought, it must have been life threatening.

And Mary was staring at Melissa. 'So, you are not keen Melissa? You like your man the way he is?'

'Well . . . . if it's what he wants to do then I would never stand in his way. But I will worry just the same as you must.'

Mary nodded her understanding and smiled, 'We all worry' she looked around shyly.

'Yes', said Wayne 'we sometimes forget the people who worry about us. We forget to reassure them and when they remind us, we take little notice. I'm sorry Hilly.' Hilda smiled and picked up his hand and held it.

Alby cut in quietly 'Jack got what he got because I messed up Melissa, and I have learned to be more careful. I nearly lost my best mate. But we are all so much better at what we do now. Wally will be alright; Jack will take care of him. Where are we gunna use him' he asked now looking from Jack to Wayne?

Wayne looked at Jack and smiled 'he could come with me in the wing, but I think you want to show him what you do Jack. So, I thought maybe, if Wally rides with Jack in the catcher and Alby rides with me. I'm always pretty close so Alby can just jump out and tie up. Is that alright with you Alby, it's a bit more running around?'

'It's fine mate.' He looked at Wally, 'you are in for the ride of your life Wally.' He grinned and his face lit up.

Wayne said thoughtfully, 'Well then after a week or two I'd like to put Wally in the truck to help Eddy.' He smiled at Wally, 'can you ride Wally?'

Wally nodded, 'I can ride nice quiet horses' he said with a grin and a shrug. He looked at Jack 'I can ride Lilly.'

Jack said, 'Ahh good old Lilly, dear sweet Lilly, where would we be without her?'

Wally smiled, 'still digging that half acre probably.' Jack chuckled and nodded.

Wayne was speaking again. 'Good place to start' said Wayne smiling, he liked young Wally and suspected he'd overcome one hell of a lot in his life. 'We'll get you out alongside Mary then. Now Hilda and Sandy have tea ready. Let's eat, my stomach thinks my throat has been cut across.'

Wally looked at the food, his eyes wide, 'I had forgotten Jack; just how good Hilda's food is.'

The talk went on as they sat round and ate. The plan they told Wally was to start getting ready to move out over the next two days. And then they'd be off to the next station which was Cloncurry Holding.

Wally felt the excitement building with in him. He could see the same excitement on everyone else's face. Everyone ate, Hilda had outdone herself thought Wayne. There was roast beef and casserole, roast vegetables and mashed potato and peas and carrots. She had also made curried sausages which was one of Wayne's favourites. There was gravy and rice as well. For sweets she'd made small cakes and a trifle. Wayne looked at Wally, she always went all out when he was around. He smiled at Hilda, how he loved her, his Hilda who loved to mother people.

Melissa couldn't believe the food and she said so. Hilda smiled at her and said 'thank you dear. You are welcome to help us out at the camp and maybe give a hand with these babies.' She looked at Jack and Mary's son Billy and the younger girl of Sandy and Alby's whose name was Susanne. Alby loved her and doted on her, she was the apple of his eye. Hilda always said she would be in the Olympics as she followed Alby everywhere. She could be seen running as fast as she could to keep up. That was when she wasn't being carted around in the crook of his arm. When she was a small baby, he would stick her in his hat, in the crook of his arm.

'I'd love to help.' Wally heard the enthusiasm in her voice and breathed a sigh of relief. He wouldn't have to worry about her being lonely and bored by herself. And he did worry about that, he wanted his wife to be happy.

That night after they had showered and got into bed Wally held Melissa in his arms. 'Are you sure Mel, are you sure you don't mind me having a go at this bull catching lark?'

'I will mind if you do to your face what Jack has done to his. Not your pretty face Wally' she kissed him all over his face.

'So, you only love me for my looks girl?' Wally set about exciting Melissa until she was quite breathless.

'Maybe you should have parked us a bit farther away Wally. The amount of noise you make. I've known you to set the white cockies to screeching in the trees.'

Wally lay himself gently on top of her, 'well as long as I am accompanied by all your noise woman, and that of the cockies, they won't notice mine.'

Melissa slapped him and he said with a soft laugh, 'Oh yeah, keep doing that woman. You know how that turns me on.'

'Well try and be quiet Wally.'

'Course I will woman, stop worrying. You think they are not all getting ready to make some noise?'

When they lay in each other's arms Wally asked her how she liked the top end so far. 'I love it Wally except for the heat. And this is winter. You will be careful out there won't you Wally?'

'You have my promise, Mel. Jack is my brother not my twin.' He grinned and kissed her good night.

That was the thing thought Melissa, about the large family of the long hut on the banks of the Murrumbidgee. They didn't see the fact that they shared no blood connection as a barrier to being family. 'It is life' Wally had told her in the beginning, 'it is life that makes you family. And then love.' And he had never mentioned it again.

It was the end of the second day, and everyone sat down exhausted to their tea. It was a cold tea of cold beef and ham with salads. Everyone was hungry and ate with gusto. Melissa loved the place, how they ate on the veranda and had an outdoor sitting area with just a roof and one wall.

Waly had noticed with much delight how Melissa had mucked in and fetched and carried all day long. Jack had noticed and so had the others. They had all decided over the past two days that Wally and Melissa were alright.

Wayne cleared his throat, and everyone sat quietly, it always heralded a speech from him. 'I would like to say thanks to Wally and Melissa here for all their help. We'll all be hoping you will stay. Just saying.'

'Thanks Wayne it was our pleasure. I for one can't wait to get out amongst it.' Wally smiled at Melissa as she nodded in agreement.

'Well anyway Wally' said Jack now, 'you'll be with me for a while, in the catcher.' Jack looked at Wally and saw the surge of excitement in his face. He smiled at the man who had always been a brother to him, one of the finest and most loyal.

Mary saw it and smiled across at Jack. She got up to help Hilda and Sandy with clearing away. Melissa got up to help though she was tired out. Wayne got up to start moving furniture to secure the camp for the weeks they would be away. This wasn't the season for storms, but it had been known to happen. Tarps were put over most of the outdoor items the rest were taken inside.

'It's good to see you again Wally' said Alby as they packed the chairs away and there was no one else around. 'She is a very nice woman your wife, and you like to do the same things. I doubt very much I'd get Sandy to come on a trip like that with me. And then to go fishing with you. You are lucky man. I've been hearing about your achievements Wally; Jack is very proud of you. He talks about you all the time and when he found out you were headed this way he was like a kid at Christmas. Of course, I didn't say that.'

Wally stood and looked at Alby knowing his face gave everything away and when Alby smiled softly, he knew it was true. Wally was choked up and his mouth worked but nothing came out. Not that you'd understand. He smiled back and said at last, 'thanks Alby, I miss him we all miss him, and we know he isn't coming back.'

Alby stopped what he was doing and cast a quick look around. Seeing no one he said softly 'I wouldn't bet on that Wally. I'd stake me life he'll go back some day.' Alby smiled and added, 'I'll be with him when he does.' Alby noted the hope that sprang to the younger man's face, 'when he's had a few more years of this mate.' Alby drew a breath, 'alright while he was single and without a family, but now I think he wants to raise that kid in the long hut. And Wayne's getting to the stage he's looking forward to retirement. And we've all made our fortune doing this and, in a few years, we'll have an even bigger fortune. I might look for a piece of land down there somewhere for myself and my kids and run some cows on it.' Alby drew a deep breath, 'unless I miss my guess, Jack will head south for a river called the Murrumbidgee. Like I said before Wally, I tell you this because I know you won't give me away. And it is only what I surmise.'

'Oh, hell no mate' said Wally slapping Alby on the shoulder, 'mum's the word. Yes, indeed and thanks again Alby.' Wally stood and his hand went to his ear, 'I do appreciate this Alby. I'll go back myself in a year or two. Yeah, thanks mate I won't be saying anything to anyone. Thanks.'

That night in the back of the land rover Wally whispered this information to Melissa. 'Why are you whispering Wally?'

'We can't let on to Jack.' Wally paused and then went on, 'Well Jack was in the same unit as me in the war.' He looked at Melissa and could tell she still didn't understand. He sounded exasperated now, 'well, if he wants to sneak about at night you won't know.'

'Oh.'

'Yeah, and Alby doesn't want him to know he told me.'

There was a silence, 'you are gossiping Wally?'

'Mel . . . . '

'Alright Wally, your secret is safe with me you know that love. You know I used to shake my head at the girls in the playground at school . . . . '

'Mel!' Wally sounded a bit gruff, he hated to think that his wife was about to compare him to a bunch of schoolgirls.

'Yes, Wally I understand the importance of being discreet. You know that has a familiar ring to it.'

'What?'

'You know "the importance of being discreet?" I can't think why.'

'Night Mel.'

'Night Wally.'

By the end of day three they were out at the camp and had it set up. Melissa had found a great happiness in minding the kids and she read them stories every day and again at bedtime. Wally sat watching her and it struck him as a bit odd that she hadn't got with child. From what he understood she probably should have. He told himself that, no matter that he thought it was lucky, Mel might feel differently. He thought briefly of broaching the subject but knew deep down he would not. Wally was pretty sure that they were both happy the way things were.

Most of the station they were on now was situated in the Northern Territory and only a stone's throw from Tom's place wally told Melissa. A giant stone's throw. 'You remember Fred and Tom that you met at the wedding.'

Melissa nodded, a smile on her face and Wally held her closer. 'Will we see them, Wally?'

'Of course, they won't be there just now. They'll be out droving, but they do come and get our bulls so maybe we will. I'd like to see them so we could call on them on the way home if we don't.'

The camp was sleeping peacefully as Wally rolled over to go to sleep, he had a big day ahead of him and he smiled in anticipation. Not a lot frightened Wally and he suspected Wayne and Jack and Alby were the same and probably Eddy as well. He liked them all and found that Bill had left a huge void. Wally was pleased that Wayne and Hilda had got together, they seemed happy.

He wondered at Wayne wanting to retire and hoped he wasn't sick. Though he had noticed the older man was showing his age. His hair was almost white now, and he had a stoop to his back and shoulders. But he was happy, and he seemed to look forward to each day. Wally liked Wayne, he thought he was very much like Dan in many ways, and he was glad that Jack had him.

Wally smiled, it was a beautiful place, though he missed the river and the birds and the kookaburras. Right on que the magpies warbled, and the dingoes howled their eerie song to the moon. It was a mournful song of need, and of love and loneliness and maybe even loss. Wally reached back and touched Melissa it was not a sound he was very used to yet. It was a mystery to Wally how that dog was able to get all of those emotions into one magnificent song. Wally smiled as he drifted off to sleep, he did count himself among the very lucky. The last thing to go through his tired mind was a memory of Dan telling him it was so.

The eastern sky was tinged with pink light from the sun and the air was heavy with dew. White cockies were getting up and had a lot to say in their ever- present excitement in the new day dawning. Wally wondered what they talked about, screeched about. Where they would feast today, who had all the bed maybe.

The little troupe of people all ate a huge breakfast that Sandy and Hilda cooked. Alby was thrilled that she worked closely with Hilda. He had seen the improvement in her cooking, and he said this very quietly to Wally now before stuffing a huge fork of food into his mouth.

Wally smiled 'I was just hoping some of it might rub off on Mel.' Alby laughed and nodded.

The men finished their breakfast and went off to sort out the vehicles. Melissa stood and watched as they were all started up again. Wally climbed in the land rover beside Jack and Alby climbed in the Willys jeep beside Wayne. The jeep was minus its doors now and it made getting in and out a lot easier.

Hilda and Sandy and Mary stood beside Mel watching. Mary went to get on her horse which she had saddled, and Mike got in the truck with eddy. They all waved goodbye and drove sedately to the gate. Mel was mesmerised by the sight and sound of these vehicles she'd never seen anything like them. They frightened her a little and she worried for Wally and Jack and all of them. All these men going off to catch beasts which could so easily kill them. Or maim or disfigure them like poor Jack. She waved to Wally, she could feel his excitement and she worried on. She watched until distance and dust engulfed him and she could see him no more.

Out in the paddock they headed in the direction of a large herd that Eddy had seen the day before. Mary followed along behind the big heavy truck; she could keep up with that. They usually followed the wheel marks and mostly ended up where a bull was tethered to a tree. Then they used the horse to encourage the bull into the chute on the truck.

Wally enjoyed the ride it was great fun until Jack smiled at Wally and pointed to the right. Wally saw what he was pointing at. A herd of cattle the like of which he had never seen before. They were all bulls and all big and strong and dangerous looking. Wayne circled back around to come up behind Jack.

And without preamble the chase was on. Jack had picked up on a large bull that was out on his own a bit. 'Hang on now' he shouted to Wally without looking at him. Jack kept one eye on the bull and the other on where the land rover was headed. That was his focus, those two places. The bull's rump and the front of the land rover. He sat straight in the seat and though his eyes darted back and forth he hardly ever turned his head.

Wally hung on; an excitement had whacked him in the midriff and a grin appeared on his face. He knew now of the excitement and anticipation he'd seen on these men's faces. Knew why they seemed addicted to it as addicted to it they must surely be he'd thought. To keep going out and do it over and over they must have been. Wally's mind was back on the job.

All else faded away as they went full pelt after that bull. Wally had to dodge or duck branches as he hung on for dear life. They hit bumps that threw them up off their seats to land back in them with a thump. Staying upright was a job and a half, all on its own. Wally was stunned at the speed and difficulty of the chase. The bull twisted and turned, and trees got in the way, small creeks and washouts, ant hills, all manner of obstacles, even the odd kangaroo. But Jack stayed with it. Then there was the other vehicle to worry about, it wouldn't be the first time they had collided. And that meant days of down time to do repairs.

Wally was astounded at the job Jack did of chasing down a wild scrubber bull. An animal that would kill you as soon as look at you. And Jack seemed so casual and relaxed as if they were out rounding a few sheep back on the Murrumbidgee. Sheep who only ever worried about which way you wanted them to go rather than how they were gunna get you out of that vehicle and at their mercy. Wally hung on, aware that last time he'd been in this vehicle Jack had taken it real easy. But this!

At last, they were cruising alongside the huge beast. It made a devil of a noise as it tried to dodge Jack. The wing vehicle was close to, right on the other side keeping the bull galloping straight ahead. The jeep got bumped and thrown about occasionally to whenever the bull caught sight of them. But the rover was his main focus, his main hate.

Jack reached down to the left, saying 'hang on Wally' as he did so. He flicked the switch and the ride suddenly got rougher. The rover was knocked about as the bull tried to buck but the arm of the vehicle had him secure. The dust these vehicles and the bull created made vision a bit hard.

The bull was bellowing his indignation and Jack steered him, fighting all the way, to a shady tree. Wally watched with his mouth open as Alby jumped from the jeep on the other side and ran towards the bull. Alby got so close to it he had to be careful of the horns. Wally held his breath, he wanted to scream at Alby to get the hell away.

Alby had in his hands, a length of rope and with an expertise that astounded Wally, he slipped the rope around both horns and secured the other end to the tree. It took only seconds, but Wally had seen just how dangerous it was. He found he feared for Alby. What Wally hadn't quite known was how much of Alby's survival depended on sheer luck, and that worried Wally.

Then it was done, and Alby jumped back, Jack released the arm from the bull's neck. Now the bull had a bit more scope and wasn't slow at trying to use it.

Jack backed up quickly as the bull made one last ditch effort to hurt somebody and Alby got out of the way entirely. Wally breathed a sigh of relief and began to relax a little.

Alby ran off and got in the jeep and they were off again at a breakneck speed. Wally's stomach was off again to. Wally had to shout as they roared off. 'And you blokes do this for months on end Jack?'

Jack laughed and said, 'you'll get your turn Wally, just watch today hay.' Jack flicked a glance over at Wally who was grinning from ear to ear, 'you'll see.'

Wally wished he hadn't heard that. He saw a branch coming just in time and ducked it only to be thrown up out of his seat two seconds later. It was madness but Wally loved it. He wondered at the work it must take to keep these vehicles going.

He'd been surprised a few years ago when he saw how much Dan loved it, but they'd caught a bull that day, and Wally hadn't. That made the difference thought Wally ducking another tree branch. Catching the bull made the difference. And it was a hell of a ride, and they would do it all day! Hell, they would do it all week for weeks, Wally felt tired.

That evening, Wally's whole body ached, he was glad it was the end of the day. A very long day. About eight hours and six bulls later Jack and Wally drove home to the camp. 'How did you like it' asked Jack?

'Well, it's bloody amazing,' said Wally. He couldn't think of anything else. 'Just bloody amazing man.'

He tried not to limp as he headed for the shower. And that night he ate his tea a little slower, savouring every damn bight. He couldn't understand why his jaw even ached. Wally wondered if he had it in him to do another day tomorrow but do it, he would. Or die trying he mused.

Wally had to refuse his wife's advances that night, 'I'm a bit bushed' he said and kissed her goodnight. Wally hated himself.

Wally got back in the land rover the next day and the first few bumps and smacks in the face were horrendous. You could duck the branch but often not the leaves, and they stung like hell. But then he found his stride and the pain faded into the distance. Wally had to be alert. He wondered vaguely if adrenalin was a kind of a pain killer, sort of like the morphine they'd had during the war. Maybe this was all an hallucination he smiled to himself. The next smack in the face told him, probably not.

Wally's mind snapped back now. The first bull they went after was a doozy. It ducked and weaved like a prize fighter and packed a wallop like one to. The damn thing twisted on its hind legs at one stage, jumped forward onto its front legs, and booted the back side of the rover throwing it off its course. They had to chase it a bit longer than any of the others. Wally couldn't believe the stamina of the animal.

'If I can't get him in a minute or so we are gunna have to leave him. He'll be getting too hot. Don't want to kill him.' Jack shouted and looked over towards Wayne who waved him off. 'Yep' said Jack waving back, 'we're gunna have to let him go.' Without slowing Jack turned and went back to the herd. Wally saw over his shoulder that the bull stopped and watched them go. I'll be damned thought Wally as he noted the victorious stance of the young bull as it tossed its head in the air.

'Another day' Jack shouted to the weary bull as they drove away.

Wally shouted back. 'You wouldn't think it would you Jack, he was so bloody agile. Twisting and turning on a sixpence for Christs sake.'

Jack laughed, 'you do get a few of them like that. We'll come back to him when he's had a spell.'

A couple of days later they saw him again and took up the chase again. And again, the bull got away. Jack had to stop chasing it because to keep going would be to cause its death.

'Aint no good to us dead Wally, and it's not very humane.'

Wally nodded and braced himself as they switched and went after a very big bull. This one dodged to the side and charged them. He got his horns under the wheel arch and threw his head back almost flipping the land rover. Wally got a fright at how close he'd come to toppling out. He couldn't imagine ending up out there with that.

He was a massive bull and Jack looked over at Wayne who shook his head, 'Looks like we are gunna leave this one to Wally. We'll need to go and pick on something more our size.'

Wally was never more pleased, and he breathed a sigh of relief. He could see how dangerous it was just to be in a paddock with these boys. They were bloody hard, and they played hard, and they had no inclination to find themselves tied to a tree.

They got seven bulls that day but didn't return to the two they had let go. Jack told Wally they would Leave them and maybe find easier targets as they drove by one of the bulls.

'He won' said Wally in awe. Wally had developed a healthy respect for these animals, they were willing to go to their death for their freedom. Jacks next words got Wally right in his heart.

'Trouble is' said Jack sadly, 'the owner will probably shoot them.' Jack had a respect for these animals to, Wally could see. Jack drove slowly for a little while as if he was deep in thought. Then he tapped his face, 'that bull that did this to my face just wanted to be free Wally.'

That night as he ate his tea Wally wondered about this business of catching feral bulls. It was bloody hard work, hard on the mind hard on the body and hard on the soul. And that was just the men, what was it like for the bulls he wondered?

Wally had seen a lot of intelligence in these animals over the last week. An intelligence he would never have suspected. They were smart and they were desperate to remain free. And after all, thought Wally, wasn't freedom a thing worth fighting for? He himself had fought alongside many others for the right to remain free, or at least he thought they had. Wally wasn't as good at the game of politics as Dan, but he suspected his fight held none of the honour of the bulls' fight, none of the simple honesty. They did their own fighting and asked for no help.

'What's on your mind Wally' asked Jack? He was a little concerned for Wally he knew the man had a soft centre and a keen mind. Maybe this bull catching wasn't for him. Jack himself had found a respect for these animals and it soured his days somewhat. He sighed.

Wally smiled at Jack 'nothing much' he lied, and Jack noticed the answer didn't match the turmoil on his brother's face. It made Jack feel sad for some reason. He smiled softly at his brother and was glad to see his face brighten.

Wally's food had all the flavour of a piece of cardboard for some reason.

CHAPTER 12

Wally had been at it for two weeks and his excitement only grew. Today he would give driving the catcher a go. They had made a bull out of dead trees for him to practice throwing the arm over it, each day after work. It was harder than he'd thought but he got the hang of it.

Jack had stood by a few days before feeling sorry for Wally, he was struggling with it. Wayne walked up and stood beside him 'do you think standing here watching is a good idea Jack' he asked kindly? He could see how much these brothers loved each other.

'I can't leave him here to try alone Wayne, I never learned how.' Jack watched Wally make a hash of another try. 'Jesus Wayne, I'm starting to think he hasn't got a chance in hell.'

'No' cried Wayne suddenly 'See Jack? It looks like he's missing by a few feet from here but for him it's a few inches. He has to get his lean right Jack, it's so much harder for him.' Wayne shook his head and watched. 'No, that'd be bloody hard and who are we to get in his way? No mate he'll be right, he's nearly there. And if I know anything he won't stop until he bloody, does it.' Wayne studied Jacks face for a few seconds, he hadn't alleviated the worry on it one iota. He smiled softly at Jack and turned back to watch young Wally as he prepared to make another pass.

They watched another two tries and Melissa and Hilda watched with fingers crossed. Sandy and Mary were pulling for him. Young Mike turned to Eddy and said 'you feel like going down there and do it for him. The poor bastard.'

'Nothing poor about him Mikey he'll get there.' Eddy went about his business and so did Mike. Each watching from the corner of their eye. Each pulling for the likeable big fellow in the rover trying his hardest.

Wally backed up and went out round to come in for another run. He drove up nice and steady, right on up to that make believe bull, hit the button and the brake, and had that bull by the neck. Nice and easy. They'd have to rebuild the bull of course.

Wayne clapped Jack on the shoulder, 'well would you look at that' he breathed, 'smooth as a babies bum, Jack.'

A cheer went up from the camp. Alby lost control and ran down pulling Wally from the vehicle. He hugged the man to him slapping him on the back. Wayne and Jack were there doing the same thing. Jack had a tear in his eye along with a tremendous dose of pride. Wally hadn't given up; he had stuck with it, and he had done it.

Melissa ran up to him 'I knew you could do it darling.' Wally slipped his arms around her and held her, he was laughing. He'd done it, he needed some more practice, but he'd bloody done it.

And so it was that the next time they went catching feral bulls, Wally had a go. He thought he'd felt excitement before, but this was more, much more. And to everyone's delight Wally caught the first bull he went after.

A few days later Wayne asked Wally if he'd drive the truck for a couple of days to give Eddy a chance to rope a few. 'Keep his hand in so to speak Wally. And I would like you to learn the truck side of it. Not as easy as you might think. They don't wanna get in that truck any more than they wanted to be tied to a tree. And having been tied to a tree they are in a very bad mood by the time they meet you.'

Wally got a surprise when he got up into the old blitz, they called Beastie. He started it up and he could feel the power of it from the word go. It was very slow but very powerful and that, he supposed, was the whole idea, considering what those bulls must weigh. Wally loved it, he preferred slow and powerful any day. And Wayne wasn't wrong about it not being easy. He had never driven anything like this for a kick off, and the bulls, well they were no easy task either but not as hard as Wally had anticipated.

And that was where Wally got to know Mary, Jack's Mary. And what he learned of her he liked. She was strong and smart and beautiful, and she was tough but loving. She cared for things that Wally had never even thought about and he thought he knew now why they called her the environmentalist. She was a lot like Mary of the shanty he thought, in her ways. They were nothing alike to look at, but their characters were alike, you could almost call it aligned. Both strong and dependable. Jack was a lucky man and he obviously adored her.

No, thought Wally by the end of the first day, Jack couldn't be still pining for Mary of the shanty. This woman was vibrant, alive and had enthusiasm in spades, that rubbed off on you. And when she left the camp to go to her property to do a bit of work there for a few days, you felt it, felt the loss. Bryce must be wrong decided Wally and felt the doubt creep into his head. He pushed it back with a blink of his eyes and a flick of his head.

Mary showed Wally how to load the bulls into the truck and by lunch time they no longer needed Eddy. Wayne was right about the bulls being in a bad mood but confronted with Mary they soon cooled down and behaved like gentlemen. He was truly amazed. Wally heard the other vehicles coming back and his stomach growled.

They all sat down in the shade of a big tree and ate their lunch. Wally had two beef sandwiches and a piece of cake with a mug of black tea. 'It's more refreshing than coffee' Mary informed him with a smile as she passed him his mug. Jack saw the rapport building between the two and was very well pleased. He wanted these two to get along.

Wally noticed, because he was watching, that Jack couldn't take his eyes from Mary. And whenever they passed each other, they would touch and pause for a moment, it was almost as if they made love with a glance. It was a beautiful thing thought Wally. How lucky he and Jack were now.

Over the weeks that followed Wally drove the truck and spent more and more time with Mary. He found that she was a lot more caring than you first thought. He got the feeling when he saw her that she immediately accepted and valued you and what she didn't like she was prepared to accept or change.

And Mary was like that about all of her surroundings and everything that came into her presence. Wally had experienced nothing like it, someone who talked and cared even about plants and their importance. Even the land and the soil and the water. The air, the weather and the quality of life. How each life depended on the other to survive and finally she talked about space and the universe. How we all belonged. She touched on pollution and Wally was flabbergasted.

But Wally had found a new acceptance, a belonging to a very large family. The family of the earth and all who inhabit her. And she told him that it was them, humans, who were doing almost all of the polluting. 'And so, it is up to us to fix it Wally so that our children will inherit a healthy planet.'

Wally couldn't believe it. It had never occurred to him that they could be ruining the planet for future generations. Wally wished he could talk to Dan and Mary.

As they went about loading bulls Mary took care not to hurt them or stress them or make this experience even worse for them. She cared about their comfort bringing them a dish of water. What was most astounding was that these animals were relaxed enough around the woman to drink it. Wally knew in his heart of hearts that they knew she loved them. And she had none of the trouble with them that the blokes had with her gentleness and with her love.

Wally was struck at how like Mary of the shanty she was. This, Wally realised now, was what he had wished she would talk about. When either one of these amazing women, Melissa included, talked about survival and such, Wally sat up and listened.

One day as they were eating their lunch alone Wally asked her about her bulls. 'I heard about that from Jack. He was amazed and not much amazes Jack.'

Mary smiled, 'I know. My bulls are really just pets. They are these same bulls that we catch Wally, but I got them when they were tiny, and bottle fed them. One of them, the youngest Caeser, still insists on a bottle if he gets upset.' Mary gave a little laugh to indicate that she knew just how silly that sounded.

She sipped her tea to cover her embarrassment.

But to Wally it was beautiful, and he realised he was staring open mouthed and shut it immediately. He had never met anybody like this woman here. Before he thought better of it, he asked softly, 'does my brother appreciate you?'

Shocked at himself he looked down at his cup, well he'd said it now. He lifted his head, 'does he?'

Mary smiled 'he does Wally in his own way. And he not only accepts my bulls, but he loves them. And he built my house for me and made me safe. I have never met anyone like Jack. Well, that is until I met you lot.' She laughed again. 'Sorry' she said.

'Oh no, don't be sorry. It does my heart good to know that you like us. Where did you get the idea and the pluck to ride those bulls. I'd love to see them.'

'I just got on them and rode them from when they were very young it was to save me walking actually. They didn't like it at first, but they got used to it. Then I decided they could cart stuff for me, and it grew from there. Next time we get a day off you and Melissa can come with me when I go to check them if you like.'

'I would like' said Wally simply and fell silent hoping she would talk.

Mary went on talking about how she cared for her environment, the habitat of so many. Their home she said, not ours. Wally listened enthralled. Then she started on about Wally catching rabbits. Wally got a bit edgy, but he listened to her as she said softly and without a sign of judgement. 'It's not that I mind, I know you kill only what you need. But it's the way you catch them, Wally. If you think about how they lay caught in a trap while their leg breaks and they lay, there for hours. In agony Wally.'

Wally heard the sob in Mary's voice as she finished. Mary went on about the way we catch things and kill things and how we could be more merciful, until Wally was convinced. 'I'm glad we had this talk, Mary. I can assure you that I will shoot them from now on. I guess what you are saying is we need to cut down on the suffering.' He finished his tea. 'What about this bull catching Mary?'

'Well, these guys seem to be about caring a bit about the animal's welfare so that's something. And sometimes it's about the lesser of two evils. So, if we don't come and do this the owners will just come and hunt them and shoot them and leave them there. This way at least some of them go on to live their lives. Some happy some not so but still . . . . And some of them die anyway so I guess I don't have all the answer, Wally.' Mary looked sad.

Wally found that his heart broke for her, he wished he could put the smile back on her face. But he was bright enough not to try.

Wally threw the dregs of his cup into the fire and was about to get to his feet when her voice stopped him. 'And this is what Jack does, it's what he loves. Someday we'll get away from all this Wally. Someday.' She lifted her head and smiled at him. 'don't get too involved in all this mate if you can help it. Go on back to the Murrumbidgee to your peaceful life. What I would give for a nice peaceful life Wally.' Mary rose to her feet. Wally noticed then how tired she looked. She was a gentle and fragile flower at that moment and Wally worried for her.

Wally smiled sadly, he was sad because she was, 'when we get home, we are going to do up a paddle steamer and live in it.' He looked down at the fire, 'It was willed to me by an old man I came to love, and I will make it a beautiful home for my Mel. I will honour the man called Clyde who was her captain on the Murrumbidgee and the Murray Rivers. I was fortunate enough to work for him for a while.'

Mary realised in that instant that she loved Wally. You couldn't help it she thought as she smiled at him. She knew that he and she were family and always would be. If she had got to pick a brother, it would be Wally. 'Come on' she said, 'back to work Wally.'

During the rest of that day, they didn't get a chance to speak very much, and Wally had time to digest some of what she had said. In fact, he found it hard to keep his mind on the job. He saw the creek just in time to stop before he went over the edge. It was overgrown with tall grass and weeds and wasn't very wide, so it was hard to see. Out of the corner of his eye he saw Mary hurtling straight for it. Wally turned the truck and though he didn't have time to stop her she slowed down.

Spotting the creek just in time she reined her horse in. She looked across at Wally and waved then rode her horse over to him. 'Thanks Wally, I guess we shouldn't have taken the short cut across to the bull. lucky the boys didn't hit it, or we'd have had some fun just getting them out. Lucky you didn't hit it to.'

'Alright Mary we'll go around.' They picked up two more bulls and it was time to go back to camp and let them go. Mary asked Wally if he would like to ride back to camp on her horse, and Wally accepted. As he rode along on the back of the horse, he got an all-new perspective on the bush. It was beautiful, no wonder the drovers loved it. It was one of the most peaceful things he'd ever done.

After he'd eaten his tea that night Wally got his writing set out and by the light of the fire, he wrote home. Home to Dan on the Murrumbidgee. He filled his pen with ink and began.

1/8/55

Dear Dan and All,

I hope this letter finds you all well and happy. It was good to hear your voice the other day Dan. Me and Melissa are okay we are on Cloncurry Holding now catching bulls with Jack and Wayne and all the others.

I don't know where to start Dan, bull catching is like nothing else. I was catching bulls myself for a few days though it took me a lot of practice to be able to catch them in that arm. It is a rush catching those monsters and tying them to a tree, I cannot help fearing for Alby as he fronts one of those beasts on foot. So many things could go wrong. Now I am driving the truck collecting the bulls which have been tied to a tree.

Our trip up here was such a beautiful thing that I can't wait to do the trip home. We are coming home Dan for sure. I would like to fish the lovely Katherine River before we leave here. The station we are on now is in the Northern Territory, almost side by side with Mable Downs.

Melissa loves it up here and she loves the people and the life, but she wants to come home to. She gets along well with everyone including Jack and Mary. Wayne is with Hilda now and the two of them are very happy. He is a very nice man and has been very kind to us. Alby has been good to us to. I really like Alby. I have so much to tell you when we get back, we'll probably come home through Northern Territory and South Australia. I would like to run the Birdsville track and fish the Coopers Creek.

We will be home at Jack's place, in about three weeks and will stay there for a few weeks. I am hoping that Tom and the drovers will come for the bulls. We have about thirty already.

Some days we might get five or six and then again, we might get two or three.

Jack's little boy Billy is a bit of a wag, he has a temper on him to. He gets along with Alby and Sandy's little girl. I have gotten to know Mary as we are on the truck together. She is the most amazing woman Dan. When you get to know her. I have never met anyone like her' Well I must go now Dan, please give my love to all. Will call you soon.

All my love

Me and Melissa

Wally folded the letter carefully, lovingly and placed it into the envelope. Hilda was going into town the next day for some supplies and the mail, Wally would give her the letter to post. Melissa was going with her for company and to help with some shopping.

Wally was overjoyed when she got back and told them that Tom had accepted the job of coming to take away their bulls. Wayne had asked her to phone him whilst she was in town. 'He said he'll try to be here in a little over three weeks so we should be about finished here' said Hilda.

'Very good, thanks my love,' said Wayne.

Jack was glad they were coming, and he smiled at Wally. 'It'll be good to see them again.'

'You'll get to meet the whole crew Mel,' said Jack. 'Their cook is a man called Ernie; you'll like him.

'A team of drovers Wally, real drovers. I can't wait. Oh, Wally this has been a beautiful trip. I'm so happy and I owe it all to you' Melissa stopped talking abruptly. She had just raved on in front of Jack and Wayne.

Wally laughed and slung his arm around her.

CHAPTER 13

Tom climbed up in the saddle and felt the twinge in his hip. He thought now that he might only have a few years of this droving life left in him. He found that he wanted to retire and just be at home with Emily every night. He had fallen deeper and deeper in love with her.

Tom had worked hard and had quite a sizeable station, just over five hundred thousand acres and had stocked it with a thousand head. He would need to get more, and he wanted to have a bit of a look at Jack and Waynes bulls. He had always been amazed at the stamina of these animals and thought they'd make good breeders. Yes, he scratched his head he was eager to retire, with a daughter and another child on the way now.

But for now, he had to get to Cloncurry Holding to take possession of the bulls there and catch up with some old mates. He wondered if Wally had made it up here yet and found that he hoped he had. He often talked to Emily about him, and his achievements and Emily was very interested. He would invite Wally and Melissa to visit them before they went back so that they could meet Emily.

Ernie watched his son swing up into the saddle and though he still did it in one smooth flowing movement which made it look damn easy, he did it a little slower. He himself was getting ready to retire he'd had enough. And he'd bought himself a small property of one thousand acres on the river on which he would run about fifty head. The lawnmower he called them. He would make a little money each year with his fifty head, and he would be not too far from Tom. The property, the stock, and the small transportable home he'd put on it had cost him over half of his savings. The cattle had cost him but they would pay for themselves in the first two years he hoped. Ernie still needed a bull, so he would see Jack and Wayne. With the money he'd get from his cattle and his savings and his small pension he would be comfortable. And he looked forward to fishing and hunting for food.

But Ernie worried about Tom, he didn't handle being away from home very well anymore. He was tired a lot of the time and Ernie wanted him to retire and relax a bit. 'Maybe take it up again a little later on' he had said one day.

Ernie was broken hearted at how his son missed his wife and child and now one on the way. Tom had replied that he wanted to go on for maybe two or three years 'Emily isn't ready to retire yet. Even so you are right I miss her and the kids. I don't want to miss so much of this next one dad.' Tom took a deep breath, 'I'll see how I'm going after this season.'

Tom knew Ernie was struggling but he wanted to be with him on these long trips. And Tom relied on him heavily. Emotionally he needed the old man with him, but he knew it was selfish. Tom sighed and straightened up in the saddle, he still bloody loved it. Loved the life and the great outdoors, and sleeping outside under the stars. And above all he admitted to himself now he loved these mates, loved knocking about the countryside with them. But he was a dad now.

They were around two days from Cloncurry Holding camp and Wayne and Jack and the boys. He still missed Bill, they had buried him about seventy miles from the homestead and about three hundred from Katherine. Tom was glad that Hilda and Wayne had each other he knew how much they missed Bill.

Tom knew this country very well and he envisioned they would reach camp at a little after midday the day after next. Tom waved to the boys to get underway, and they moved the four leader bulls out of camp and onto the trail. He would use these bulls on his property. Tom and the boys had obtained another hundred thousand acres next to Tom, for the boys Jimmy, Nevil, Charlie, and Jack. Herbert was not interested as he had bought a home with his wife in Darwin.

The boys had a thousand head and they would operate their station out of the home they had near Tom. The properties were next to each other, and they had built the homestead buildings on the boundary. The buildings were a large communal kitchen dining area with a sitting room and all individual sleeping quarters. And some of those had a small kitchen and sitting room. They were all set.

Fred rode up next to Tom 'are you okay little mate? You go and sit in the truck with your dad if you're not too well mate we'll be alright.' Fred waited for Tom to smile and say no thanks. Fred was worried about Tom he worked altogether too hard, and he wished there was more he could do.

Tom smiled and said, 'thanks Fred, I think I will'.

As Tom rode away Fred made up his mind that he and the boys had to have that little talk with Tom. Fred had his little holding near Damper Creek where he intended to retire with Janet, where he hoped to retire with Janet. She had been acting a little strange lately, a little cold. Fred shrugged his shoulders and switched his thoughts to the two thousand acres he'd just bought next door to his property. He could run a few dozen head on it and a few chickens as well.

Fred had started building a house on the place and he and Janet lived in the finished half. He hoped against hope that things were alright between the two of them. She hated how much time he spent away from home he knew that. Fred worried about the age difference; he was almost twenty years older than her.

Fred had loved all these years he had worked for Tom; he had found nothing in the man that you could gripe about. They were all treated as equal partners. His years of droving had been like a long holiday to Fred.

He had spoken to Jimmy about it and Jimmy had been wanting to retire also. Those blokes all had a property a very big property and they would make a good living out of it. Ernie had his and so did Tom. Tom had been very fair. They had wanted Fred to go in with them, but Fred wanted only for peace and Janet and his small holding near the river.

Fred decided he would broach the subject with Janet when he got home. Try to clear the air.

Wally was over at the wood heap chopping up some wood he'd dragged home earlier, they liked to keep a fire going all night. Not many of them slept out on the ground now. He also cut up wood for the makeshift barbeque. The girls were making steak egg and chips for tea. Wally's stomach growled at the thought. A shout went up and Tom rode out of the scrub followed by Fred and the boys Jimmy, Charlie, Nevil, Jack, and Herbert. They were followed by the four bulls. The barbershop quartet as Fred called them. They only used these bulls for jobs like this one where feral bulls were involved. These were Tom's own bulls.

Next came the truck pulling the great trailer behind it and Ernie at the wheel.

Jack and Wayne had been checking the fencing around the holding yard. A couple of the bulls had had a fight the day before and cracked some of the poles. You didn't just walk in and put a stop to a bull fight, they pretty much went at it until they were done. And the victor was the new boss in the yard, effective immediately.

They dropped what they were doing and so did Wally. They were joined by Eddy Mike and Alby.

The drovers swung down from their saddles and the handshaking, the back slapping and the loud conversation had begun. Ernie got down out of the truck and shook hands with Wally. 'Congratulations on your marriage young Wally I am very happy for you. I'm sorry I didn't make it mate too bloody old.'

'I understand Ernie and thanks.' '

'Is the young lady here mate?'

'Yeah' Wally turned around and yelled, 'Mel'. Melissa walked over and smiled at Ernie; she knew straight away he was special. 'This is my wife, Melissa' Wally announced with pride.

Ernie smiled at the young woman, 'she is delightful Wally, lovely.' Ernie shook hands with Melissa briefly sensing that she was very shy. 'I am very pleased to meet you, Melissa.'

'Oh, thank you.'

'This is Ernie, Melissa,' said Wally. 'Tom's father.'

Melissa smiled and turned to Tom and said 'hello again Tom. Oh, and Fred . . . . Hello Fred.' Melissa was introduced to the rest of the boys. Melissa was, as ever struck by the niceness of these men, the gentleness of them. She had never known such loving people and she felt very safe with them.

Fred took Melissa's hand and smiled at her, and she blushed. Has to notice thought Jack standing by. He stepped forward to rescue Melissa. Was there a woman who didn't fall for his charm? Fred even made his Mary blush and he had also made Mary of the shanty colour up. Jack studied Fred, what was it about him, it's not like he's particularly good looking? Must be the damn waist coats, or vests, Fred always wore. Some of those were just Geordie. Jack smiled, he liked the man.

It was good to be together again, there was quite a bond between these men now. Ernie spoke when they were sat around with a coffee. 'I have heard from Tom and Fred that your long hut is an amazing place, Wally. When they described it to me, I told myself I must see it someday. To build such a place out of refuse material. And they also tell me it is a beautiful spot there on the river, and the children are always happy and polite. It is a credit to Mary and Dan and all the rest of you.' Ernie smiled softly at the young man now, 'I've heard that even the roses and the daisies grow almost as tall as a man. And that every year the ladies plant sun flowers and the birds flock to them. Is all of this true Wally?'

Wally shrugged, nodded and grinned, 'yes, it is, and you would be welcome there anytime Ernie.'

Tom smiled up at Wally now, 'and Emily would like to meet you before you go back. She can't come over with us as she is busy with her eatery.' Tom looked down for a bit and looking back up at Wally he said 'Emily and the girls also do the sunflower thing now. They started this year.'

'Yes, I have heard about her food Tom, apparently it is legendary. And after hearing about how she started her business and what happened to her, she is one lady I would like to meet. It is largely thanks to you and your Emily that I got started on the road back Tom. We'll call there and see her on the way home. We had always intended to.'

'When are you intending to head off back Wally' asked Fred?

'Well, we'll probably leave here after Christmas sometime and take a slow ride home. Explore a few places.'

'Sounds good.' Tom wanted to look at the herd, so they all went with him. 'Nice little lot' he said at length, 'should bring in a pretty penny.' He turned to Jack; he sensed Jack had become their leader. 'Any chance I could buy one or two of these?'

'Of course,' said Jack and looked at Wayne. Wayne smiled and nodded. A deal was struck for a couple of half-grown bulls with the idea that Tom could quieten them down a bit and the ladies could do the rest. Well brought up cows did not suffer these louts for very long.

'One's for dad' Tom said, he turned to his father now, 'You happy dad?'

Ernie nodded, 'yes I am and thank you.' He was looking over the two bulls 'I won't need him to start producing for a couple of years anyway. No, he's bloody perfect.'

That night the drovers and the bull catchers sat down to steak eggs and chips together, and for afterwards Hilda had made steamed pudding and custard. The men all complimented her on her food and the other ladies as well.

When the eating was done and they had cleared away the men and women and the kids sat down at the fire to talk over old times, what they were doing now, and into the future. The cockies came into roost along the waterhole, and as the sun went down, peace descended on these people. Bound together by only their common love for each other and this Australian bush, their voices hummed into the night with many a sprinkling of laughter, at many a tall tale.

The two older men Ernie and Wayne sat talking with each other. They touched on the subject of retirement and Ernie said how he looked forward to it. Fred chimed in with how he wished he was retired right now. Charlie said, 'you are, aren't you Fred' and they all laughed including Fred?

Tom had been gazing into the fire light deep in thought. He stood up now and said 'who among us is ready for retirement right now. Who would be ready for retirement tonight?'

At first nobody put their hand up and everybody looked thoughtfully at the fire. Then slowly they all did except Jack and Wally and Mike and Charlie. Charlie was just plain frightened of his missus. All of these drovers and their wives had already moved into their new homes on their new property.

Jack stood up; it was like a meeting of the council now. 'I know you blokes' he nodded at the drovers 'have been at this for a long time, what's it now Tom, twenty odd years? It must be hard being away from home for so many months of the year. I guess you could retire and do maybe one or two jobs a year. One of those jobs would be our bulls of course.' There was laughter at that. Jack went on 'you blokes will still be doing what you love, you'll still be working with cattle and there will always be the mustering. You all have the next phase of your lives mapped out and almost ready to walk into.' Jack shrugged and looked at all of them in turn.

Ernie stood up as Jack and Tom sat down and looked beseechingly at Tom, how he loved this man, but it was now or never. 'Tom' he said with a shaky voice 'I love you with all my heart and I would follow you to the ends of the earth. We all would, you know that son, we have.' He shrugged, 'but I haven't got too many trips left in me. I need to get started on my little herd son; I look forward to it.' Ernie sat down almost overwhelmed with feeling.

Wayne stood up and cleared his throat, casting a glance at Hilda he spoke. 'As much as I love this life Jack and Alby, I am gunna have to hand over the keys to the wing vehicle.' He stayed on his feet but was silent for a moment then 'I have enough to buy a place and would need to have a conversation with you blokes soon.' Wayne sat down and looked around at the faces some smiling, some nodding, all understanding. Hilda took his hand and held it as she smiled softly at him.

To everyone's surprise Alby struggled to his feet, these men all felt there was enough love here, enough trust here to speak what was in their hearts. Without fear of recriminations or contradictions. Alby put his shoulders back and shoved his thumbs in his pockets, 'I would be agreeable to retirement, I am ready to buy me and Sandy a home with some cows or some such. I'm not saying I want to stop now; I'm just saying I don't want anyone to go on because of me. And I don't want my face to end up like Jack's.' Everyone at the fireside laughed and some clapped Jack on the shoulder and said things like 'me neither' and 'hell no'. Alby went on, 'I'm just trying to say that I'm okay with whatever, whenever, wherever.'

Ernie looked up at the big man a smile on his face, 'well said Alby mate, well said.' He knew how much he was going to miss these two men, Jack, and Alby when they went back to the south country for go back, they would he knew. He also knew that parting would rip at their hearts the same as his and the rest of the drovers.

Alby looked pointedly at Jack, 'now having poked shit at Jacks face, I will stay beside you Jack. If you work, I'll work and if you retire I will. And I will go wherever you go. You are my family now Jack and so is everybody here.'

Jack nodded at the man and smiled 'here, here Alby, I feel the same mate.'

Jimmy got to his feet as Alby sat down. 'I'm fucking ready for retire. I think my wives are getting restless.' There was much laughter 'you may laugh but you don't know my wives when they are restless. Ooh is very bad thing, very bloody bad.' There was laughter and applause as Jimmy sat down shaking his head.

To everyone's surprise especially Jack's, Wally stood up. 'Why don't we call it like this? Whoever is ready to retire just do it at the end of this year and hand over to any who wish to keep going.' He looked at the drovers, 'seems to me like you all got it worked out and are waiting on the others hay. And nothing much is gunna change like Jack said you'll still be working stock and you'll still be together. Good job we had this little meeting. And as for me? Well, I'm already bloody retired.' Wally flicked his eyes at Jimmy who grinned widely. He had to speak up above the laughter as he said, 'I'm nobodies bloody fool.' The laughter went on as he sat down. No one got up. Wally glanced at Melissa and said, 'it's the river for me.'

After the laughter subsided and the jibes, Tom got to his feet. He looked at Ernie, 'dad I'm about ready to chuck it in myself.' There it was said.

Ernie nodded now 'I know son, I know. Those kids need you and so does Emily.'

Fred got to his knees and looked across at Ernie and said, 'you didn't stand up Ernie.'

'I know son, I know.' Ernie waited for the laughter to die down 'we'll get it sorted son' he said to Tom. 'Wally had a good idea, thanks Wally.'

Wayne sat back and stretched his legs, obviously totally relaxed. He said, 'I'm glad we had this talk to, I am about too old for this now.' He squeezed Hildas hand, they had made plans some time ago. Hilda reached up and kissed his cheek.

Laying in his swag beside Melissa that night Wally couldn't sleep. He was afraid he was in on the beginning of the end of an era. He didn't know what was coming next, but he'd just witnessed some very fine people trying to let go of a way of life that they loved. He hoped they'd all be happy. He had a sudden urge to be alone on a riverbank with Melissa, away from the world and all its cares. To just be there on the riverbank with only the cockies for company and make sweet love to Mel.

Also on Wally's mind was the fact that Tom had asked him if he would like to go droving with them. Wally told him that he thought the bull catchers needed him for a bit longer and Tom had smiled. 'Okay Wally, we'll be back this way again soon. We usually do a job over here taking cattle to Mount Isa. It's usually the last job we do and it's around the end of October. We'll swing by and pick you up if you like. I'll give you a ring a couple of weeks beforehand.'

'Thanks Tom I'd love to come with you. And about Mel?'

'Bring her Wally if she will come. She might like to give Ernie a hand. Can she ride Wally?'

Wally shook his head. Tom went on 'well she can learn, or she can stick with Ernie it's up to her, I'll leave it with you Wally.'

Wally found that the idea of droving cattle had stirred his blood. A dingo howled and Wally fell asleep.

The next morning Ernie and Hilda cooked breakfast with the help of Mary and Sandy. Melissa was engrossed in taking care of the children. She dressed them and supervised their washing and teeth cleaning. Then after she helped with the dishes, she would take on their lessons. They did need to learn some songs and some stories. Billy was over four years old, and she had begun to teach him letters and numbers. Susanne was not yet four, but she was very bright and took to learning better than Billy.

When the men came home with the bulls, you'd find Billy sitting on the top rail of the holding pen with his hat on and dressed in jeans and boots. It was like it was calling to him. Mary had told Melissa she was glad she was trying to teach him something.

Wayne and Hilda had talked for a bit the night before and Wayne had asked her if she was ready to give up this life. Hilda had smiled softly and said 'I do love it out here and I'd rather be here with you than at home without you. However, I am getting tired love. I wouldn't change a minute of the life I've had with you. Except that I wish we had gotten together years ago. No, I'm happy with the plan love. Let's do it. Do you want to head South still; just a little way so it's not so humid?'

'And the land is a smidgen cheaper right now. As soon as bull catching is over, we'll start looking' Wayne had agreed, and he made love to Hilda to the tune of cockies who were still objecting to being kept awake.

Everyone sat down to breakfast with a certain feeling of having cleared the air. So that when it was time to get up and go the drovers had heavy hearts and so did the bull catchers. These men knew on the one hand that droving was coming to an end regardless. On the other hand, they had a life to look forward to better than most and it was because of all their hard work, their hard life and their sacrifice. And every one of them was glad it had been brought out into the open. Everyone without exception had hugged at their parting.

Tom led the bulls from the yard as usual and the act had an air of finality about it. But it didn't cut Tom to the quick as it might have done. It was Wally who had made him see. Wally and Alby. Tom only knew that he would have to maintain a relationship with all these people, he couldn't do without it. They had opened his eyes to what he had, in them and in his family and in his pocket.

Fred knew when he pulled out, there might not be many more trips for him. He was tired and slowing down. He would need to find out what was wrong with Janet, he couldn't lose her. Could he? He'd get to work on that bloody house to and get it finished.

They disappeared quickly into the bush and Wally knew they were good friends. Like Tom he was determined to stay friends forever. Alby stood beside Wally; he had realised that they were a lot alike, and they both loved Jack. Everyone was glad that they had made a gift of two bulls of their choice to the drovers.

The drovers and the bulls gone, the bull catchers had to pack up their camp and move to another site. They would move about two hundred miles away; clear across the station. They would leave early in the morning and hopefully strike camp the night after next.

It was decided that the girls and the kids would ride in the two land rovers Jacks and Wallys. As they pulled out you couldn't tell where they'd been, they always dug a trench for toilets and rubbish. Mary had insisted and these bull catchers now took pride in the way they left their sites.

Wally had already been designated to digging the trench when they got where they were going. And they would all set up camp and start again. Another camp, another herd.

There was an excitement about the move, Wally felt it and realised that this was another dynamic to the bull catching. It was the moving about from one water source to another. Another patch of dirt another clump of trees and another set of neighbours. New dingoes, new cockies, new joys, and new problems. And Wally loved it.

Best of all he could see that Melissa loved it to, he could see they all did. And the kids? Well, they had a new back yard a very large one, one they would spend days and weeks exploring.

They spent four weeks at that camp and ended up with thirty more bulls, it had been a very good season. Their total bull count for the year had been sixty- seven. And they still had more to go. The boys had made close on seventy thousand pounds after expenses they'd be left with around sixty thousand.

If they did as well off the last station, they should clear about eighty thousand pounds. A fortune. They would need to pay more expenses which would include wages after which they would be left with around twenty thousand pounds each. Mike and Wally would be paid a wage and so would Hilda.

After they had finished on Cloncurry Holding, they would pack up and move on. They would go home and spend a week or so and then on to the next station.

CHAPTER 14

When the bull catchers were finished on Cloncurry Holding, they went back to town to their property there. The first night back everyone went to the pub for tea. All except Mary, she had left from the camp to go to her property and check on her bulls and her two cows as she often did. Wally had had to drive the truck back, so he and Melissa didn't go with Mary, saying they would go with her next time. Jack had to bring the chaser back for a few repairs. Wally worried a little as she left and then asked himself who would be more capable of looking after themselves than Mary?

But Wally didn't have the same faith in bulls as Mary did. He found them to be devious, self-serving, and downright hostile for the most part. Wally wouldn't get in the yard with one for all the tea in China. His feeling of doom escalated all through the afternoon though he tried hard to quell it.

He sat at tea with Melissa and worried, he worried so much his heart was pounding, and his neck throbbed. Wally refused to play pool with Jack who wasn't concerned about it much because Wally didn't play pool very often. 'Mugs game' he usually replied when asked to play it.

People tended to overlook Wally with his crook arm, but Jack knew he was a capable enough player of the game. Jack smiled down at Wally and went off to the pool room.

Jack's little boy Billy had stayed with Jack, and he now sat at the table with Wally, Melissa, and Susanne. The boy suddenly threw himself back in the chair, gave a yell and started to cry softly the tears streaming down his face. Melissa went to him and got him to quieten down. Jack and Alby came into the room and Jack took the boy with him to the pool room. 'Come and watch dad beat the pants off Uncle Eddy mate.' The boy looked at Wally begging him to understand with his eyes.

Alby looked at Wally as he went to follow Jack, then stopped. 'You go ahead Jack I'm just gunna sit here with Wally for a while.' Alby sat across from Wally, he noted the pale pallor, the sweat, and the heightened breathing. 'What is it, Wally?' Wally stared wide eyed at him. 'Can you tell me mate' asked Alby gently; the big man was starting to worry him. It looked like a panic attack, but Alby wasn't sure.

Wally swallowed and Melissa worried. 'Go on Wally tell us what's wrong baby.'

Wally dropped his eyes and lowered his head. 'It's nothing Alby but I am a little worried about Mary. She's out there alone.'

'She often is Wally.'

'Yeah but . . . . I dunno Alby. I got a bad bloody feeling is all. And that boy just suddenly went all wide eyed and terrified like, and then started to cry. You know like his heart was broken or something. I dunno Alby. Something doesn't sit right in here.' Wally banged on his chest with his fist. His anxiety was ramping up now and Alby reached across and touched his arm.

Alby sat looking from Wally to Melissa and back again. Melissa looked worried as if she was picking up on what Wally felt. 'Damn it,' said Alby. He put his elbows on the table, he'd had a bad feeling all day. He stood up then said 'let's go home and talk to Wayne. I'll go and tell Jack something.' Alby got up and hurried off trying to collect his thoughts. Sandy hadn't come into tea with them she'd stayed home to get some sleep.

Jack asked what's wrong and offered to come. 'No mate' said Alby and found his heart was breaking for the man. So, he had to say something and get out of it. 'We're just gunna take Melissa home, her and Wally are a bit tired and me to. I'd like to take the opportunity to check on Sandy as well Jack. Be back a bit later mate you get on with your game.'

When Wally, Melissa, and Alby told Wayne about Wally's feeling, Wayne kept his eyes on Wally. He looked as if he'd seen a g . . . . Suddenly Wayne was struck by the same anxiety, and he had to know if Mary was alright out there. He couldn't bring himself to head off to town and tell Jack any of this. Anyway, it would be wasting time, maybe precious time at that. 'Come on' he said, getting quickly to his feet grabbing his torch and his rifle. 'we've got to get out there. Will you sit and wait with Hilda please Melissa? Just in case she wakes up.'

'Of course.' Melissa looked at Wally, at the anxiety on his face and couldn't think of a damn thing to say.

'I'll see you soon baby' he said softly to her as he kissed her and left. Wally had to force himself to get in the rover, he felt sick.

The three men set off on the two-hour trip to Mary's place armed with torches and guns. No one spoke much on the way, but Wayne stated at one stage he felt it to. He looked at Alby and new immediately they were right to come. No matter the outcome, and they all hoped they were just on a fool's errand, but they had to come.

It was the longest two hours, each man deep in his own thoughts and fears and not one of them game to give voice to them. By the time they reached Mary's gate they were all but jumping out of their skins. Not Mary: God in heaven not Mary they thought. Each man knowing what it would do to Jack. Each man knowing what a loss it would be to all of them, and indeed the world was a better place with Mary in it.

On the way up the drive Wayne gave voice to it. 'There are no lights on that I can see, and I reckon we know what we are all thinking. Straight to the cattle yard gents.'

Wayne parked the rover with the headlights on the yard. All three men saw it at the same time. On the ground just inside the gate, Mary's favourite bright orange shirt, Mary would never drop that on the ground and leave it there.

Alby let go a sob and opened his door. 'Mary', he shouted and ran to the woman lying on the ground.

Wally was right behind him, and Wayne grabbed a rifle and followed. Mary was dead. 'Not Mary, oh God no not Mary. Why? Why?' Wally couldn't make it out why this woman? Why someone who was so good as Mary was? So good through and through and so beautiful.

Wally dropped his head in his hands for a moment, then he noticed Wayne was looking around on the ground with a torch. Pulling himself together he went over to him. It had just dawned on him that they could be in danger here themselves. They didn't know what had happened to Mary. Didn't know if fate had the same thing in store for them. Wally stood gathering his wits.

Alby followed sniffing and wiping at his face with his hand. Alby had loved Mary, loved her with all his heart. Why? Everyone loved her. Why her? Alby was numb.

Wayne said 'look gentlemen. There are signs of a fight here. Did Mary find herself in the middle of a bull fight?'

Alby knew she would if one of her bulls was in danger. He squinted at the ground and back at Mary. She looked trampled but he couldn't say that. Wayne said it. Then, 'do we think this was Mary's bulls or . . . . '

Alby swung his torch around, 'look Wayne, on the ground there. That looks like Caeser.' A form on the ground on the edge of the torch light.

They rushed over to it and found it was Caeser. Wayne said now, 'well, what the hell happened here? The other bulls? Maybe they were all fighting, and Mary went in to... '

The three men jumped in fright as a loud, angry bellow rang out from just over to their left. Wally swung the torch around and the eyes, the red eyes with illuminous light brown centres near frightened him to death. He knew it wasn't the devil, but it was a devil of a bull, he was sure of that. It took a moment for his eyes to focus on the rest of the bull. He was a monster with great long horns, and he was as black as the night. And he was pouring the bloody dirt!

It let out another blood curdling bellow and came straight at them from about fifty yards. Wayne had the rifle to his shoulder and let off a shot, but he only slowed him up, the bull stumbled. It was enough for the men to run for the fence, which they tried to climb over. Wayne and Alby made it over but not so Wally.

The bull started playing with Wally it had him on the ground and was pushing him along. Wally had the presence of mind to curl himself up into a ball and wait. He was terrified. Every time the bull snorted Wally got hot air and snot in his face.

Wayne let off another shot which dropped the beast which dropped its head on Wally's. Wally succumbed to the blackness, the peaceful blackness. Alby ran over and lifted Wally carefully out from under it and passed him up to Wayne on the fence. There was no time to check Wally first, the bull may have just been dazed. Alby was kneeling beside

Wally talking to him when they heard a land rover coming in the gate. It was Jack! Wayne left Alby reviving Wally while he ran to Jack.

'Jack no' he shouted 'no Jack don't go there. No mate please.'

But Jack had seen the orange shirt. He ran to Mary looking over at Wally. Alby shouted that Wally was okay. Jack sank to his knees beside Mary. How could he believe what he was seeing? How could he survive this? His beautiful Mary all trampled into the dirt. His Mary who would never look at him again would never love him or laugh at him again. Would never speak to him in her beautiful sing song voice. No, he couldn't stand this.

Wayne was kneeling beside him now; Jack came to his senses a little. 'I heard a shot, Wayne. Was it Caeser?'

'No mate, we shot the bull that we think killed Mary. I think Caeser is dead to Jack we think the other bull killed him.'

Jack sat in the dirt and lifted Mary into his arms and rocking her gently he cried until he was empty. That was it he thought, that's how he would do this. Running on empty. Jack didn't have the option of putting a gun to his head this time, he had a son.

'What happened to Wally' he asked when the crying subsided?

'There was a strange bull here, a mad bull Jack. He got Wally but Alby reckons he's just out to it.'

'Well check him would you Wayne?'

Wayne did so and told Jack that Wally was coming round. Wayne felt suddenly tired, so tired. He looked at Jack and then at the rover.

Wayne went now to his rover the tears almost blinding him. He reached for his radio he needed to speak to Hilly, he would hold it all back until he'd spoken to her. Some one answered his call and he asked for her. When he heard her voice, the dam burst, and he cried until he was empty to.

Wayne heard her dear sweet voice asking him what is the matter darling, what is it? Wayne tried but his throat wouldn't work. It felt paralysed. He managed to say her name a couple of times and then she told him to cry, to just cry. Hilda was hoping he wouldn't say the words she knew he must. Hilda was filled with dread, poor Mary, and poor bloody Jack.

At last Wayne said, 'We have lost Mary. We were too late Hilly. We were too bloody late.' She looked at the sleeping Billy and her heart began to break in two.

Hilda with the help of Eddy, Sandy and Melissa took charge. She got the police to go out to Mary's place. Then she rang the doctor. When Jack got back, he would be in shock, he would need something. The doctor came over with some sedatives. He told Hilda to get him to the hospital if she was worried and told her what to worry about.

Hilda let Wayne know and he was still hardly able to speak. She was glad she had got extra sedatives for them they would all be in shock she thought. The doctor had thought it a possibility to.

Hilda was shocked and concerned when she saw Jack, he was like a ghost. There was a hollowness about him, and his eyes were hard to read. Alby was shaking from head to foot and showing signs of shock. Wally told Hilda and Melissa he had let his brother down. He should have gone out there when he first felt it.

Hilda had held Wayne and then given him the sedatives with a coffee laced with some whiskey. She did the same for the others and Jack. She sat and watched Jack the whole night through. He looked like someone who was dying, and she kept her all-night vigil in prayer for him. Now and then he reached for her hand and cried.

Later, the doctor had said he thought that Mary was probably killed outright. She had taken a horn to the brain he'd said, and death was instant. It was a relief to know that Mary had suffered very little, and the doctor had indicated that the other injuries were done posthumously. Jack was the most relieved to hear his Mary hadn't suffered. It would help them all to deal with their grief, just knowing that.

The good doctor would be the only person who would know the truth. Him and Sergeant Billy Judd.

The funeral was set for a weeks' time and Jack had to tell his little boy he would not see his mother again. The boy had cried in his arms and after he stopped, he said, 'you won't leave me will you dad?'

'No kid, you have my promise. We'll go on from here little mate and we'll stick together hay.' Jack thanked God; the boy had not gone with his mother. He may have lost them both.

The little boy, Billy had put his arms around Jack's neck and Jack held him. They had stayed like that for a long time.

Two days after the terrible incident which had taken Mary's life Tom and Ernie arrived. 'The others are coming they'll be here in a couple of days.' Tom told Hilda. 'Where is he?'

Tom found Jack out at the table with his head hanging down on it. Tom sat beside him and slipped his arm around him. 'Jesus Jack' he said softly. He cried there with Jack he didn't like the look of him. The man looked as though he'd lost his soul. His little boy looked the same, 'Jesus, mate' Tom said again and pulled him into his arms.

Tom looked at Ernie, he had taken this bloody hard, and Tom hoped he'd be alright. He had refused to stay at home.

Hilda came out and got Billy and carried him inside, she wondered if this would kill the lot of them. Wally was no use he was struggling with his own shock and grief. Everyone knew he had gotten close to Mary; they were kindred spirits she thought. Jack himself wanted to go to Wally, but he couldn't do anything.

Ernie sat on the other side of Jack and together the three men sat without words. When they had sat a while Jack said, 'thanks for coming.'

Tom said 'Of course, mate. I dunno what to say.'

Just then Hilda came out and took Jacks arm 'I'm sorry Tom' she said, and Tom and Ernie sat back. 'Come with me Jack' she said softly. Jack found a great degree of difficulty getting up and Ernie got up and helped her, as she helped Jack to his feet. She led him into the phone and held it out to him.

'No' said Jack. 'I don't want to.' Tom and Ernie looked at each other in the doorway.

Hilda held it to his ear. 'Jack. Jack, are you there little mate? Jack.'

Jack grabbed the phone with both hands and put it to his ear 'Dan....' was all he could manage.

'Jack I'm on my way. I'm in Melbourne now and I will see you in a few days okay mate. You hang on Jack, I'm coming. I'm sorry mate, so sorry.'

'Dan? Coming? Please?'

'Yeah, mate I'm coming. I love you son, I'll see you soon. We'll be okay son we'll get through this together hay. We'll be okay boy I promise. I'll be there as fast as I can son, I'll be just a few days. Hang on Jack. Tell Wally.'

Jack passed the phone back to Hilda and almost smiled. He'd do that, he'd hang on and wait for Dan to come. In the meantime, he had to see to Mary, he had arrangements to make. Jack turned and went to see Wally; he knew Wally was suffering. For all his strength and toughness Wally had a soft centre and that centre was broken. He put his arms around Wally, 'Dan is coming' he whispered in Wally's ear. 'He told us to hang on mate.' The two men ended up in each other's arms, comforted. They held onto each other. 'Yeah, we'll hang on Jack' wally sobbed, 'we'll wait for Dan.'

Mary's funeral was at One o'clock on a Monday. Her grave was just across form Russell's. It was a solemn affair and Dan had just made it. He stood beside Jack at the grave and held him and Wally stood next to Dan. Wayne stood on the other side of Jack with Alby and Ernie. Tom stood with Ernie and Fred and the rest of the drovers. Mike and Eddy stood with Billy and the women on the other side of the grave.

Wayne had rung the station manager at Bidialpar and told him they would be a bit late doing the bull catching this year. 'I'm sorry but it can't be helped' he ended. Wayne, in actual fact didn't know how they were going to do it, but he knew they must.

The manager had asked what was wrong and Wayne told him. 'We have lost one of our number and we have a funeral to attend.'

'Who' the manager Joe came back? He'd heard the tremor in Wayne's voice and had known him to be a very stoic man.

'It's Mary. Mary Kingroy from Kingroy station. You know, she married Jack.'

'No bloody way Wayne. How?'

Wayne told Joe and the man told him to take all the time he needed. 'My condolences to you Wayne and to your large family.' There was a pause, and his voice went on 'I do know how you all loved her Wayne. I am very sorry.'

He had fronted up to the funeral and had left along with some of the other guests. Most of the mourners didn't go to the pub out of respect for the bull catchers and drovers who they knew were good and loving people. There were hundreds of people from town and stations round about attending the funeral for the much-loved Mary and it would have been a crush in the pub.

Wally stood silent as Melissa pushed in and put her arm around him. He vowed he would never forget what Mary had taught him. He would teach his children and his children's children. He would carry her loving ways into the future, he would never forget her. And Wally had a litany of writings, a wealth of information for his new journal. He'd need a new journal.

The funeral was at an end and the company of mourners retired to the pub for the wake. The hotel had put on a spread in the dining room. Nobody ate much, and so they went into the bar. Jack stood contemplating his future, his bleak and dismal future without Mary. Dan had given him strength, but he needed to find it in himself now, for Billy. But he was struggling, helplessly. Why hadn't those bloody bulls just run over him and killed him? Please God why hadn't they? Jack tipped another beer down his throat.

The publican himself took care of the bar. He clapped Jack on the shoulder and said 'I'm real sorry mate. Let me know if there's ever anything I can do hay.'

Jack thanked him and checked Dan was still with him. Dan was talking to Ernie and Wayne; he told them he would stay as long as he was needed, and they nodded their gratitude. Dan had made a huge difference; Dan always made a difference. Dan was the only father Jack had ever known, and he was more like a father than a big brother.

No one noticed the smallish, non-descript man who came in and sidled up to the bar just along from them. There were a few others not belonging to the party in there, the bar had been left open to the public. Everyone had heard of the tragedy, and everyone offered the barman money. 'For these good people.'

Jack ambled away from the bar and now stood beside Alby. Alby checked Jack, he had a bit of colour in his face now and Alby had seen him smile just before. It was a start. Alby flicked his eyes around the bar, he was uneasy, and he didn't know why. He looked at Wally who was also studying him. Shit, Wally felt it to! Alby looked around, his scrutiny taking in everything and everyone.

His eyes came to rest on the stranger at the bar, he was a smallish bloke with a suit and a big wide brimmed hat on. He didn't really stick out because most of the blokes there were in suits and Akubra hats. Alby thought he'd seen him at the funeral, he was sure he had. It was what happened when the man saw him looking at him that began to disturb Alby. He started and looked like he tried to shrink into the background, quickly. He had his hat pulled down over his eyes and he lifted his glass to his mouth. Alby wondered what he should do, he checked Wally who was talking to Jack now.

Alby decide to keep an eye on that bastard, he was decidedly peculiar, shifty in fact. But he didn't want to upset everyone farther by making a bad call.

Jack stood out on his own and spoke to Hilda at the table, but he didn't go to her. Jack turned back now and looked at the smallish man at the bar who had now stepped away from it, and with his hand in his pocket he spoke pointedly to Jack. Yelled at Jack.

'You let her die you bastard. You couldn't be bothered to look after her. You didn't deserve her ya mongrel. She was all I had.'

Jack looked into his eyes and realised with a chill that the man was mired in pain and madness. His eyes were bright and wide almost popping out of his head. His mouth was hung open and slack lipped and his skin was tinged with grey. A chill ran down Jack's spine, the man was sick. Worse, the man was insane.

Jack found he didn't care what happened to him in fact he'd welcome it. He agreed with everything the man was saying. Then he heard Billy laugh and fear took hold of him, Billy was playing with some other kids in the beer garden. He watched mesmerised as the man's hand came out of his pocket holding a small gun. He found himself staring down the barrel of a gun and felt nothing. Though he was scared he had no inclination to try and save himself. Who was this bloody bloke?

Everything happened in slow motion, even the screams as the gun went off were long and drawn out. Jack felt a pain in his head and a searing pain to the side of his midriff and went down, stiff legged, on his back side. His world darkened. He relaxed as his head hit the floor; he'd be with Mary again, soon. It was all he could think, God how he wanted it. Needed it. He mouthed the word Mary as he pitched sideways.

He heard someone shout and then Billy screamed. Poor Billy thought Jack as he let go, poor little bugger. Jack tried to fight the blackness just then. But to no avail.

Alby, he was vaguely aware, had put something lovely and soft under his head. His world got blacker and then he was brought round momentarily by somebody turning him on his side and his head hitting the floor. Just like dear sweet Alby he thought dimly, to put his head on something nice and soft then tip him off it. Dan was by his side, 'you'll be alright Jack we got that bastard under control. The ambulance is coming mate, just hang on.'

Jack was annoyed at all the talk; he didn't want to know. He wanted to be off to Mary and the wonderful peace he now knew she and Caeser had found. But which Mary? Jack was suddenly sickeningly confused. Was he looking for Mary his wife or . . . . Oh God! Then Jack was gone, he was at peace at last. Swallowed up by the blackness.

Jack's peace didn't last long, and he found himself fighting his way through the blackness with a blinding pain in his head. His side ached like hell to. Not again he thought, he couldn't go through this again. Days of pain and suffering weeks of pain and suffering. Shit no! He got his eyes opened, and the light was blinding him. Gradually he made out a nurse who had her back to him. Why was he still here anyway?

Jack remembered the nice morphine he'd had last time and decided to ask, no demand, some. His throat wouldn't work. He looked beyond the nurse with her back to him and saw the doctor at the front desk who was reading something.

Well, he decided he'd wave to the man. But he couldn't move a muscle. A terror like nothing he'd ever felt struck Jack as he realised, he was probably in a coma. One of those comas where you can see and hear but you can't talk or move, and nobody knows your there and you can't shut your eyes. Mary, he said in his head, I'm coming. Please God let me go. If his spirit was freed, where then would he fly? To heaven or the Murrumbidgee? Well, he was bloody sick of this.

Jacks' muscles began to work when somebody beside him he hadn't seen, touched his arm and made him jump. He slanted his eyes to the side and breathed a sigh of relief. 'Dan' he croaked in a whisper which hurt.

'I'm here son' Dan was smiling! 'Thank God you're alright we all got quite a scare Jack.'

'You got a scare? You got a scare?' Jack screeched inside his head. But no words came out, Jacks mouth was moving but he made no sound.

The doctor was by his side and knew who he was. He knew what today was for Jack and knew what he was doing when he got shot. 'Don't worry Jack, your voice and your movements will all come back very soon. We'll just give you something for the pain.'

The nurse shoved a needle in his arm, and he felt better almost immediately. The doctors voice went on. 'You were hit by a bullet Jack, and it bruised one of your ribs. It also cut your skin and some muscle, so you will have a little pain there for a few days, maybe even weeks.'

Jack reached up and touched his pounding head as the doctor went on. 'I will let Dan here tell you what happened there, Jack' he touched Jacks head. 'I wasn't there so I didn't see it.' He smiled reassuringly at Jack and stepped back.

Jack looked aghast at the blithering doctor then turned his eyes to Dan. Dan smiled, 'I know your head hurts mate but if Wally hadn't knocked you flying, you'd have been killed for sure. The bloke was lining you up to shoot you when Wally hit you in the head to knock you out of the way. One day we shall have to talk to Wally about how strong his right arm is.' Dan smiled, 'well anyway your head then hit the floor and knocked you senseless. Your throat doesn't work because they gave you a general anaesthetic to look at your rib and stitch your wound. You've had ten sutures Jack.' Dan picked up Jacks hand, 'you can come home shortly if you like mate.'

Jack went home that day, still unable to talk very much. Hilda put him to bed out in the guest area of the outdoor living area where he could be with everyone. She'd made up a camp bed for him and put a swag on it. Jack got into it and accepted one of Hilda's "coffees for special occasions".

Wally sat beside him, and Jack said, 'I believe I've got you to thank Wally, for my headache.' Wally laughed and Jack reached out and took Wally's hand in his, 'thanks for saving me Wally.'

'Do you mean that Jack? You said Mary with a smile on your . . . . '

'No Wally, I am grateful to you. My son needs me now. Where is Billy?'

Hilda spoke up from the table 'he's playing with Susanne and Tom's little girl. He's alright Jack, we are watching him for you. I'll go and get him, and you can have a talk with him. Maybe reassure him a little Jack.'

Jack nodded; he would do that. He would care for his and Mary's son. When Billy came in to see Jack, everyone left them to it. They had things to sort out. Jack spoke softly as he told Billy he loved him, and he always would.

'But I . . . . I miss mum dad. I miss her so much I feel sick all the time.'

'Yeah, me to son me to. But look, we'll manage you and me. And you have all these people here who love you.'

'I know dad. But you could have '

'No not me son. Others have tried. Much bigger and much stronger. I'm here son, I'll always be here. And Dan here is your grandfather. He'll be here to.'

Billy looked at Dan and Dan smiled at the boy who was a lot like Jack, 'that's right son. You can call me Grandpa if you have a mind to. And me and Mary will always be here for you. I know we live a long way away, but we are there should you ever need us.'

Dan held his arms out to the boy who stepped into them. 'Is that a promise pa? Do you love me?'

'Oh yes young man. Haven't I told you that?'

Billy shook his head and smiled. 'Well, I do,' said Dan.

'Can I call you pa? That's what Johnny Dodd calls his grandfather.'

'Pa would be just fine Billy. Pa would be bloody amazing.' Dan kissed the small boy on the forehead and was rewarded with a great smile. One of the kids outside started yelling and Billy looked towards the sound.

Jack spoke softly to the boy, 'you go ahead Billy and see what's going on. But a hug for your old man first.'

Billy left to play with the kids, there were a couple of kids from a station here and they were kicking a football around. Jack settled back and smiled at Dan. He saw Dan relax. 'Thanks Dan' he said now.

'Everything will be all right Jack; we are all here for you. You are badly hurt my son, deep inside where it is slow to heal, but heal you will. And you have a fine and loving boy, and we love him, Jack. Just as we love you. Cast your mind back occasionally Jack to what we all came through and survived. And find strength in that and know that we will always be there for you Jack. And I promise you we will all come through this to.'

And they were all there, the drovers the bull catchers the kids. All Jack's family and he knew he should be grateful. Knew he would be grateful, soonish. All the people of the Murrumbidgee who rang every day, they were all there. And Billy was there, Billy who looked like his mother.

Jack smiled at Dan and Wally came and sat down with them. The three men were comforted by each other. They were family and they had come through a lot together. Wally's heart broke for his brother, and he put his hand on Jacks arm. 'You gave me a fright man. I don't know what to say Jack.' Jack heard the sob in Wally's voice.

Jack smiled at this man who next to Dan was his best friend. Wally had always been there, Jack realised in that instant, he'd always had his back. Even in his darkest days Wally had stayed by his side. Why hadn't he seen that before? 'That's okay buddy, neither do I.'

The two men laughed, and Alby sat down next to Wally. Dan was glad Jack had him.

Jack decided it was time to shake off the self-pity and he surprised everyone.

CHAPTER 15

It was four weeks since the funeral and Wayne knew they had to get back out there. The boys were getting restless, including Jack, especially Jack. When Wayne spoke to Jack about it, he'd replied that if we wait for me to get better, we'll go bloody broke.

And at last, they were ready to go back to work. They had everything packed up and the vehicles checked and loaded. Wayne sat with Jack at the table. Dan was there to as Wayne wanted to talk to both of them.

He told Jack now that if he needed more time, they would be able to manage without him. Tom and the drovers had left a few weeks ago as they had a job waiting. So, they had said their tearful goodbyes and promising to return soon, they left.

'No Wayne I need to go. If I stay here, I'll go mad.' Jack looked at Dan, 'do you wanna go home Dan?'

Dan sat looking at Jack and smiled. 'I do son, but I need to know you'll be alright lad. I have always needed that, Jack.' He turned to Wally 'and you Wally, are you going to be alright?'

After much reassurance on both sides, they came to a decision. Dan missed his home down in the southern lands and he missed his wife. Dan and his two boys came to a mutual arrangement.

Dan booked a flight for two weeks' time and Jack said someone would take him to Mount Isa to the train. So, Dan was off to the bull catching camp with Jack and Wally and the boys. Dan wanted to be there when Jack went back to camp, it would be pretty hard on him. He would miss Mary all over again.

Wayne had tried to ask Jack what he planned to do with his and Mary's property, but Jack had gone quiet. It would fetch a decent price because it had water on it. A great creek ran through the top corner of it which fed a kind of Billabong which had water in it all year round. Wayne wondered if he wanted to sell it or retire on it. But he left it alone, Jack would talk when he was ready.

So, the bull catchers once more set sail for the heart of Australian bushland to catch some wild scrubber bulls. Dan was excited though he was homesick now. It seemed like such a long time since he saw Mary. He felt a sudden attack of guilt when he reminded himself that Jack would never again see his Mary. And from what he'd learned from Wally, she was a sad loss to the world. Dan suddenly wished he'd got to know her, a woman so far ahead of her time he thought.

The first morning Dan got in the catcher with Jack he was so excited he had butterflies in his stomach. He worried a little about how well Jack was able to do his job, whether he was ready to do such a dangerous job. Maybe all this was too soon, every one of these people had lost someone they loved when they lost Mary. But Dan understood it was necessary for them to keep going.

The girls Sandy, Melissa and Hilda had taken over mothering the boy though he was filled with sadness. These people would be alright he thought, they had each other. But to come out here and do this? All Dan could do was hang on tight and hope for the best.

Then the first bull was sighted, and Jack went after it. It took Dan's breath away, the suddenness of the chase; cruising one minute, hurtling through the scrub the next. This was in earnest, this was real. They flew through the scrub ducking branches, bouncing off bumps and swerving to miss stumps and trees.

Dan hung on for dear life as they hurtled after a monster scrubber bull. And he was a monster with a mostly black coat and long sharp horns. He looked a fright, and he sounded a fright. Dan felt the thrill go through him to his boots, his farmers boots.

Dan almost left the vehicle when they side swiped a young tree and bounced off it. 'Hang on now' Jack shouted as he leaned to the side. Dan had been this far before and he knew what to expect as Jack deployed the arm and secured the bull. The land rover shook and rattled as Jack brought the bull, puffing and bellowing to a shady tree.

As Dan watched in horror, Alby jumped out of the other vehicle and ran towards the bull. Right there in front of him Dan watched Alby tie the bull to a tree with a piece of rope. Dan knew he would, this is what he did, but seeing was believing. Alby very quickly and expertly tied the rope then jumped away and Jack let the bull go. Dan couldn't believe how smoothly that had gone but he also recognised the myriad of things that could go wrong. He worried for Alby now, and Jack.

When they were cruising again Dan said, 'and Wally does this?'

Jack grinned now, 'Wally is probably better than me. But Wally is so good with getting the bulls in the truck that he seems to have got the job. For now.' Dan worried now for Wally and did Wally love this enough to want to stay. How would he stand it?

After a few days of riding in the catcher vehicle Dan decided to help Wally in the truck. Wally had told him how Mary treated these animals and Dan was curious. He was not disappointed; he was amazed at how Wally was able to control these wild scrubber bulls. He never once hit or kicked the animals or even shouted at them. He had to use a loud voice because the bulls were a rowdy bunch.

They were eager to let their indignation be known. Alby gave them water which they seemed very grateful for and drank it noisily.

One day in the truck, Wally asked Dan how the small jetty had turned out. Dan had smiled and after a moment of silence he said, 'I think we got a bit carried away son.'

Wally grinned at the man he loved most in the world, 'how so Dan?'

'Well, we planned on a twelve-foot-long jetty which is now more like twenty. We planned on six feet wide which is more like twelve. You could make it your sitting room Wally. We just need to put a roof on it. We also attached floaters to it which are just drums so that if the posts ever give way you will stay above water. We did this so we can fish off it.'

The two men laughed, and Wally said, 'thanks Dan, Mel and I really appreciate it. I can't wait to get started on it.'

Dan was comforted by this statement and said quietly, 'I have some bad news for you Wally I didn't say anything before now because things were sad enough. I'm sorry Wally but . . . . but . . . . '

'Clyde?'

'Yes son.' Wally wiped his eyes and Dan put his hand on his shoulder, 'we got notification a week before I came up that someone would be bringing the Murrumbidgee Princess to our jetty in November. I am sorry mate.'

'Thanks Dan and thanks for leaving it until now, it was a good call Dan.'

'I can't bloody wait to see it. I mean to be able to get in it and have a good look at it. And Wally, I will need a letter from you saying that I can take possession of it.'

'Of course.'

'Are you going to gut it Wally and start again?'

'Yep, take everything out. I know exactly how I want it. That's if Mel agrees.'

'Would you like me and Ben to get started on that? Take all the fixtures out?'

'Yeah, that would be good Dan, whatever you can do would be great, and thanks.'

Dan left for home and Wally and Jack felt the loss. Jack looked at Wally that evening and said, 'what am I gunna do when you go Wally?'

'You'll go on as before and anyway we are staying indefinitely so we will go when you are ready.'

'Thanks Wally,' he sighed and went back to eating his tea.

Wally leaned in close 'you can come with us Jack. And stay a while down there. For the wet you know.'

Jack smiled 'thanks Wally, I'll be okay. One day I shall return to the lovely Murrumbidgee. She saved us Jack her and Mary. I would like to raise my son there in the long hut and send him to school in Balranald. I'm saving money so as I will be able to maybe buy a bit of land or even just build a house there.'

Wally glanced at Alby who nodded his head. A tear made its way down Wally's face and Jack smiled 'did you think I could stay away forever Wally? From all the people I love. What about you?'

'Well, we own the houseboat now and Mel and I will do it up to live in. Dan has built a somewhat magnificent jetty for us to tie up to on the riverbank.' They laughed together. 'Dan says we just need a roof on it, and we can fish there no matter what the weather's like.'

The two men were quiet for a time and Jack asked Wally, 'how long do you reckon you'll stay Wally?'

'Well, me and Mel want to go explore the Territory for a bit. We'll do that after we finish here, dunno if you're interested in coming to Jack. You and Billy?'

'Hell, yeah Wally, are you gunna call in and see Tom?'

'Well, that is something I would like to talk with you about Jack. When Tom comes to get the herd, he's gunna let me come back with him. Just to see what it's like droving cattle. We'll be finished catching then Jack why don't you come to? We could all come back in the land rover.'

In fact, when Tom took the final herd bound for Darwin, Wayne came as well, and Hilda drove Jacks vehicle. Wayne and Hilda wanted to stay a while in Darwin, pick up a new land rover and head off on the way to Alice Springs to look at a couple of properties.'

Wally loved the life of the drover and knew why they were always a happy go lucky lot. Jack loved it to, and he and Wally got very much closer over their time with the drovers. Wally loved riding though he got thrown a couple of times but soon learned to stay in the saddle. Ernie was glad of the help from the two women. Melissa did a few days droving the cattle but mostly stuck with Hilda.

Fred was delighted to eat Hildas cooking for a while. Ernie took a few days from the cooking to get back in the saddle and he loved it. It was lovely to get out and ride along with Tom.

Alby told them he and Sandy would meet them in Darwin.

All too soon they were in Darwin. It was just before the beginning of the wet and the boys were officially finished work for the season. They hung up their saddles at the end of the drive. They had enjoyed one another's company and the trip brought them all closer together.

Jack had loved it to and found himself wishing the profession of droving wasn't coming to an end. He knew he would take it up if it wasn't. He had found an appreciation for why these boys didn't want to give it up. Knew now why they were so happy all the time.

When they reached Darwin, the bullocks were taken to the cattle yards and counted in. Jack was a bit surprised at the greeting Herbert got, it seemed he was well liked and well respected. Herbert informed Jack that he would be coming back here to work when the drovers retired. 'Me and my wife are building a house, a very grand house and we will live there. Anytime you or yours are in Darwin you are welcome to stay with us.'

While they were in town, they were introduced to Herberts wife, and they all liked her. The two of them seemed very much in love and Fred was happy about it.

Over the course of the next week Jack and Wally and Wayne and the girls met Sue and her cattleman husband. Tom introduced them and did nothing to hide his contempt for her.

Sue took Herbert aside she could never believe the man he had become. 'I can't believe you are that scrawny cheating swine I knocked arse up in the hotel foyer all those years ago.' She looked him up and down, he was tall and strong looking. His face, suntanned now, had filled out and was quite handsome. But mostly it was the air of assurance about him now, that made the difference.

Herbert watched her eye him up and down and smiled, 'and you my dear are as beautiful as ever.' With that he turned and walked over to Fred, him and Fred knew. They knew what she was underneath, and they wanted no part of it.

Fred had watched the exchange and he wondered if Herbert still carried a torch for her. She was a very beautiful woman, he himself still felt a little something. But this woman was nothing like his Janet and he was glad of that. Fred breathed a sigh of relief, Herbert seemed glad to get away from her. Fred noticed that Sue went immediately back to her cattleman giving Alby the once over as she did.

One night at tea in the dining room at the pub they met up with a couple called Bradly and Lilly. Jack had met these people, but Wally was fascinated to meet all the people who made up Jacks social calendar now. He hadn't met anyone he didn't like. Wayne had known Bradley for years and had met Lilly more recently. Wally knew their story and he liked them.

Wayne told Jack when they got a moment of his plans to buy the acreage, they were on at the homestead they had built. 'We can put it in everybody's name but me and Hilda can be a bit more secure' he said.

Hilda said now 'are you sure Jack? You don't mind?'

'No Hilda I'm bloody thrilled. I don't really know what I'm going to do with Mary's place. I don't really want to get into raising cattle out there. Well not right now, no I just need to hang on to it. Have you made enquiries Wayne?'

'No not yet but I know he'll sell, he said when we leased it, he'd sell it to us if we wanted.'

Hilda got up and came round to hug Jack. Jack fell into her arms, it felt good, a woman's arms around him. Then it was over, and he smiled down at her and winked, 'Why'd you get involved with this bloody old reprobate. You'd have been better...'

'That'll be enough of that. Unhand my woman, Jack.' There was much laughter.

Hilda smiled but she didn't laugh 'I always liked you, Jack. You are a lovely man, and you deserve to be happy.'

Jack looked sad now 'I remember that first night I got to the station Hilda. I was feeling a bit bewildered and very nervous about the whole thing. And then I met you and I knew I'd be alright, knew Alby would be alright. I don't know how or why but I did.'

'I have a feeling that you will end up happy Jack and you have a lovely little boy. Anyway, we will all get back to normal when we get home, I can't wait to see him off to school Jack. I think Wayne and I will go on a bit of a holiday somewhere after we have spent some time on the new rover. Wayne is going to do it out the same as yours Jack and yours Wally. You are happy with your little homes, aren't you?'

Jack and Wally both nodded. Wally said now, 'Mel is happy with the back door. I just knocked the window out made the opening bigger and put a small door in it. It saves getting out in the rain to move somewhere and it is a little safer to be able to just slip into the driver's seat without getting out.'

'Yes, I like that idea Wally,' said Hilda. 'And I am very glad that we have had this time with you Wally and you Melissa. You are a lovely couple, and Jack is lucky to have you Both.'

CHAPTER 16

Wally, Melissa, and Jack along with Billy toured about the Territory for the next month. Alby and Sandy joined them for a couple of weeks and then went on home. Jack found his heart had eased some over the course of their droving trip and now the trip around Arnhem Land with its magnificent ranges and creeks and waterholes. The reds and the greens, the deep blue sky, nobody could think up such colours. It was an ancient, timeless land home to a beautiful but odd population of creatures. Creatures who absolutely suited this place of timelessness and mystery.

The two men Jack and Wally sat on the bank of many a water source and fished for their dinner. Both men comfortable and comforted in each other's company.

'Remember when this was do or die' Jack asked one day as they sat and waited for a bight? The two men always let the two dogs off when they fished to let them know if any danger lurked in the murky waters.

'Shit yeah, when we fished the Murrumbidgee for dinner,' said Wally. 'It was a bit more important back then. If we didn't get any, we went hungry.'

Jack laughed 'yep, made it all the better when we did Wally.'

Wally decided to take a punt and drew a deep breath, 'you were pretty gone on Mary for the longest time hay Jack.' Wally kept his eyes on his line.

Jack looked sharply at Wally a retort forming quickly on his lips. But Wally turned his head, he had a stupid grin on his face and a knowing look in his eye. He squinted at Jack, there was something else in his eyes.

'You to Wally?' Jack was flabbergasted. It had never occurred to him that others may have been so afflicted. He was too busy hiding how he felt. Well, he thought he was anyway.

Wally's grin got wider 'yeah mate but we got over it a bit quicker than you.'

We?' Jack was amazed, he asked again. 'We?'

'Yeah, even poor little Bryce.' he laughed at Jack now. 'Thought you had the monopoly on pining for Mary huh?'

'Shit. I suppose I did Wally.' Jack laughed, 'why didn't I know about this' and the two men laughed. It felt bloody good. He leaned to the side and flung his arms around Wally. Wally was a wonder, and he'd set Jack free in a way. In a most tremendous way, he had.

'Who else' he asked Wally now?

'Oh, only the males Jack.' And they were off laughing again.

'All of them?'

'Yeah mate, pretty much. All those who could see. Well, she isn't just a beautiful woman she's a hero and our saviour.'

'I 've had a wonderful time these past few weeks Wally. Thanks.'

'You are welcome my brother, and you have a bight.'

Jack reeled in an old beer bottle, 'that'd be about right Wally.' The two men laughed again they felt like boys again and it was wonderful. Jack had never felt so carefree. Not that he could remember, and it was all thanks to Wally. Jack knew that he and Billy would be okay, he just had to work out where? He figured there was no real hurry for that either.

Wally squinted at Jacks line, 'Oh I don't know Jack, I think it's still got the top on it. Well, go on, reel it in Jack. It's a bottle of beer.' Jack started to reel it in a little faster, and it dropped off. 'See Wally? The one that got away.'

The next day they moved on to Kakadu and had a bit more luck catching barramundi there.

After the trip was over and they were on their way home they called in to have dinner at a little place called Damper Creek where Wally finally got to meet Emily for the first time. She smiled at him, and Wally saw just how special she was. And when she turned and walked towards him, he was stunned. He grinned at her.

Tom stood back and smiled at Jack. The two men walked out on to the veranda where the tables were with Melissa. Inside Emily walked in her characteristic shuffle right up to Wally and extended her right hand. Wally took it and they both laughed.

'I am proud of you Wally.' Said Emily. 'I have heard all about your achievements from Tom. I have been waiting to meet you for a long time.'

'And I have been wanting to meet you. I owe you and Tom a debt of gratitude. Tom told me one day "Wally if you want to catch bulls you can catch bulls" he said. "And if you want to be a drover, go droving". That is what he said to me Emily and then told me about you. And I have never looked back.'

'Yes Wally, and Tom told me you excel at bull catching and droving and Tom doesn't just shell out such praise, willy nilly. You deserve it I know. Come Wally, let's get you seated you must be hungry.'

'Well, yes, we have been looking forward to trying some of your food Emily, we've heard all about it and not just from Tom.'

After tea when the dishes were cleared away Eric the trapper arrived with his accordion. He began to play and after a while people got up to dance. Wally was astounded. He was farther astounded when Emily stood up and asked him to dance with her.

Wally laughed and stood up, there wasn't much else he could do. 'I don't know how' he said simply.

Emily smiled 'then I will lead Wally. Follow me.'

Tom got the very shy Melissa to get up with him and they all had a damn good night. A love of music and dancing was born in Wally, and he wished he had gone to those dances with Jack all those years ago. This was fun and when he looked over at Melissa she was laughing and having the time of her life. Wally was glad and Tom was laughing at something she said. It was a great night. He looked over at Jack, his face was shining as he laughed at something Billy did.

He had always told Jack that he couldn't see any point to going to a dance and asking a girl to dance with him when the outcome of that would be a rebuttal. Jack's answer to that had made no sense to Wally either when he'd said 'the girls will all wanna dance with you Wally. You are hurt.'

Jack got up to dance with a girl called Rose and Fred got up with Janet. He still hadn't had that little talk with her, and she was more distant now than ever. And to his growing dismay she was looking stressed and ill.

Fred held her to him tenderly and danced over into a corner with her. Looking into her eyes he asked her, 'what is it woman? Just tell me love, I'm a big boy now.' Fred really didn't want to be a big boy right now though. 'Are we over?'

Janet looked into his beloved face and smiled sadly 'I guess we are love. Over.'

'Fuck! Why baby? Why?'

'Well let's just call it a conflict-of-interest hay.'

'No, let's not Janet and call it what it is. You don't love me and don't want to be with me anymore. Be honest Janet, you owe me that. I married you girl; you owe me that much.'

Fred let go of her hand and walked out onto the lawn where he sat down heavily. He was surprised when Janet sat beside him. He didn't speak, he couldn't.

Janet put her hand on his shoulder, 'Fred, you want to retire and live a nice quiet life down by the river. Just spending your time with a few cows, fishing and enjoying the peace and quiet. That is not in my future Fred. It's not for me. Not now it's not.'

'But I thought you wanted that to. Jesus Janet just go away love. Leave me alone for a bit hay.'

Janet sat looking at him and then slowly rose to her feet. His voice stopped her, 'then what do you want woman? Please! I can't bloody handle this. What did I do Janet?'

'You have done nothing; I want the same as you Fred but it's not going to happen. You see Fred something has come up and I must let you go. I had to choose between you and the baby, and I chose the baby.' She walked away to finish doing the dishes.

Janet made it to the middle of the lawn when she was stopped, Fred turned her to face him. She was crying and tears ran down her cheeks. 'Jesus Janet. Are you pregnant? Is that what you're telling me woman? You're going to have a baby? How long?'

Janet nodded and looked up into his face. He was angry she thought, though his face swam in the tears. 'I'm sorry Fred.'

'Well, you didn't get that way by yourself did you woman? Come here honey . . . . ' Fred drew her into his embrace and held her as she cried. 'Why are you crying woman' he asked at length?

'Because I love you and I didn't want to lose you.'

'You are not going to lose me. I don't know Janet; I didn't want this at my age. I'm too old woman. But you are having a baby and I think you have a right to be happy about it. But me and nappies Janet? I don't know love.'

'I love you, Fred.'

'I know.'

They stood that way for a while and presently Fred bent his head and kissed her long and passionately. Janet kissed him back matching his passion. 'Come on woman, let's go home. I just want to lay in your arms. That's all I ever wanted you know.'

He took her hand and started to walk away but Janet stopped him, 'we haven't finished the dishes.'

'Bugger the dishes.'

That night as Fred lay in her arms he smiled and told her how much he loved her, couldn't live without her and how he would just need a little time to grow into a father.

Janet smiled back, 'make love to me Fred.'

'But the baby.'

'Never mind that, I need you, Fred.'

Fred was never a man to shirk his duty and he wasn't about to start now. But Jesus, a baby! Fred was a father. 'I'm sorry love I just need a little more time here.'

Next day when everyone turned up for breakfast Fred announced the baby news.

Janet sat with her mouth opened along with everyone else. So, for the most part everyone was a little slow to react. Tom, who knew what this news would mean to Fred stayed quiet. Fred had never wanted children and they all knew this. Wally, in his ignorance, clapped the man on the shoulder and said, 'congratulations Fred, you to Janet,'

'Yes', said Jack who did know the facts here. 'I'm er . . . . I'm happy for . . . . '

Fred cut in, 'I know I have been less than receptive to the idea of my child coming into the world in the past. But now . . . . well I'm getting used to it. And it clearly makes Janet happy so . . . . ' Fred shrugged and smiled at Janet, yes, he thought she is happy. And if his little problem cleared up soon, he would probably be happy to.

Emily sat forward in her chair, 'well you have a little while to adjust Fred, it is not arriving tomorrow.'

Fred looked at Janet, his face said panic stricken. 'How long do we have?'

'Six months, I didn't know how to tell you.'

'Shit! I'd better get to work on the bloody house. Six months!'

Wally, Melissa, Jack, and Billy said goodbye to the drovers at Damper Creek with Wally saying he hoped to meet them again soon. Fred and Janet and the trapper Eric and Harry were there.

Wally turned to Emily 'we'll come back for the food. I can see how you made such a success of it here Emily, but I can't imagine how you managed all on your own.'

'Yes, well it wasn't long before I needed help. You dance really well Wally, and I can tell you love it. Keep going Wally, the sky's the limit, you have achieved so much. I remember learning to drive a car was my biggest challenge and here you are driving everything there is to drive. And you ride horses, catch bulls, plough crops shear sheep. And you dance beautifully Wally. You come back soon.'

'I know all this would have been bloody hard Emily, but you did it. And Tom is very proud of you, and I can see why he would be.'

'She is a marvel' put in Harry: 'but she is responsible for the lot of us having to think about diets.' He patted his stomach, and everyone laughed.

'Harry was my first customer; he is the reason I did all this.' Emily smiled at him, and he smiled back.

Ned had come across to see the drovers and the bull catchers off, he liked them. All of them. Emily turned to him 'and you drove me to get my food and we have chairs and tables because of you Ned and then you taught me to drive' Emily turned now to the trapper Eric. 'And you with your beautiful music give us an escape. A beautiful, happy place Eric, where we can sing and dance.'

'Well thank goodness they were there, hay.' Wally grinned at Harry, Eric, and Ned.

Emily moved on and said goodbye to Melissa and Jack. It was then that Wally got his first good look at Toms daughter, and she was the dead spit of Tom. Tom introduced her, she was five years old and had light brown hair and freckles and a cheeky grin. 'We call her little Fred because she looks nice and speaks softly and for the most part she is like an angel. But make no mistake she is a bit of a demon. She rides about as well as Fred and I do and has her mother's temper.' There was much laughter. Tom picked her up and sat her on his hip.

The bull catchers all piled into their cars and waving goodbye they left the little hamlet of Damper Creek, a stone's throw from Mataranka. They would take two days to make the trip back to Camooweal.

Billy had wanted to ride with Melissa, so Wally got in with Jack. Jack was glad Billy had someone but what would happen when Melissa left with Wally. Jack said this now to Wally.

'Come with us Jack. We won't be leaving until next year. You could come down home for a few months, get out of the rain.'

Jack smiled widely at Wally; he had always liked the man. Wally was a good man, the salt of the earth. He put his hand on Wally's arm and nodded. 'I'd like that Wally, let's just see what happens hay.'

Wally grinned and sighed deeply 'well I hope you do Jack.'

'Maybe after the next season Jack, maybe this time next year. I still need a little more money.' Jack drew a deep breath, 'you know how much land costs down there, Wally and where can I make this sort of money?'

Wally nodded 'I understand Jack. But you said yourself you are no good at growing anything, so why buy land?'

'Well Jack I was thinking more along the lines of transporting some of the bulls down there, buy them, ring them, and feed them on the good pasture for a few months. Then I'd sell them on. Probably a bit more profit than we get now, maybe a very tidy little profit hay Wally. I could buy bulls here every year.'

'That's a bloody good idea Jack.'

'Yeah, I got the idea from a bloke I met about a year ago. He ships them to Thailand and sells them on at quite a profit. See nobody wants them much because they are tough but a few months easy living and they are a different animal. Are you interested Wally? Or we could fly up here for the bull catching as usual, and then go home for the rest of the year. Think on it, Wally. Our own bulls so we wouldn't have to buy them. I mean we could sell some up here and the rest down there. We'd have to pay road trains but probably just two or three. Something to think about mate.'

'Oh, I am mate I am. Sounds like a good lark. Yeah, by Jesus why don't we? You wanna talk to Wayne and Alby. Alby will go where you go Jack.'

And back at the hut, Jack, and Wally, with Wayne and Alby and the women sat down to tea and another idea was born. Everyone agreed. Wayne said he would do three months and that was all. 'That will do nicely,' said Jack.

The boys sat well into the night hammering out the problems. 'Even if we just do two stations' said Wayne.

'Yeah' said Jack 'which two Wayne?'

'Well, I think Scotty wants Cloncurry Holding so we can give him that and keep the other two. I like the managers on the other two especially Robby on Mable Downs.'

It was agreed that they would keep those two stations. 'There's a lot to be done' said Jack as he rose to his feet and yawned. He picked up his little boy Billy and went off to bed.

It struck Wally that Jack was the boys' mother now as well as his dad. And he was doing a bloody good job. Wally thought again how lucky he and Mel had been that they hadn't found themselves expecting before this. He hoped that Mel was happy.

Over the next week a lot of talk went back and forth and a phone call was made to Dan. Dan thought it was a great idea and he would have both his boys back for the best part of the year.

Wally said to Jack 'you know mate there are a lot of house boats going cheap now why don't you get one of those for the months you are down home.'

A grin spread across Jacks face 'you know that's a bloody good idea Jack, I'll think about it. Might have a look at some when we go down.'

Alby jumped in he liked the idea, but they had a small child who did not yet swim very well.

'Well anyway' said Jack, 'we'll need someone on the block of land with the bulls. So, if you wanna volunteer Alby, I for one would be grateful. And together we should be able to buy a bloody decent size of a block. Maybe get three or four hundred head on it.' He thought for a while 'maybe Dan and Mary could come in on it to.'

The boys were excited, 'we can lock the vehicles up here while we are away' Jack put in.

'Well Hilda and I will spend a lot of time here we can keep an eye on things. What do you say Hilda?'

Hilda smiled at this man she loved, 'sounds good dear. I will still get my usual fee for cooking?'

Wayne cleared his throat and looked aghast at her. Jack smiled at her he knew how she negotiated with him, put the squeeze on him might be a better term for what she did to him. 'And what may I ask is your usual fee, Hilda' Jack asked quietly?

Hilda tapped her nose, and everyone laughed as Wayne's face went red.

Wally looked at Melissa 'we might as well leave the land rover here for when we're here and take the plane home. We can get another vehicle for down there. What do you say Mel?'

'Of course, Wally if this makes you happy then I am to.' She gazed at him for a moment, 'you have always looked after me Wally and I love you for that.'

Jack said, 'I think I'll do the same, though now it's just me and Billy I need to make the vehicle into two singles instead of a double.'

He glanced at Billy who was sleeping in a lounge chair. 'He kicks like a mule all night.'

Wayne cleared his throat now, 'When I make our rover into a home like yours, me and Hilda can go off on trips round the place. Maybe even go and have a look at the Murrumbidgee we've been hearing so much about.' He smiled at Hilda 'and take a look see at this long hut. I want to see that.'

That night as Wally held his beloved Melissa and gave thanks, he still had her, he sighed deeply. 'Are you happy about these arrangements Mel? I mean it'll be busy. But I think we will make a good amount of money.' Wally had been impressed with what these blokes had paid him for his work with them. He hadn't expected anything, and he protested this. But when he opened his envelope and counted the money his jaw had dropped. In his hand he had nine hundred Pounds.

'Well, I think it is the best idea for Jack. He can still do what he loves and still be a part of his family down home. And it will keep him busy, he needs to be busy Wally. I for one am excited to go home, I am. We can start on the houseboat. Did Dan say anything about it last time you spoke.'

'Only that he and Ben have got it ready for the build. Tomorrow we can draw a sketch of what it is and what we want hay. I think Jack will be alright now Mel and when he gets his home sorted out down there, he'll be a lot better. I hope he does get a houseboat and lives next door on the river.'

'Yes, Wally and we can get started on . . . . '

'Enough talk woman.' Wally kissed her long and lovingly, then he lifted his head and smiled, 'I have been talking for days.'

Wally wasn't so tired that he couldn't give thanks for all that he had after he had made love to Mel. He thanked God for her.

CHAPTER 17

Jack got on the phone and made reservations on the plane for seven people. Alby and Sandy were coming to, Alby wanted to see the place on the Murrumbidgee. It would be his new home, and he would bring his family with him. Alby found he wanted to meet Mary.

Wayne was happy with the arrangements because he would still be making bloody good money and he and Hilda would still have time to do what they wanted during the wet. Head south Wayne said and experience the dry summer.

They would fly down to the Murrumbidgee after Christmas in the new year. Wayne and Hilda had decided not to go on this trip as they had the business of their home to sort out. It was decided that Wayne would start making the arrangements this end and the boys Wally, Jack and Alby would look for land down south.

They spent Christmas at the long cabin, or tin can as Waynes sometimes called it. This was where Wayne would live permanently and he would be there from time to time amongst travelling, to keep an eye on the place. Everything was ready for the next season; the vehicles had been repaired and oiled and greased ready for July/August. They would catch bulls during the months of July and August and September.

Hilda and Sandy prepared a beautiful Christmas table, and they'd all gone to Camooweal to shop for presents for everyone. They had stayed the night in Camooweal and Jack had gone to spend some time in the cemetery. Then he had gone to see Sergeant Billy Judd at the police station.

He learned that the man who had shot him was a man called Jeffrey Rowe. He was Mary's only living relative and she his. He was doing time for what he'd done to Jack and a couple of other indiscretions.

'Where's he doing his time Sarge?'

'Down in Brisbane, why you wanna see him, Jack?'

No' laughed Jack. 'God only knows what he'd try and do to me.'

'So how are you coping Jack?'

'Yeah, all right thanks mate. Well at least now I know it was personal. Anyway, I gotta get back to the pub we're staying the night. We'll be heading down south in January.'

'Are you coming back Jack?'

'Yeah, mate it's a long story. Tell you what if you're in the pub tonight I'll buy you a beer and tell you all about it.'

The sergeant Billy Judd arrived in the pub that night and was amazed at the plans these blokes had made. 'Shit! I can see this working. Yeah, I envy yous.'

'Well Eddy has left us, so we'll need another bloke. You in sarge?'

'Hell yeah. My long service is up this year so I 'll be getting out of the force.' Billy was fifty-two years old, but he didn't look it. He'd been in the force for thirty years and he'd had enough.

Wayne and Jack were pleased at this turn of events, the sarge was six foot seven and built like a brick shit house. He was slightly bigger than

Alby and had a reputation of never being bested in a fair fight and not being afraid of anything. Yeah, he'd do nicely. Jack told him this now and he let out a below of a laugh.

'Not sure I'll be kicking bulls in the balls Jack, even though it has given your face a certain what shall we call it, panache.' He leaned forward and peered at Jack with a crooked smile 'yeah gives it character.' He took a swig of beer 'nope you can have that Jack, I'll be keeping my face out of it.'

Jack laughed good naturedly 'the ladies like it alright.'

The sarge looked at Hilda, 'nice to see you again Hilda. How are you these days? Married to this one here they tell me. I was glad to hear of it Hilda.' He smiled.

'I'm fine thanks Billy and I'd like to thank you for all your help that time to.'

'My pleasure Hilda.' The big policeman shrugged and looked into his beer. Wayne looked from one to the other and shrugged.

Billy had to work through to the middle of April so he would start with the bull catching season in July.

Wayne suggested at the Christmas table now, that they put him in the truck. That would leave Jack and Alby in the catcher and Wally in the wing and him, Wayne, in the camp on a stretcher reading. It was later decided that Wayne would ride along with Billy for a while.

A renewed interest in the bull business was born. Sergeant Billy Judd they all thought would be invaluable with permits and such things.

'You've out done yourselves girls' Wayne said as he tucked into his Christmas dinner. He looked at Jack, he worried about Jack. He was temperamental, but now he would have Wally and Alby beside him. And he would get to spend a considerable time with Dan. He worried a bit about him spending any time with Mary. Wayne was no fool, he knew the embers still burned low in the poor bastard. He needed to talk to Jack, he would do it tomorrow, he wanted to let Jack know that he would always be here. And Wayne promised himself he would be going down South a lot. He'd nearly lost Jack once and a shiver went through him every time he thought of it.

Hilda sat beside him and slipped her arm around him. Wayne smiled softly at her 'what did I ever do without you woman? And what did I do to deserve you?'

'You did just fine my love' she said and smiled at him.

'Nay woman, never.' Wayne smiled mischievously at his plate. 'Mind you the amount of money I pay you . . . . '

It was Hilda's turn to go red as she stared wide eyed around at them and Jack let out a below of a laugh.

As Wayne stuffed his mouth, he promised himself he would stick by Jack. Jack and his little boy Billy. Wayne wondered what sort of a bull catcher they would be able make out of the sarge. He knew Billy Judd from when they were boys and the man had always had a keen sense of justice and a ton of guts. He would only be an asset.

On Monday the third of January the seven people boarded the plane for Melbourne. Jack rang Dan from the airport as they waited, and Dan knew a contentment he hadn't thought possible. His boys were coming home. And with them was Alby and Sandy and their baby, the newest members of the family.

When he hung up the phone he smiled at Mary and slipped his arms around her. 'They are on their way Mary. They will be here tomorrow. I will get Ben and young Philip and we'll go down to the riverbank and put the tents up. I never dreamed of this happening Mary when they left. First Jack and then Wally. This is perfect. Are you sure Mary that we can afford the land across the river? It is good land and a lot of it, but it is also pricey.'

Mary smiled 'if they do take Bryce in with them it'll be worth every penny. Have you told them?'

'Not yet Mary I wanted to tell them face to face. That land will do several hundred head for short periods. It runs right back up into New South Wales and the Darling flows right through it. Can't wait to take everybody out there to see it.'

Dan left Mary and went off to get the tents up. It would be nice and cool on the riverbank and Wally could sleep on the houseboat if he wished. He and Ben and the boys had cleaned it and put a coat of paint on it, so it looked great even now.

Dan rubbed his chest as he walked, he got breathless a lot lately. He knew he'd have to slow down a bit and now he would be able to. Wally was back to do the ploughing. He would be able to spend more time sitting with Mary watching the grass grow. He smiled at the thought, how he loved her and loved this life they had. But Dan was just over fifty and told himself he had to slow up.

Dan had gotten to know Wayne and liked the man a lot. He was an honourable man and Dan had a deep respect for him the same as he had for Tom and Ernie and Fred. And now they had been told to expect a visit from a giant of a man called Billy Judd. Dan had met him, and he'd had a drink or two with him. He liked him also and was ready and willing to welcome the man into his home.

Ready to welcome the man into his family, he was another fine and honourable man from the top end.

And adding to Dans happiness was Bryce was coming. He loved the bulldozer and Dan didn't know if he would want to throw in with the boys. He was pretty certain he would for Bryce had talked, ad nauseum of his desire to go bull catching. Dan thought he'd probably have more trouble trying to stop him.

That afternoon the three men got the tents up, they were big old army tents, roomy and strong, Dan had bought them for just these occasions. Then they put the beds up and the women arrived with the bedding and made them up.

When they had finished, the tents were closed and laced up to keep out weather and animals. Ben had made a fireplace and they put table and chairs on the jetty they had made and they had put a roof on it.

Bryce arrived home on the morning of the fourth of January with his fiancé. He was set to marry her in April. He was excited about Jack and Wally coming and bringing Alby with them.

He looked over the tents that Dan and Ben had put up and smiled. He remembered the tent days though vaguely. He also remembered how good it had been to have a house to get in and food to eat. He would often stop what he was doing and thank Mary whenever she was nearby. He would never forget what Mary of the shanty had done for them. Mary of the shanty was their matriarch, their saviour, and their hero.

Dan sat now telling him that the boys had offered to take him in with them on their venture. 'You mean catching bulls' breathed Bryce?

Dan smiled and nodded 'what do you say son?'

'Well shit! Yeah. I say yes. Me dad? They want me to go in with them?'

'Of course, Bryce, but they asked us first because there is a danger attached to it. You will need to take care boy and do your apprenticeship. Do you understand?'

Bryce stared from one to the other, they were all there, the people of the long hut and Mary. Mary of the shanty was watching this. His chest puffed out and a grin spreads across his face that touched Dan. 'Of course,' Dan said slowly, 'we will understand if you want to stay on at the mine. It is a good job Bryce, a good and steady job with good and steady pay.'

'No dad, no. I have dreamed of this, but I never thought it would happen. Dad, I know that block of land you're talking about I went and did some work out there once. It's a lovely block but it'd be a bit pricey, wouldn't it?'

'Yeah, well me and Mary want to pay our way into this enterprise.'

'What about me dad I've got bugger all money?'

'No son you don't need any, but you'll have to work for wage at first. From what Wally says they pay well. He said they paid him more for six weeks than he could make in six months at the mine. No take it son if that is what you want.'

'Thanks dad, you to Mary of the shanty. Mum.'

Mary was surprised at his calling her mum. She ran to him and fell into his arms and cried. Bryce held her to him; he had told Wally that he was over her. But he was no more over her than Jack was. Hell's Bells, he'd just called her mum.

Everybody was seated at the table finishing their dinner when they heard the vehicles turn up. They all rushed outside to greet them all, Dan went straight to Wally, he was back. He was back, thank God and so was Jack. Dan embraced them both then shook hands with Alby. He held the girls even Sandy to him and kissed them on their cheek. The girls cuddled him they loved Dan.

Alby could not drag his eyes away from the long hut. It was a magnificent building with wide verandas all around and small dwellings all about it. It was all painted a creamy white and there were chairs all up and down the veranda. Of course, the great logs that had been their outdoor setting for years were still there. The front door had been widened into two doors and were open most of the time. In the summer they put streamers across to keep the flies out.

The river was just off to the South and almost right where the Murrumbidgee flowed into the mighty Murray. Alby noted the gardens just away to the right of the building and he knew it was their market gardens. It was pretty bloody impressive he thought.

The kids all poured out the doors and milled around excitedly. They kept their distance from him, but they clamoured for Jack and Wally's attention. Yeah, this was a family he thought as he stared at the people all loving each other. Alby recognised it as a paradise and knew why Jack and Wally always headed back here. Hell, he would to if it had been his. And now, he smiled inwardly, it was. This was his new home, his and his family. He felt a contentment dispel his nervousness as he smiled at Dan and said, 'good to see you man.'

Dan introduced Alby to Mary and Alby turned and grinned at her. He saw what all the fuss was about and felt he was glad he hadn't grown up to close to her. Yes, he had escaped the complications of wanting and loving this woman thank Christ, he had an idea it would be a hard one moving on from her. Then she put her arms gently around him.

'It is good to meet you at last. And this must be Sandy, how are you, Sandy? Welcome to our humble abode, the long hut.'

He was introduced to Bryce who was grinning from ear to ear and instinctively knew he liked him. He shook the younger man's hand and smiled 'so are you coming in with us Bryce? Gunna catch a few bulls?'

'Hell yeah. Wild horses couldn't keep me away.' '

That's the spirit lad.'

Once they were seated in the kitchen, they were given some of the best food Alby had ever tasted. 'I love the place' he blurted out as his face went red. The laughter that ensued was a friendly loving sound and Alby was home. He looked at Sandy and she stared wide eyed about her, a wide grin on her face, she was home.

They were taken down to the tents at the river to look over the houseboat and put their gear away. They were all given the choice of where they wanted to sleep, and they all fell in love with the tents on the riverbank.

Dan talked as they walked, and Alby was surprised to hear that Dan had already found a property to hold the bulls on. Dan went on to say that they would all pitch in and build a dwelling on the place. He told them that he would like them all to have a sturdy warm dwelling by winter. 'We know what it's like in a tent here in winter.' He smiled and most of the people nodded and smiled with him.

Dan went on talking excitedly about the new property they had bought, 'it's only about a half an hour drive from here so you are welcome to stay here Alby and you Sandy.' Dan went on, 'if you decide to stay alongside us, we can build you somewhere here.' He turned to Wally, 'and you Wally, are you happy with the houseboat here?'

'Yep, thanks Dan. Me and melissa are gunna get reacquainted with Matilda and go a waltzing for a little bit along the Murrumbidgee. I have been longing for this.'

Wally couldn't believe his eyes when he entered through the front door of the houseboat. 'Shit Dan, you've done a bloody good job thanks. It won't take long to get a home in here.' He smiled at Melissa then turned to Dan, 'Jack is gunna look around for one of these for him and Billy.'

Dan smiled at Jack, 'just as well we made a good size jetty huh.'

Jack looked around for Billy and smiled when he saw the boy playing cricket up at the hut with some other kids. A distant look appeared on Jack's face as he remembered the games they had played there with the kids in days gone by. It seemed so long ago, yet it seemed like only yesterday.

Dan saw the smile 'do you want a game son? Feel like getting a beating from an old man?'

Jack nodded and grinned at Dan, 'you can try old man, you can try.' Jack and Dan laughed together as they walked side by side with Alby and Wally. Bryce joined them and Alby nudged him with his elbow. 'You, me and Wally hay? I reckon we can take these two even if they get Bradman to help them.'

The men all laughed as they went up to play cricket with the kids and Alby was glad, he had come. He was glad to be part of the long hut community on the bank of the Murrumbidgee River. He was glad he was part of the large family, the very loving family on the Murrumbidgee, a stone's throw from the Murray. And Alby was glad his kids would grow up here.

Dan was overjoyed that Alby had come, Jack obviously had quite a bond with the man, and he could see that Alby needed Jack. Wally had quite a bond with both of them, but that was Wally. And when sergeant Billy Judd got here, he would be welcome also.

And Sandy watched her beloved Alby, and she was glad for him. And come what may she knew they would always be safe here and forever be a part of a great love. A family love. She missed her parents, but this was her place here by Alby's side. And she would go and see her parents every year when Alby went back. Sandy was especially glad because her children would be settled and educated. They would go to school along with the other children and be happy.

She just wished Mary was here, she knew Jack still missed her terribly. He needed to be here in the loving bosom of his family. And she had noticed a shift in Jacks behaviour since getting back, he was more relaxed.

Mary stood beside her now and smiled kindly at her. 'Do you think you'll be happy here love?'

'Oh yes, I do. And Alby is happy here and he could never be separated from Jack.'

'Well, you and Alby are very welcome. We have room and food to spare and plenty of love to go round.' Mary was touched by the tear that rolled down the young woman's cheek and she put her arm about her shoulders. 'We have plenty of room for more children especially. When are you due my dear?'

THE END

ABOUT THE AUTHOR

ROSANNA MARY SEATON

Born Rosanna Mary Seaton in Pemberton WA in 1954 to parents Maida and Arthur Seaton. The daughter of a rabbit trapper (returned war vet) I grew up travelling all over Australia. By school age I had lived in all the mainland states of Australia.

I was raised mostly in the arid outback of Australia, through the red Centre in Northern South Australia, Northwestern New South Wales and in the Southwestern areas of Queensland which included the Simpson Desert. We also lived for a time in WA and spent a couple of years out on the Nullarbor which is a vast expanse of sparsely populated land which includes the Great Australian Bite to the South and the Great Victorian Desert to the North. It occupies an area of around 200,000 sq. kilometres. I can remember one time; my father pulled the caravan up under one of the very few trees out there. He got out of the car, looked about and said, 'there's your back yard kids, now go and play in it.'

I, along with my family, inhabited a very isolated and severe region which was mostly semi desert and desert areas. It is mostly referred to as the red centre, because of the red soil and rolling red sandhills. Add in the green spinifex bush and deep blue skies which gave it a beautiful and vibrant contrast of colours. Then after the rains in summer came the wildflowers of yellow, white and other colours. Then here and there are the old grey green mulga trees with their gnarled and twisted beauty adding a certain charm to the bush which it inhabits. And then there's the unique strangeness of those who live there, the majestic yet stern emu, the comical kangaroo and the exquisite brolga whose dance is a thing of beauty.

The great outback of Australia has a timeless yet ancient splendour about it, Gods own country indeed.

This country was largely given to cattle stations. We relied on the yearly monsoons for what rain we did get, and water was usually a problem. Many dangers lurked in the bush, ready to snare any careless inhabitant who dared to treat her without due respect. And she could deal a swift and deadly blow. Many good men, strong smart men, were taken to her breast and held there for their carelessness.

My father was a rabbiter, (shooter) mostly though he worked at excavation and station work now and then. He was a boundary rider on the dingo proof fence on the NSW and QLD border for a while. He would also get work on the railways from time to time, 'to tide us over' he would say. He was a returned serviceman and ex commando, and it was from him that I learned to hunt and to survive in the lovely but harsh Australian bush. And I soon learned and afforded her the respect she demanded.

My mother was my teacher mainly, though we did go to school whenever there was one nearby. At age fourteen I was packed off to boarding school, I think, because I was becoming as wild as the red desert hills I roamed and was no longer interested in books. Well, that did the trick, but I hated every minute, every second of it. How I missed my beloved sand hills, but with a broken heart I embraced the world of books once more. Most of us at the dreaded boarding school felt the same as most of the other kids were in there for the same reason as me. We had become too wild. Anyhow my mother was a good teacher, but her competitor was the ever changing, adventure ridden bush. We mostly lived in a caravan and tents and travelled all over the country, so she had her work cut out.

I have lived in South Australia and raised my children there in that state. Thankfully they have had a bit more stable life than me although I would not swap my childhood for another. I can say that with absolute certainty.

I wrote a book some years ago about my life growing up out there in the Never Never, called Tales from The Sand Hills. I love writing about the bush and the characters who inhabit it and gain much pleasure in sharing it.